D1528602

WOMEN'S ROLES IN ASIA

Recent Titles in
Women's Roles through History and Women's Roles in American History

WOMEN'S ROLES IN ASIA

Kathleen Nadeau and Sangita Rayamajhi

Women's Roles through History

 GREENWOOD

AN IMPRINT OF ABC-CLIO, LLC
Santa Barbara, California • Denver, Colorado • Oxford, England

Library of Congress Cataloging-in-Publication Data

Nadeau, Kathleen G.
    Women's roles in Asia / Kathleen Nadeau and Sangita Rayamajhi.
        pages cm. — (Women's roles through history)
    Includes bibliographical references and index.
    ISBN 978–0–313–39748–6 (hardcopy : alk. paper) — ISBN 978–0–313–39749–3 (ebook)
1. Women—Asia—History. 2. Women—Asia—Social conditions. 3. Sex role—Asia—History. I. Rayamajhi, Sangita. II. Title.
HQ1726.N33   2013
305.4095—dc23   2013006741

ISBN: 978–0–313–39748–6
EISBN: 978–0–313–39749–3

17 16 15 14 13   1 2 3 4 5

This book is also available on the World Wide Web as an eBook.
Visit www.abc-clio.com for details.

Greenwood
An Imprint of ABC-CLIO, LLC

ABC-CLIO, LLC
130 Cremona Drive, P.O. Box 1911
Santa Barbara, California 93116-1911

This book is printed on acid-free paper (∞)

Manufactured in the United States of America

We dedicate this book to all
those who dream and believe in gender equality.

Contents

Series Foreword

Women's history is still being reclaimed. The geographical and chronological scope of the Women's Roles through History series contributes to our understanding of the many facets of women's lives. Indeed, with this series, a content-rich survey of women's lives through history and around the world is available for the first time for high school students to the general public.

The impetus for the series came from the success of Greenwood's 1999 reference *Women's Roles in Ancient Civilizations,* edited by Bella Vivante. Librarians noted the need for new treatments of women's history, and women's roles are an important part of the history curriculum in every era. Th us, this series intensely covers women's roles in Europe and the United States, with volumes by the century or by era, and one volume each is devoted to the major populated areas of the globe—Africa, the Middle East, Asia, and Latin America and the Caribbean.

Each volume provides essay chapters on major topics such as

- Family Life
- Marriage and Childbearing
- Religion
- Public Life
- Lives of Ordinary Women
- Women and the Economy
- Political Status
- Legal Status
- Arts

Country and regional differences are discussed as necessary. Other elements include

- Introduction, providing historical context
- chronology
- glossary
- bibliography
- period illustrations

The volumes, written by historians, offer sound scholarship in an accessible manner. A wealth of disparate material is conveniently synthesized in one source. As well, the insight provided into daily life, which readers find intriguing, further helps to bring knowledge of women's struggles, duties, contributions, pleasures, and more to a wide audience.

Acknowledgments

We would like to express our appreciation to the editors, especially Kaitlin Ciarmiello, Nicole Azze, and Erin Ryan, with ABC-CLIO, the copyeditor, Sarah Wales McGrath, the team in PreMedia Global, and ABC-CLIO for making this book possible. We thank our families, friends, colleagues, and students whose love for equality and collegiality keep us growing.

—Sangita Rayamajhi and Kathleen Nadeau

Chronology

3100–1700 BCE	Indus Valley civilization
1766–1122 BCE	Shang dynasty (China)
1700–500 BCE	Vedic period (India)
1122–480 BCE	Zhou Dynasty (China)
7000 BCE	Queen Vispala of India is a warrior woman of the Rigveda. Friend to the twin horsemen, she loses a leg during battle that is replaced by an iron leg. She then returns to the fight.
500 BCE–CE **50**	Mauryan Empire (India)
800 BCE	The essentials of Hinduism begin to be preserved in a collection of prayers, hymns, and rituals in the Vedas.
500 BCE	The Indian prince Siddhartha Gautama, founder of Buddhism, begins preaching against less enlightened Hindu beliefs and rituals. He rejects the caste system and beliefs in the gods. He teaches that the path to enlightenment is the renouncement of all worldly desires.
336–321 BCE	Alexander the Great takes over north India, and India becomes part of Macedonia.
312–60 BCE	Seleucid Dynasty (Asia)
221 BCE–CE **220**	Han Empire (China)
135 BCE–CE **240**	Kushan Empire (India)

39–42 BCE	Queens TrungTrac and TrungNhi lead a revolution of 80,000 people who push the Chinese invaders out of Vietnam.
CE **320–550**	Gupta Empire (India)
551	The birth of Confucius, founder of Confucianism, marks its beginning.
581–618	Hua Mulan is a legendary figure from ancient China, who fights in many bloody battles for love of country before being summoned to court by the emperor, who wants to appoint her to a high office. She humbly refuses and asks for a horse instead.
589–618	Sui Dynasty (China)
618–907	Tang Dynasty (China)
625–705	Empress Wu Zetian rules during the most glorious years of the Tang Dynasty in China.
907–1279	Song Dynasty (China)
939–1407	Dai Viet (Vietnam)
1030–1151	Ghaznavid Emirate (India)
1157–1247	Important period for Tomoe Gozen, a famous Japanese samurai who fights alongside Minamoto no Yoshinaka. Today, she often is re-created in anime.
1206–1368	Yuan Dynasty (China), the period of Mongol rule over the Han people. New ideas about women, marriage, and inheritance are introduced during this period.
1206–1526	Delhi Sultanate (India)
1336–1573	Ashikaga Shogunate (Japan)
1350–1767	Ayutthaya Kingdom (Thailand)
1368–1644	During the Ming Dynasty (China), the Han people have different perceptions of women than did the Mongol people. Foot-binding becomes more widespread during the Ming Dynasty as a symbol of a women's beauty, position in the social hierarchy, and fidelity to the family.
1492–1905	Russian expansion into Asia
1526–1765	Mughal Empire (India)
1531–1581	Taungoo Empire (Myanmar)

1603–1867	Tokugawa Shogunate (Japan)
1644–1911	The Manchu Qing Dynasty (China) implements the same form of government used during the Ming Dynasty, with the exception that each post is held by one Han and one Manchu, with the Manchu official having the most power. A new dress code is introduced. Men are required to shave their heads and wear a long pigtail, while the Han custom of binding women's feet is prohibited, albeit nigh impossible to enforce, so the law is soon disbanded.
1765–1947	British Raj (India)
1790–1945	European colonization in Southeast Asia
1879–1904	Raden Ayu Kartini, pioneer women's rights advocate in Indonesia
1895–1945	Japanese expansion in East Asia and the Pacific
1911–1949	Republic of China
1914–1918	World War I
1926–1927	Communist uprising in Dutch East Indies
1929	Kingdom of Siam is renamed Thailand.
1931	Women are granted the right to vote and stand for election in Sri Lanka.
1932	Women are granted the right to vote and stand for election in Thailand.
1935	Women are granted the right to vote in Burma (called Myanmar since the military junta in 1988).
1937	Women are granted the right to vote and stand for election in the Philippines.
1939–1945	World War II
1941–1945	Japan occupies East Asia and Southeast Asia.
1941	Women are granted the right to vote and stand for election in Indonesia.
1946	Women are granted the right to vote and stand for election in the Democratic Republic of Korea (North Korea). Women are granted the right to stand for election in Burma (or Myanmar).
1945–1989	The Cold War

1945	Indonesian Independence
1946	Philippine Independence
1947	Women are granted the right to vote and stand for election in Japan.
1948	Women are granted the right to vote and stand for election in the Republic of Korea (South Korea).
1948	Burmese Independence
1949–	People's Republic of China
1950	Women are granted the right to vote and stand for election in India.
1950–1953	Korean War between the Democratic Republic of (North) Korea and the Republic of (South) Korea causes horrific suffering for countless innocent Korean victims. The war is largely caused by the arbitrary drawing of the 38th parallel line by the occupying allied forces after World War II, which divided the previously unified nation and gave rise to the Cold War between the communist Soviet Union and anti-communist United States and its Western European allies.
1951	Women are granted the right to vote and stand for election in Nepal.
1953	Women are granted the right to vote and stand for election in Bhutan.
1954–1975	Indochina wars
1955	Women are granted the right to vote and stand for election in Cambodia.
1957	Women are granted the right to vote and stand for election in Malaysia.
1958	Women are granted the right to vote in Loas (Peoples Democratic Republic of Loas).
1960–1965; 1970–1977; 1994–2000	Sirimavo Bandaranaike serves as Sri Lanka's first woman prime minister (she is the first woman in the world to serve as a prime minister and served three terms). She succeeds her husband as premier in 1960 after he is killed by a Buddhist monk.
1963	Women are granted the right to vote and stand for election in Afghanistan.
1965	Federation of Malaysia: Malaya, N. Borneo, Sabah, and Sarawak, and Singapore

1965–	Republic of Singapore
1966–1977; **1980–1984**	Indira Gandhi is the first woman prime minister of India, She was the only child of Jawaharlal Nehru, who ruled India from Independence in 1947 until 1964. She was assassinated, during her second term in office, on October 31, 1984.
1971	Bangladesh, formerly East Pakistan, becomes an independent nation state after a nine-month war for liberation against West Pakistan.
1972	Women are granted the right to vote and stand for election in Bangladesh.
1976	The Socialist Republic of Vietnam is officially proclaimed.
1976	Indonesia annexes Portuguese East Timor.
1979	Vietnamese troops enter Phnom Penh and end the murderous Pol Pot regime in Cambodia.
1986–1992	Prodemocracy campaigner Corazon Aquino takes over the presidency from Ferdinand Marcos in the Philippines. She is the widow of opposition leader Benigno Aquino, who was assassinated in 1983. She is Asia's first female president and the second woman in the world elected as a nation's president.
1988	Military junta takes power in Myanmar.
1988–1990; **1993–1996**	Benazir Bhutto is the first prime minister of a Muslim country, Pakistan. She is the daughter of former ruler Zulfikar Ali Bhutto, who ruled Pakistan from 1971 until 1973 and served as prime minister from 1972 until 1977. He was overthrown in 1977 and executed by the military regime of general Zia ul-Haq in 1979. Having graduated from Harvard University and Oxford University, Benazir Bhutto restores democracy to Pakistan in 1988, but her rule is tainted by corruption and she is twice ousted by presidential decree. She served a second term from 1993 to 1996. She is assassinated in Rawalpindi on December 27, 2007.
1989	Vietnam withdraws from Cambodia. This is the first time for a half-century that Vietnam is not involved in any war.
1990	Aung San SuuKyi leads the opposition party to a landslide victory in election in Myanmar (Burma), but the military

1990 (*cont.*)	regime refuses to relinquish power. Daughter and only child of independence hero Bogyoke Aung San, who was assassinated in 1947, Aung San Suu Kyi has mainly lived under house arrest since her return to Burma in 1988. She is the recipient of the 1991 Nobel Peace Prize.
1990–	Age of globalization, the rise of mulitnational corporations, trade liberalizations, advances in communication —especially the computer—and increasing interconnectiveness of all parts of the world.
1991–1996; 2001–2006	Khaleda Zia is the first woman prime minister of Bangladesh. She is the widow of the late president Ziaur Rahman, assassinated in 1981. She serves a second term as prime minister from 2001 to 2006.
1994–2005	Chandrika Kumaratunga is a female president of Sri Lanka. She is the daughter of Sirimavo Bandaranaike, the first female prime minister of Sri Lanka and the first female prime minister of the world.
2001–2004	Megawati Sukarnoputri is a woman president of Indonesia. She is the daughter of Indonesia's first president, Sukarno, who was replaced by one of his generals (Suharto), who kept him under house arrest until his death. Megawati Sukarnoputri co-led the Indonesian Democratic Party for Struggle that overthrew the Suharto dictatorial regime. She, subsequently, was democratically elected into the office of the presidency
1996–2001; 2009–	Sheikh Hasina Wajed is female prime minister of Bangladesh. Her father (President Sheik Mujibur Rahman), her mother, and three brothers were murdered during a 1975 military coup. Abroad at the time, Sheikh Hasina Wajed returned home in 1981 to take over her father's party and won a 1996 election.
1997	Asian economic crisis
2004	An Indian Ocean tsunami devastates much of coastal South and Southeast Asia, killing around 283,000 people.
2006–2007	Han Myung Sook is female prime minister of South Korea.
2008–2009	Global banking crisis leads to a world recession.

2010   Prodemocracy leader and Nobel Prize laureate Aung San Suu Kyi is released from house arrest in Myanmar (Burma).

2011   Yingluck Shinawatra becomes the first female prime minister of Thailand.

Introduction

Asia is a geographically and culturally diverse part of the world with a wide variety of ethno-linguistic groups, political and economic systems, and religions. This book looks at women in South Asia (Sri Lanka, India, Bangladesh, Pakistan, and Nepal), East Asia (China, Japan, and Korea), and Southeast Asia (Myanmar [also known as Burma], Thailand, Cambodia, Laos, Vietnam, Malaysia, Singapore, Brunei, Indonesia, and the Philippines). These countries have varying ecological, historical, social, and cultural circumstances. They have been influenced by local beliefs and practices as well as influences coming from other countries of Asia and the West. We cannot do justice to all of their cultural and historical specificities; readers may refer to the selected bibliography for additional readings on this subject. This book will give a broad understanding of some of the similar cultural patterns in women's experiences in Asia, although their idiosyncratic and individual differences are equally important, as is how they are influenced by globalization.

STEREOTYPING OF ASIAN WOMEN

Western media present conflicting images and stereotypes about Asian women. Value judgments on *purdah* (hiding women from the view of men) in some Islamic communities and *sati* (wife burning) in India portray these women as being backward in relation to Western women. In some popular stereotypes, Asian women are depicted as being mysterious and

Bangladeshi girls from one of the poor areas of Chittagong. (Sharon
Panackal, all rights reserved)

hypersexual, and their sexuality is connected to some overly exotic and mystical past. Edward Said, in writing about the Middle East, referred to this kind of stereotyping as Orientalization. That is, Orientalization is the way in which the early Europeans, including those from Europe and North America, came to dominate, control, and restructure the societies and cultures of Asia by reimagining them into their own culturally biased and fictitious images. The European colonizers used violent and duplicitous means to bring the people living in Asia with whom they came in contact into submission, which ignited resistances and further perpetuated the stereotyping of Asia by the West. Later, in translating and interpreting the culturally diverse and different Asian religious and philosophical texts, Western scholars made some gross generalizations based on mistaken notions about the inherent character traits and personalities of the people living in Asia. This led to more distorted stereotyping of the people and cultures of the wider region. The chapters in this book challenge stereotypical images of exotic Asian females by appropriately contextualizing cultural practices in the social and historical contexts in which they are grounded.

WHEN THE COLONIZERS CAME, WOMEN'S WORLDS CHANGED

By the fifteenth and sixteenth centuries when the colonizers came to Asia, local people already were trading with other royal polities along the vast and expansive sea lanes and the Silk Road, and they had been doing so for centuries. Marco Polo's (1254–1324) *Description of the World, or the Travels of Marco Polo*, offers an early glimpse of some the riches and splendors of life in the various cultural and religious communities living within the contexts of the robust economies and societies interspersed within the connecting centers of these ancient trade routes. He is considered to be the first European to have travelled along the Silk Road as far as China, although a few friars before him travelled back and forth along the Silk Road to Mongolia through Turkey, Iran, and Afghanistan. Polo was befriended by and became a personal confidant of Kublai Khan (1214–1294), son of Toluia and Sorghaghtani Beki, and grandson to Genghis Khan, who conquered China and founded the Yuan Dynasty (1271–1368). Daughters of the great Khan (King) Genghis played especially prominent and powerful roles in ancient Mongolia. Anthropologist Jack Weatherford explains that one of the ways that Genghis Khan was able to keep control over his vast and huge expanse of kingdom was by arranging marriages between his daughters and faraway princes, who couldn't refuse, while writing into their marriage contracts that his daughters—not their husbands—had the right to rule.[1]

Mercantile traders brought silks, precious porcelains, iron implements and tools, and other products to island ports around Southeast Asia in exchange for gold, pearls, resins, medicinal herbs, beeswax, rattans, exotic flowers, different kinds of woods, rich forest and sea products, and textiles and other handicrafts. One of the earliest known maritime kingdoms was the Sri-Vijaya Empire coming out of Indonesia, which controlled east-west trade through the Strait of Malacca for 400 years, from 700 to 1100 CE.[2] The Chinese have done business in this zone since at least the Tang and Sung Dynasties of the tenth and eleventh centuries.[3]

European colonization often led to the decline of earlier prosperous economic and political centers due to lack of any real incentives for the local people. Literary critic and historian Resil Mojares[4] explains that in the case of the Philippines, Spanish colonizers attempted to monopolize all of the local routes of trade by mandating that all goods first pass through Manila before being exported around the region and back to Spain and the European mainland via the Mexican trade route. They worked under the auspices of local headmen who helped the merchants exploit their followers as servile laborers. This strategy destroyed the criteria governing the pre-existing follower-to-leader system. Precolonial leadership roles were subject to contestation and change, even when inherited, because they were part of autonomous communities that could oust those who fell out of favor. Local leaders were frequently like heads of large households who earned their positions by means of attracting a large group of loyal followers. Like the British in India, the Spanish, later Americans who came to the Philippines, and Dutch who came to Indonesia undermined and dismantled local leadership systems by using the military to put their own puppet heads in positions of power to do their bidding and took out any who would oppose them.

The colonizers negotiated the terms of their agreements mainly through the agency of male leaders, while females were displaced. The ancient Asian regimes differed from those of Europe. In island Southeast Asia, for example, differences in gender roles may have been merely differences in work patterns that complemented each other within their respective spheres. Anthropologists Cristina Blanc-Szanton[5] and Shelly Errington[6] explained that the ideology of gender differences around the islands was complementary, that is, the opposite sexes complemented each other rather than competed against each other. In East Asia, contrarily, gender relations were—and to a large extent still are—hierarchically based on the patriarchal system of Confucianism, which ranks men over women. Euro-colonial policy attempted everywhere to change gender roles in accordance with their own preconceived notions about what men and women should do. Undoubtedly, the expansion of the European colonial and economic powers into Asia had a disintegrating and transformative effect on the pre-existing structures family and state.

ORGANIZATION OF THE BOOK

Women's status and roles in Asia involve social, cultural, political, and economic interactions, negotiations, and change. This book takes a thematic and chronological approach that compares and contrasts women's changing status and roles in relation to the particular histories and regions in which they are situated. Women's roles concern negotiations about which gender does what work in a particular place and time in history. Gender relations are culturally construed. By their nature, they are multidimensional. What are believed to be appropriate behaviors for men and women can be reinvented and transformed in relation to the political, economic, social, and cultural environment. Normative kinship roles and social relationships can be changed in response to colonization, modernization and development, globalization, and encounters with world religions. Each of the chapters in this book provides an overview of some of the ways to approach and interpret this subject.

Chapter 1 provides an overview of women's roles in religion in precolonial, colonial, and postcolonial times. Colonization in Asia dramatically changed women's status and position in most societies of the region. Prior to colonialism, women held important roles of political influence and prestige in Asia, especially as mothers, daughters, and wives of important political figures by participating in politics as peacemaking go-betweens and behind the scenes, or as in the case of Mongol queens, wielding power and authority over whole nations. Religious dancers and courtesans, geishas and concubines, female shamans, healers, and midwives were esteemed. However, European colonization, with its patriarchal structures of religious control and dominance, largely took away their political and economic basis of empowerment. Religion is an aspect of culture, and the different world religions (Hinduism, Buddhism, Confucianism, Islam, and Christianity) as well as indigenous religious spiritualities today continue to exert a formative influence over Asia. Each religion has different theological traditions and denominations within itself, ranging from conservatives to progressives, and women religious leaders past and present have played roles in women's emancipation movements as well as environmental justice and peace movements across the region.

Chapter 2 examines the role of women in agriculture and domestic activities, with a focus on their participation in revolutionary movements. Revolutionary movements for national liberation swept across Asia for most of the second half of the twentieth century. Women's involvement in revolutionary movements was pronounced. Until recently, most Asian societies were predominantly agricultural; today, even in the rapidly urbanizing and industrializing countries of China and India, or the Philippines and Indonesia, the bulk of the local populations directly or indirectly continues to be involved in agriculture, especially subsistence farming. European colonialism and later capitalization of agriculture and farming brought many changes to women living in traditional Asian peasant societies. Increasing hardships have forced many women to migrate to cities and abroad in search of paid employment. Many look for work in the informal sector because they lack a high school or college education and networks needed to apply for better paying jobs that require certain skill certifications and training. In poorer countries that have more people looking for employment than available jobs and where teachers and civil servants are not paid a living wage, educated women often migrate abroad to take comparatively better-paying but lower-status jobs for which they are overqualified. Many educated women in Asia today, however, have successfully broken through the glass ceiling and can be found at work in all professional and occupational fields.

Chapter 3 discusses women's roles in the realm of family and kinship structures. The sociocultural norms and values of countries like China, Japan, Korea, Malaysia, Indonesia, and many countries of South Asia are seen to be directed by the various religions or religious philosophies through the centuries. Confucianism, Buddhism, Islam, Hinduism, and Christianity are viewed as the influencing factors in the construction of social hierarchies and norms and values. In ancient family regimes, men and women responded equally to the call of circumstances. Women, like men, held positions of power as strong independent queens or political leaders, embodying innate human dignity. But as histories merged, boundaries fluctuated, and political alliances forged with and without the support of colonizers, roles of women too began to change.

The patriarchal order was prevalent throughout South Asia, where women's roles encompassed aspects of subjugation and denial of self. With the fifth-century advent of Confucian philosophy, which considered the family as an important social institution, societal norms and values related to women became stringent. As the philosophy moved across East Asia, it took with it these harsh realities for women. With Buddhism, there was a certain relaxation in society's perceptions toward women, but Confucian values remained steadfast and continue to do so in many of the traditional communities and families of East Asia even today.

For South Asia and Southeast Asia, it was also religion that directed social norms and values. Islam, Hinduism, Buddhism, Christianity, and indigenous spirituality are the main religions that actively mold the perceptions of the various societies of South and Southeast Asia. Women in this region are at the center of the family structure, at least performing managerial roles within the house, if not cooking, cleaning, and washing. Young girls are venerated and even worshipped because of their feminine qualities of chastity and innocence, yet as they grow into adulthood and move from one role to another—from daughter to daughter-in-law, mother, and mother-in-law—the girls are perpetually under the watchful gaze of their mother, elders, and society. Girls in South Asia from their very birth are in a vulnerable position of segregation, marginalization, and oppression. When boys are born much celebration ensues, especially in countries such as India, Nepal, and Pakistan. When it is time for their education, boys in the home are given priority with quality of schools and higher education. When a girl is married, she has to juggle her roles as mother, wife, and daughter-law, and (if she has a job outside her home) career.

Throughout the pan-Asian region, times are changing, especially in the urban centers where increasing numbers of married and single women are opting to live independent lives as career women. Today, women are less bowed down by the burden of patriarchy and tradition, and perceptions about women continue to change for the better. Yet the changes seem to be taking place in urban settings, allowing traditional conservatism to prevail in Asia's rural areas.

Chapter 4 is concerned with women's roles in politics and their positions of power. Asian women have been at the forefront of political movements and revolutions. In spite of the low economic development compared to the countries of the West, fewer educational opportunities for women, and poor political participation at the national level, Asia has had several women political leaders in the twentieth century. In many ways, these women—who have been heads of states or government, or opposition leaders—all in one way or another have had kinship ties with male political power holders, either their fathers or husbands. And these female leaders come from elite Asian families, are well educated, and move in elite international political circles.

But the struggles of women have emerged from the need to demand rights to social justice from the grassroots level, from among the unskilled and uneducated women demanding rights to education, electoral rights, and right of access to unbiased civil laws. Women's rights advocates have participated in all women's protest demonstrations or colluded with the men in national movements and struggles. But slowly, many of these women's protest groups that initially struggled for social and economic rights veered toward political activism and ideology, eventually working under male political patrons. Corazon Aquino of the Philippines, Indira Gandhi of India, Benazir Bhutto of Pakistan, and Sirimavo Bandaranaike of Sri Lanka are some of the staunch female political leaders of Asia, who have also helped to bring down dictators or else are remembered for their political prowess. At present leaders such as Sheikh Hasina and Khalida Zia of Bangladesh, Sonia Gandhi of India, and Aung San Suu Kyi of Myanmar exercise political power in their respective countries.

Chapter 5 examines women's contributions to literature. A major corpus of literature written by women emanated in the form of resistance (or in retaliation) to the contemporary norms and values as well as the oppressive belief systems that prevailed around Asia. Theirs was a voice in search of an individual identity, a need to understand the self, and a modus operandi to find a center stage where men had been operating all along. Tied to this particular aspect of the self was women's involvement in national struggles, political upheavals, and struggles against imperial powers. Out of this history of revolutionary struggle emerged strong literature about women and written by women. It was mainly poetry and songs that carried the oral tradition of folk tales through which women initially expressed their dissatisfaction with their own status in the family and society. Next was story writing, short stories as well as longer fiction, which was another way to either capture the trauma and travails of the revolutions and political struggles or to express their own deeper feelings that otherwise went unexpressed in real life. Magazines and periodicals were other mediums through which women from different walks of life could interact and initiate discussions on issues important to them. In the last decades of the twentieth century, the specific themes of women's writings slowly began to shift so that together with expressions of the self, these female writers began to incorporate broader subject matter. In their writings, they prioritized the diaspora, feminism, psychosexual dilemmas, and marginalized communities. Thus women through literature have been effectively rewriting their roles in literary history.

Finally, Chapter 6 focuses on women's changing roles in relation to the broad sweep of history and the impact of postmodern globalization. Many women in Asia have had personal experiences of living in areas adversely impacted by conflicts and wars, impoverishments and environmental degradation, and tourism of the culturally insensitive sort. They have participated in independence movements and then liberation and human rights movements, some of which have successfully toppled abusive and authoritarian dictatorships. Women decision makers in Asia today, and throughout history, have had to interact and come to terms with the issues and concerns of the historical period in which they are situated in culturally unique ways and in relation to their circumstances. The consumerist mentality of global capitalism and media notions of what it means to be in love have introduced new forms of culturally attuned courtship rituals and ideas about women and marriage to some traditional communities, while internet dating is transforming local marriage practices across the region. Modern globalization and cultural change have brought many new challenges and opportunities to women in Asia. They endured much suffering during the twentieth century and yet have gone on to make tremendous strides for women's emancipation and empowerment.

NOTES

1. Jack Weatherford, *The Secret History of the Mongol Queens* (New York: Crown, 2010).

2. Patricio Abinales and Donna Amoroso, *State and Society in the Philippines* (New York: Rowman and Littlefield, 2005).

3. Kathleen Nadeau, *The History of the Philippines* (Westport, CT: Greenwood, 2008), 23.

4. Resil Mojares, "The Formation of a City: Trade and Politics in Nineteenth Century Cebu," *Philippine Quarterly of Culture and Society* 19 (1991): 288–95.

5. Cristina Blanc-Szanton, "Collision of Cultures: Historical Reformulation of Gender in Lowland Visayas, Philippines," in *Power and Difference in Island Southeast Asia*, Jane Atkinson and Shelly Errington, eds. (Stanford, CA: Stanford University Press, 1990).

6. Shelly Errington, "Recasting Gender and Power: A Theoretical and Regional Overview," in *Power and Difference in Island Southeast Asia*, Jane Atkinson and Shelly Errington, eds. (Stanford, CA: Stanford University Press, 1990).

1

———∞∞∞———

Women and Religion

Moral theologies and legal codes governed precolonial social relationships of power and dominance in early Asian civilizations. These societies were mostly based on open and closed systems of slavery in which people were in and out of debt to one another. However, slavery in Asia was not the same as the Euro-American transatlantic slave trade, which treated human beings as if they were commodities. By contrast, Asian slavery modes were social organizations working in terms of their religious moorings. While the institutionalization of slavery may have nothing to do with Buddhism and Confucianism, for example, as envisioned by the founders Buddha and Confucius, they still advocated a specific social order of hierarchy, namely that of serving the king. While Buddhism diverged from Hinduism, it continued to be informed by Hindu cultural ideas and practices. The Buddhist occupation with merit making and harmonious coexistence with all living entities, coupled with Hindu notions of caste and hierarchy, coalesced with the open system of slavery as practiced in ancient Thailand. In comparison, the Chinese Confucian interest in following lines of authority through kingship that ranked people according to age level and that placed ancestors over the living, seniors over juniors, males over females, and male scholars over commoners fit nicely with the closed system of slavery in Vietnam.

Historian James Watson explains that an open system of slavery is one in which a person of slave status has some opportunity to move either out of slavery in terms of freedom or out of slavery in terms of becoming part of the kinship group.[1] Ancient Thailand (Siam) provides a typical model of this system, which partially still exists, albeit in distorted form. This system is commonly thought to be the result of having an abundance of land but too few people. This creates a need for laborers to work the land as well as the need for a broader selection of spouses and sexual partners. This limited supply of people, explains Watson, usually results in a system of slavery that is open because the slaves may eventually be incorporated into the dominant group, and the division of the available land resulting from this inclusion is not an issue of concern.

In contrast, a closed system of slavery is one in which there is practically no opportunity for a change in status. A closed system refers to a situation in which land is considered a highly valuable resource such as in China prior to the nineteenth century. This system is controlled by the dominant lineages. Because access to landed inheritance is restricted, the status of slaves is more inclined to remain stationary; they are not accepted into the controlling kinship lines under any but unusual circumstances (e.g., adopting a male heir). It is this stationary position of status that most definitely marks a closed system, explains Watson.[2]

This chapter provides an overview of women's roles in Hinduism, Buddhism, and Confucianism, and then examines some of the precolonial religious and social roles performed by Asian women: (1) as temple dancers, courtesans, concubines, and wives by way of examples coming from ancient India, China, and Thailand and (2) as shamans in Korea and the Philippines. While Confucian government officials in Korea perceived shamans to be a threat to their authority and down casted them, Spanish colonizers in the Philippines viewed shamans as competitors and demonized them for the made-up crime of witchcraft. But European witch lore diverges from that of Southeast Asia when it comes to matters of sex and gender, which also is discussed in this chapter. The conclusion is that sex and gender relations are socially and culturally constructed, and must be situated in the historical contexts in which they are grounded and against which women's liberation can be theorized.

WOMEN IN HINDUISM

Hinduism is the oldest major religion in the world. Its earliest known history is found in the Vedas, which are ancient Indian scripts that date back to between 1700 and 900 BCE. The Vedas recorded the history of a warlike North Central Asian people known as the Aryans, who first arrived in India around 1500 BCE. Over time, gradual overlays of incoming Aryan migrants pushed the majority northern Dravidians south where today, the Tamils of southern India remain the largest population of indigenous Dravidian descent. The Aryans eventually occupied the whole subcontinent except for the south. Their Vedic poems were memorized and sung through the generations, until the development of the Sanskrit writing system in the 500s BCE. The Aryans modified many pre-existing religious beliefs and customs to make

Krishna conversing with a lady in a pavilion, Malwa school, 17th century. A subplot of the Hindu epic Mahabharata is the appropriate conduct between men and women. (Stapleton Collection/Corbis)

them their own. They changed the caste system (a pre-existing way of organizing work groups) into a more rigid hierarchical structure, probably to further buttress themselves into upper-caste leadership roles. The caste system is mainly composed of the four following groups. At the top are the Brahmans, or priests, who advised kings in the old days, while today, they work in various occupations and professions. Next are the Kshatriyas, or nobles and warriors; below them are the Vaisya, or craftspeople and merchants; and the final caste is the Sudras, or servants and laborers, who were most likely Dravidian during the Vedic era. While today caste discrimination still exists—for example, it exerts a formable influence on local marriage arrangements in India—the scheduled caste system, like affirmative action in the United States, mandates equal opportunity for all, without consideration of gender, religion, or caste affiliation. For example, universities and parliament have reserved seats for women, minorities, and lower caste groups.

Ancient Hinduism is replete with major and minor gods and goddesses associated with nature. Gods and goddesses in the religion of Hinduism are considered to be role models of what it means to be a virtuous human being. While there are multiple gods and goddesses in Hinduism, at root, it is still a monotheistic religion because all gods and goddesses are considered to be mere emanations of a single godhead, Atman or Brahman, according to the most ancient Hindu scriptures written in Sanskrit. As the anthropologist David Kinsley explains, the Rig-Veda is the oldest and most important text for the study of female goddesses in Hinduism.[3] Seven major Rig-Veda goddesses are (1) Usas, goddess of dawn; (2) Prithivi, goddess of earth; (3) Aditi, goddess of mothering presence, who interestingly has no male consort; (4) Sarasvati, goddess of a particular mighty river, the name of which has been lost to history; (5) Vac, goddess of speech; (6) Nirrti, goddess of the dead and undead; and (7) Ratri, goddess of the night. There are numerous other minor goddesses named in the Vedas. Early goddesses are almost always hidden aspects of nature, as the following description of Usas illustrates:

> Usas, the goddess of dawn, reveals herself with coming of daily light in the world. A young maiden pulled by a horse drawn chariot, she is followed by the sun, Surya, who urges her onward. She is asked to chase away evil demons, to send them far away. As the dawn, she is said to rouse all life, to set all things in motion, and to send people off to do their duties. She sets the curled up sleepers on their way to offer their sacrifices and thus renders service to the other gods. Usas gives strength and fame. She is the light, which impels life and is associated with the breath and life of all living creatures. She moves with rta, cosmic, social, and moral order. As the regularly recurring dawn she reveals and participates in cosmic order and is the foe of all chaotic forces that threaten the world.
>
> Usas is generally an auspicious goddess associated with light and wealth. She is often likened to a cow. She is called the mother of cows and, like a cow yields its udder for the benefit of people, so Usas bares her breasts to bring light for the benefit of humankind. Although Usas is usually described as a young and beautiful maiden, she is also called the mother of the gods and the Asvins, a mother by her petitioners, she who tends all things like a good matron, and goddess of the hearth.
>
> Usas observes all that people do, especially as she is associated with the light that uncovers everything from darkness and with rta, moral as well as cosmic order. She is said to be the eye of the gods. She is known as she who sees all, but she is rarely invoked to forgive human transgressions. It is more typical to invoke her to drive away or punish one's enemies. Finally, Usas

known as the goddess, reality, or presence that wears away youth. She is described as a skilled huntress who wastes away the lives of people. In accordance with the ways of rta, she wakes all living things but does not disturb the person who sleeps in death. As the recurring dawn, Usas is not only celebrated for bringing light from darkness. She is also petitioned to grant long life, as she is a constant reminder of people's limited time on earth. She is the mistress of the marker of time.[4]

Productive and regenerative powers of the universes are a constant theme in Hinduism.[5] From ancient times to the present, Hindus, like Buddhists, have venerated and revered the sacred linga, or phalli, symbols of creation. Architect and Asian studies specialist Nelson Wu explains that a tiny mound of sand molded in the form of a phallus by the hands of a holy Brahman in a roadside shrine is as sacred a sign as a column or phallic-like temple of a linga.[6] The linga, however, is not the actual and real iconic object of worship for Hindus. Rather, it serves as a visual aid for their further reflection upon that which is unseen and beyond the physical plane in which we live.

Linga also represents the Lord Shiva, the god of creation and dance. Lord Shiva and his consort, a devadasi dancer, a subject discussed in detail later in this chapter, together dance creation into being. Worshippers venerate the lingam of Shiva as a treasure of sensual love. They imagine it in the form of the father and mother embrace, or Siva Linga, which rises from the yoni (vulva) base. The uniting of Siva (male) and Sakti (female) bring together the divine and human, that which can be seen and unseen, as when the rain from the sky fertilizes the earth, It is the meeting of the creative principle of life with the productive forces of the universe, symbolically reflected in the sacred act of intercourse as cosmic union.

By contrast, the female partner, Yoni, derives from the Sanskrit term *yauna* (water) and translates as "vagina." It is the female counterpart of the lingam, or phallus, in indigenous South Asian Indian, Hindu, and Buddhists contexts. The word according to ancient sacred Vedic and Bhagavad Gita texts is used variously to refer to vagina or vulva, womb, birth canal, source or point of origin, place of birth, fountainhead, fertility, bountiful harvest, place of rest, repository, receptacle, heavenly seat or abode, and home. The original meaning of yoni in astrological terms is divine passage. A child was considered to come from a yoni, or constellation of stars, that prevailed in the heavens during the time of the child's birth.

Hindus believe in reincarnation, or the cycle of death and rebirth, and in this context, yoni refers to a life form, be that a plant, insect, fish, bird, animal, or human. Life begins at death, when the soul takes its journey to rebirth. A person's station of rebirth is contingent on whether they lived meritoriously during their lifetime. A meritorious life consists of acts of compassion or good deeds for others, whether fellow humans, animals, or any other living thing. A human birth occurs based on having acquired good or bad karma (deeds). It is believed that before a person is born, they have passed through many cycles of yoni (or previous lifetimes) as, for example, an insect, fish, bird, or animal. A human being who reaches enlightenment breaks the cycle of death and rebirth to attain Nirvana, eternal bliss, or union with Brahma, the god of creation.

Yoni also refers to an empty space, or void, enclosed by a system of walls. It is the opposite of lingam, or solid. This enclosure of space, as in a sacred cave, is indicative of the intense concentration of emotion it takes for proper worship to occur, in contrast to the open and unharnessed space of the outside world. Yoni also refers to the base of the Siva Linga, the father-mother embrace in which Brahma, Siva, and Vishnu are embodied and emerge—Siva being the destroyer, Brahma the creator, and Vishnu the sustainer of life in accordance with the ancient Hindu trinity of one god. Yoni, the female principle, contains these three powerful deities as the root of Sakti, or the creator of all living things.

During the medieval period (550–1500), despite women's power and freedom as expressed in the ancient Rg-Vedas, and later Bhagavad Gita, her status began to go down. India suffered many invasions during this dark period. The great Muslim invasions, beginning in the eighth century and culminating in the eleventh century, brought different and opposing cultural ideas about women's roles in family and society. From the early Muslim perspective, women had no free will because they were always considered to be the personal property of their father, brother, or husband. Indian scholars Babita and Sanjay Twari explain that early Muslim ideas influenced many Hindu attitudes about girl children and women in traditional Indian society.[7] Indian fathers and husbands wanted to protect daughters and wives from being kidnapped and thrown into harems by the invaders. In an effort to better protect them, local women began to wear the veil (*purdah*) and to cover their bodies. Women were no longer free, like men, to walk about and work outside the home.

Modern Hindu women, by comparison, are freer to make their own decisions and work outside the home in accordance with their individual and familial circumstances. They often enjoy many of the freedoms that come along with their responsibilities as contributors to the family. Still, they face many challenges in the context of a traditionally patriarchal Indian society. While the role of women in Hinduism has undergone tremendous changes since ancient times, the position of the female goddesses in relation to male gods continues to have a positive influence on women's status today.

WOMEN IN BUDDHISM

Buddhism is a rich and culturally diverse set of beliefs and practices that revolve around the teachings of the historical Buddha, who first articulated his message of salvation in the sixth century BCE. Since the formation of the earliest Buddhist communities in India, this religious view and way of life has been constantly changing as it continues to spread and take hold of new values and customs. There remains, however, great similarity between the practices of the geographically varied and historically disparate Buddhist societies and cultures.

As with all major world religions, there is no singular and definitive definition of Buddhism. It needs to be examined within the contexts of the cultures in which it took root. Buddhism continues to grow today, especially in East Asia, Southeast Asia, Central Asia, Central Mongolia, and the United States and Europe, as it offers believers alternative approaches to ecology and society.

Traditional accounts of Buddha's life and teachings have been widely disseminated through various media, including art and architecture, song and dance, and ritual and scripture. Most of these accounts are didactic. Buddha was born the princely son Siddhartha of a Hindu king and queen who surrounded his preciousness with all the pleasures and delights of this world. One day, Prince Siddhartha stepped outside the palace gate for the first time and encountered ordinary people suffering from sickness, disease, old age, and the final stages of dying. Deeply puzzled, he began to reflect upon the question of how to solve these problems of sickness and suffering in the world. Leaving home against the wishes of his bereaving and beloved wife and family, Siddhartha spent the rest of his life developing a more egalitarian religion than Hinduism, one for ordinary people. He studied many yogic disciplines ranging from techniques for entering mystical states to severe bodily chastisements and concluded that self-mortification would not solve the problems of birth, sickness, aging, and death. At the age of 34, he sat and meditated under a Bodhi tree all night long. After fending off attacks by Mara (the world of illusion) and his army, he awakened with the dawn to a new and transcendental state of wisdom and enlightenment (nirvana) that allowed him to become the Buddha.

During his lifetime, Buddha's teachings spread throughout north India, neighboring kingdoms, and beyond. He broke all boundaries of caste; disciples included kings, priests, nuns, merchants, farmers, outcastes, yogi mendicants, robbers, and thieves. He led by virtue of his illustrious example. His majesty awed kings, while his compassionate heart allowed him to comfort the sick and downtrodden. Ever mindful and calm, the Buddha directly faced adversities and dangers with composure and wisdom. He taught a widening circle of lay followers, as well as a core religious community, or Sangha, of nuns and monks responsible for spreading his message.

Buddha welcomed women monastics only after his aunt Mahaprajapati, who had raised him from birth, asked that she and an accompanying group of female companions be allowed to shave their heads, put on the robes, and take the vow of poverty to join the inner sanctum of Buddha's followers who had completely renounced the world. Religious studies professor Rita Gross explains that at first the Buddha refused their request but eventually gave way and allowed the institution of the nuns order to be established.[8] However, the nuns were required to accept eight special rules as a precondition for their admission to the order. These rules subordinated the nuns' order to the monks' order. Many female monastics, during his lifetime, attained nirvana. Nirvana, or the extinction of worldly desires and cravings that brings an end to the seemingly ceaseless cycle of rebirths, is the goal of early Buddhism. These women's stories sung in the form of eloquent poems were collected in the Therigatha verses of the elder nuns. This cannon was preserved in the form of Theravada Buddhism, which is the form of Buddhism found in Southeast Asia today.

The Buddha, Prince Siddhartha Gautama, died at the age of 80 in the home of a benefactor who inadvertently served him a meal made with poisonous mushrooms. Even dying, he reached out and consoled his friend, thanking her for the meal that allowed him to enter into nirvana's eternal bliss. It is said that Buddha instructed his followers to cremate his body and distribute his ashes among the various groups of his followers, who were to enshrine them in stupas (relic mounds). These South and Southeast Asian sites have become places of pilgrimage for Buddhists, as they represent places where Buddha is present. Early texts and archaeological records are replete with records of worship at stupas connected with key places in Buddha's life, such as the sites of his birth, enlightenment, first teachings, and death. However, stupas are also found in places that predate Buddhism.

By the seventh century, the practice of enshrining the sacred relics of the Buddha was no longer evident in the archaeological record. It was replaced by the practice of enshrining small tablets engraved with a four-line verse believed to be the culmination of Buddha's teachings:

> Of all those things that from a cause arise
> Tathagata the cause thereof has told
> And how they cease to be that too be told
> This is the doctrine of the great recluse

While the exact interpretation of this pithy saying has been widely debated, Buddhist generally agree that it contains the essence of the four noble truths that the Buddha taught during his lifetime.[9]

Many contemporary engaged Buddhists participate in new social and religious movements that call for world peace and ecological replenishment of the planet. Their actively nonviolent involvement coincides with Buddha's this-worldly teachings. Cultural tolerance, religious pluralism, and the feminist concern for human, animal, and environmental well-being are common themes in these new movements. Buddhism continues to take many forms in many places as it adapts to specific cultures and changes in accordance with local situational contexts and in relation to global processes. While some Buddhists make a conscious decision to retreat from the human world in an effort to escape from suffering, others—as exemplified later in this chapter—choose to get involved in social action work, even at great risk to themselves. Buddhism of this latter sort is best understood as a living process that traverses religious and political boundaries, intersecting with a wide ecumenical array of humanitarian movements.

WOMEN IN CONFUCIANISM

The founder of Confucianism, Confucius, was born at a time when China was threatened with disintegration, known in Chinese annals as the "Spring and Autumn period" (Ch'un Ch'iu), from 722 to 481 BCE. The golden age of the Chou Dynasty had fallen apart, and conflict and disruption had set in, threatening the rule of the emperor. Feudal princes, inspired by greed and the lust for power, were warring against each other in contradiction to ancient ethical codes of how to behave honorably. Corruption in governance was rife, and massacres and bloodshed were rampant throughout the land. In the province of Lu, where Confucius was born in 551 BCE, the reigning duke was harassed by dissentions, and lesser members of his house threatened to take over his royal power. It is likely that living in this time of war and turmoil led Confucius to develop a lifelong appreciation for the importance of social and family order and civility.

Early twentieth-century journalist, museum curator, and scholar Francis Ruth Grant (1896–1993)[10] reiterated the popular ancestral narrative of Confucius's life. He was born of the illustrious Kung family, which could trace its roots back 18 centuries to the founder Hwang Ti. In the days of Confucius's grandfather, political turmoil forced the family to leave their homes and settle in Lu, where the father of Confucius, Kung Shu Liang Hih, was born. Confucius's father became famous as a military officer who exhibited strength and courage under fire. During the siege of Pihyang in 562 BCE, a group of his men were about to be trapped by a dropping gate that he caught and raised, enabling all of them to escape. Notwithstanding his many feats, he had nine daughters but no son to carry on his family name. At 70 years of age, Shu Liang Hih approached the royal house of Yen and asked to marry one of the three daughters. Yen's two eldest daughters refused to marry such an old man, while the youngest, Chiangste, replied, "Merely designate your wish, father." Thus Yen gave his youngest daughter, Chiangste, to the warrior. Grant explains that, especially before the rise of Maoist China, Yen modeled traditional family fidelity from the male oriented Chinese Confucian perspective. However, most modern Chinese young adults, today, have a say in who'll they'll marry, even when their marriages are arranged. Feeling pressure from her responsibility to produce a son, Chiangste climbed the sacred Mount Ni and prayed for a son from Heaven.

Legend has it that auspicious omens accompanied the birth of Chiangste's illustrious son, who is popularly believed to have been born in a cave in Mount Ni. Two dragons are said to have appeared in the heavens, together with five sages, at the time of his birth. Music floated through the atmosphere when Confucius's mother went into labor. Upon the body of her son were 49 marks signifying his unique destiny, and his head was shaped like Mount Ni. While there are many legendary renditions of the birth of Confucius, invariably they report that he grew up in humble circumstances. Despite not coming from a wealthy family, Confucius's mother persisted in her efforts to give her son the best possible education.

Confucius's father died when he was only three years old, entrusting him to the care of his mother. It is said that his favorite childhood games were imitating ceremonial rites, which are fertile expressions of religious and cultural traditions. His passion for knowledge absorbed him, and at 15, he became an assistant teacher. At 17, apparently in need of material means, he sought employment to help to support his mother. He obtained a local position as a director of agricultural works; it is said that the harvest was bountiful and the cattle thrived under his watch. At 19, he married the daughter of a noble Sung family, and the couple had a son and two daughters. By the time his son was born, Confucius already had established his reputation, for the Prince of Lu sent him a symbolic gift of a carp. Confucius, aware of propriety, named his son Carp (Li). Thereafter, explains Grant, there is scant information in the historical record about his family.[11]

Confucius's mother died when he was 24 years old, and in accordance with the profound significance attached to mourning for the dead, Confucius removed himself from public life for three years. He meditated and studied ancient ceremonial and political texts. Emerging from his reclusive retreat, he began teaching. Throughout his life, Confucius humbly insisted that he was not an original thinker. Rather, he was a great synthesizer. He honed and developed his precepts from the literary and historical record left by ancient sages. He believed that his scholarly pursuits were mandated by heaven. Heaven from the ancient Chinese perspective can be likened to a creative life-giving spirit that is immanent everywhere in nature and the human world. Like his predecessors, Confucius was a keen observer of nature, and he believed in the sacredness of all natural life. Accordingly, the sage considered that his destiny was to lead men and women back to a love of their fellows. He thought they could best serve heaven by serving each other. In a period when anarchy threatened to disrupt civil society, Confucius imparted to his students the ideals of justice and order that typified the ancient Shang and Yu kingdoms, which can be traced in the archaeological record to the twenty-fourth century BCE.

Confucius thought that it was important to put scholarly ideas into practice for the future benefit of society. Therefore, he traveled for most of his life in search of a high political position that would enable him to serve his fellows to the best of his ability. He wanted to make life comfortable for everyone. Confucius yearned to implement ancient philosophical principles, ethical doctrines, and political economy into the prevailing structures of government.

In 517 BCE, the political factions that threatened to disrupt the kingdom of Lu broke out into chaos and anarchy. Realizing the futility of remaining in his native province, Confucius traveled to the neighboring kingdom of Chou. He hoped that the local prince would offer him a government post. However, the ruler offered him only a pension. Perhaps the prince thought that if Confucius were given real power and authority, he would expose the already corrupt government. Refusing the pension, Confucius devoted the next 15 years of his life to teaching and research. His thoroughness in every field of knowledge is remarkable. According to legend, he is reputed to have studied philosophy with Loa Tze, music under Chang Hung and Su Hsiang, and politics under Tang Tau. Although it is not likely that Confucius was mentored by these ancient and legendary masters, the legends point to the reverence Chinese people have for his thorough and well-rounded education.

The ancient teachings of Confucius have continued to influence the people of China, Korea, Japan, and Vietnam into the present period. The philosopher Joel Kupperman explains that although Confucian attitudes toward gender, family life, and hierarchy were probably around during the time of Confucius, they most likely gave way for women's individual self-expression and mobility at the marketplace as well as decision-making power within the farm household.[12] Also, peasant women in pre-Maoist China have enjoyed more economic independence in terms of working outside and participating in household decisions than did their upper-class sisters. Confucianism as a system of governance mandated by the state was not officially instituted as part of the established order until the Han dynasty (206 BCE–220 CE). Kupperman speculates that much of the (neo-Confucian) rhetoric that belittles and subordinates women probably was added on long after Confucius's lifetime.[13] Nevertheless, he explains that older sisters were never allowed to play the role of older brothers in the ritual ceremonial life described in the *Analects of Confucius*.

The *Analects* is one of the most reliable works on Confucius's life. It is a concise collection of his sayings and activities, written by his disciples. It is said that Confucius wrote *Spring and Autumn* and edited the *Book of Poetry or Songs*, the *Book of Rites*, the *Book of Records*, and the *Book of Changes*. Later during the Sung dynasty (960–1279), scholars brought together the *Analects*, the *Mencius*, the *Ta Hsueh* (Great Learning) written by Tseng Shen (a disciple of Confucius), and the *Chung Yang* (Doctrine of the Mean) written by Tzu Ssu (the grandson of Confucius). They named this collection Four Books. The Four Books together with the Five Classics (collected, organized, and edited by Confucius) became the basis for education in China from 1313 to 1912. They formed the basis for the competitive civil service exams that were mandatory for approximately 600 years. Even today, the effects of this examination system are visible in the national college-level entrance examinations of Taiwan, Japan, and Korea.

From the perspective of modern times, it is difficult to imagine that during Confucius's lifetime, all formal communication between the emperor and his people took place through the form of flowery oratory and musical ballads. Ancient emperors listened to the heartbeat and pulse of the nation through the folk poetry and songs of their people. As stated in the *Book of Rites*: "Each five years, the Son of Heaven makes progress through the kingdom and the Grand Music Master is commanded to lay before him the poems of different states."[14] These alliterated poems by the common people were studied by royal scholars, for through them, and between the lines, in the absence of a press, the condition and well-being of each province in the kingdom was articulated. Ancient Chinese rulers were aware that the singing of poems provided a safety valve for the people to relieve their stresses.

Poetry also was an important part of the performance of religious and governmental ceremonies. No ceremonial ritual was complete without the recitation and singing of poetry. The cultivated person was knowledgeable in poetry. Confucius wrote in the *Analects*: "A man may be expected to act well in government service after he has mastered 300 lyrical poems."[15] Men, not women, in ancient China were allowed to compete through rigorous examination for government posts. It is said that the itinerant teacher Confucius collected over 3,000 poems throughout the various provinces of the country, out of which he selected and used only about 310 poems in his written works. These poems covered diverse subjects from tributes to heaven or the emperor to love poems and poems about the beauty of nature.

Master Confucius attracted a large following of disciples from different social, cultural, and economic circumstances. It is said that he attracted several thousand avid students in his lifetime. He refused no seeker his guidance, no matter how humble their origins. He was known to say to his students, "I was born with knowledge. I am the only one who has given himself to the study of antiquity and am diligent in seeking for the understanding of such studies."[16] During his journeys, Confucius drew parables based on his personal experiences and observations of real social life that corresponded to the ideals of past scholars about familial and social life. His hierarchical model of family and society will be deconstructed from a feminist perspective later in this chapter.

Finally, explains Grant, Confucius and his students walked mostly on foot across China.[17] They underwent many hardships, including starvation, humiliation, and persecution. At one point, an assassin almost murdered Confucius. However, Confucius always showed himself to be an exemplary leader of impeccable moral character. He encouraged his disciples to strive to become better human beings by living virtuous lives. This ideal was epitomized in the life and teachings of Confucius.

At the age of 68, Confucius was invited back to Lu by the sovereign ruler, where he spent the rest of his life editing the classical texts and continuing his teaching. Despite his ardent desire to transmit his political theories into the structures of government, Confucius recognized that legitimate power and authority did not come from a high-sounding official title. When one of his students resented Confucius's not holding a high political office, Confucius replied: "You remember the Book defines a good son as being ever-dutiful, and a friend of his brothers, thus, giving the example of good rule. This, too, is to rule. What need, then, of office?"[18] In 479 BCE, Confucius died at the age of 72 and was buried in his hometown of Chufu.

INDIA'S *DEVADASI* AND COURTESANS

The term "devadasi" (temple dancer) derives from the root word "deva," which means a being of light, one who radiates or shines. Deva is another word for god, and devadasi literally means one who is married to the gods.[19] In precolonial times, a devadasi was a woman dedicated to caring for a temple and learning the sacred poetry and music of India. Scholars have traced the devadasi tradition back to the Chola period (850–1300 CE), as most of the Vishnu scriptures containing reference to them were written during this period.[20] The devadasi dancers were supposed to bring forth the order of the universe that their husband, Shiva, was supposed to introduce in the universe as Natraj, the god of dance. While epic stories of India were inscribed on temple walls and popularly danced out in music and song as a way to propagate Hinduism, especially to those who could not read or write, it was only the devadasi who, symbolically, married a god. Her marriage was re-enacted in many and various ritual forms at the different community levels, which accorded her a special place in the gender hierarchy. She could never marry a man and for this reason was considered to be a most fortunate woman who would never suffer the pains of widowhood. Unlike widows and other unlucky women who were not allowed to participate in auspicious ceremonial rituals, the devadasis were always invited, especially to weddings, for they were believed to be always fertile and unaffected by the biological cycle. They could form long-term sexual relationships with high-caste men who supported their temple communities, and it was this sexual aspect of their lives that caught the attention of the British colonizers.

The British overlords greatly degraded the formerly high status of the devadasi to that of a common prostitute. Sociologist Jogan Shankar explains that in 1882, social reformers and Christian lobbyists began to pressure the British administration to abolish all ceremonies that dedicated girl children to Hindu shrines.[21] They organized conferences and rallies to create public opinion against the devadasi system. Feminist historian Philippa Levine states that "from the 1860s, convictions for the dedication of girl children to 'temple harlotry' under section 372 and 373 of the Indian Penal Code became increasingly common."[22] Further, the devadasi's secular counterpart, the courtesan who entertained only high-caste men in precolonial times and was part of royal courts, suffered a similar fate. They, like the devadasis, were labeled "nautch girls" by the British authorities who, under pressure from puritanical abolitionists and reformers in England, initiated a series of antinautch campaigns that worked to abolish this occupation. These incessant campaigns largely contributed to the massive dislocation and impoverishment of the devadasis and courtesans. Many, not all of whom were out of work, were forced to work as common prostitutes.

The British colonial population in India consisted predominantly of male soldiers and officials, overseers and businessmen, and laborers. Prostitution developed locally among the disenfranchised and poor after the colonizers entered the scene. Prostitutes appeared around British colonial installations and encampments, after which brothels emerged. These brothels were legalized and monitored by British health officials, who stigmatized and criminalized prostitutes as the source of sexual disease among the troops. The British viewed prostitution as a necessary "evil" to service the soldiers who were instrumental in maintaining the imperial order. Levine states that "for nineteenth century European colonialism, male desire was a necessity for the maintenance of empire, and a powerful means to separate maleness and femaleness. But though such desire was marked as a driving force, it was female greed and native promiscuity that were seen as destructive, while male desire was regarded as harnessable and productive."[23] She goes on to explain that while this notion that prostitution exists outside of history to "cater to men's desires" is still around today, in practice prostitution is influenced by cultural mores and value systems of the dominant group.[24]

THAILAND'S CONCUBINES AND SECOND WIVES

Thai history is largely informed by the social teachings of Hinduism and Buddhism. Unlike in China or India, where genealogical links were traced largely through the male lines, in Thailand, genealogies are traced bilaterally through both male and female sides of the family. It is Thai daughters who are expected to care for parents in their old age. This horizontal status accorded to both sexes is offset in so far as Thai females are always considered the property of either the father's or husband's household. Historian Craig Reynolds explains that within the household, a woman's position is subordinate to that of a man, and the conjugal power of the husband was codified in an 1805 family law: "he managed the property held jointly by spouses and he could sell his wife or give her away, and he could administer bodily punishment to her, provided the degree of punishment was in proportion to the misdeed."[25] Female slaves were valued for their contribution to sexual reproduction and as second wives and concubines. Although a father or husband could sell his daughter or wife into slavery in times of starvation or financial crisis, he could keep her at home as long as he paid the interest on the loan. Also, according to historian Andrew Turton, a free man had to demonstrate that he was undergoing severe hardship before he could legally sell any member of his family into slavery, or he would be punished according to law.[26] Slaves had some legal rights against owners who abused them. They also could own property, and some were held positions of authority over other slaves and free clients.

Historically, Thais practiced an open system of slavery that was oriented around Buddhist theological ideas of a galactic order, and even the king of Siam considered himself to be a slave to Buddha. The ancient system of slavery in Thailand, like the Philippines, was a form of debt bondage, and men and women could buy their freedom. The king held most of the slaves and divided them between princes and leading monks in exchange for their loyal service in governing the kingdom. Slaves, courtesans, and second wives were a sign of luxury and wealth, but slaves worked alongside free persons. Free persons were self-sufficient farmers who also worked the king's land and could be called upon to provision food and labor on construction projects for the kingdom.

CHINA'S CONCUBINES AND SECOND WIVES

China has long been influenced by Confucian social teachings. Unlike in Thailand, where the family tree is traced bilaterally through male and female lines, genealogical links are recorded over the generations through males in China, Korea, and Japan. Chinese females typically are perceived as outsiders in the patrilineal context of the East Asian family system, and although this practice may be changing for some, it is still widespread, even in the diaspora. Chinese females are not named in ancestor rituals, so their primary role in the context of the traditional family system is to produce a male heir. During the communist period (1949–1977), Mao Tse Tung tried to eradicate some of the excesses of the Confucian family system that badly discriminated against women. The communist-led government banned the practice of foot-binding and called for greater equality between men and women. "Women hold up half of the sky" is an old saying popularized by then chairman Mao, but nevertheless, even today female fetuses are still the first to be aborted in favor of boys under modern China's one-child policy.[27]

Traditionally, especially before World War II, a Chinese woman could enter into domestic service as a maid or child servant, the latter of whom might be adopted as a sister or become part of the family. Or she would be arranged into an exogamous marriage, sometimes as a child bride. While the bride-price for the first wife was high, it was transformed into a dowry, and the marriage rite marked the transference of certain rights and privileges to her. In contrast, the primary role of second wives was to produce sons, and concubines were for pleasure. Matchmakers arranged the sale of maids, brides, concubines, and prostitutes behind private doors.

Watson explains that slaves in ancient China found themselves in a closed system.[28] As a rule, slaves were born into that state or purchased as children, and the wealthy purchased concubines. While the potential for slaves to change their status was open in Thailand (in ancient times called Siam), that opportunity was limited in China. China is a patrilineal society, and any inclusion of males who are not members of the lineage would threaten existing heirs because there would be further division of property at the death of the clan head. Therefore, male slaves who were not purchased as children for replacement heirs were in a permanent slave status, although eunuchs were accorded a high status because they were considered more loyal and powerful. In contrast, female slaves had more opportunity for improving their situation through marriage. Chinese women were and often still are considered to be outsiders, rather than members of the family, even when they marry inside the lineage group. Because they did not have any inheritance rights, they were considered non-threatening and therefore had some potential for social mobility.

China created its own supply of slaves from within by creating stratification within its social structure. The stigma attached to the status of slaves also marked their descendants. This was partially due to the practice of ancestor worship. The Chinese viewed their lineage as a requirement for being considered civilized. Because males were the carriers of the lineage, even the poorest farmers resisted selling their sons until all their daughters and even wife were sold. This attitude resulted in fewer males on the market, and the price of male slaves was higher than that of females. The practice repeatedly broke the male slave's line so that his hereditary line remained unknown, although in some instances, a new ancestral line might be bought in an effort to conceal lack of ancestry. Once a slave was purchased, the master was responsible for his upkeep and welfare. Females made up the largest portion of slaves; however, females and their children through marriage could lose the stigma of being a slave. Hence the Chinese system of concubines, courtesans, and second wives was based on use value, not exchange value, and slaves contributed to the total reproduction of the

A South Korean shaman performs an annual ritual dance ceremony to chase away evil spirits and pray for good luck for an old cargo ship embanked on the Han River, which flows across Seoul (2003). (AFP/Getty Images)

society. However, by the nineteenth century, this system began to be subsumed and transformed by the influx of colonial capitalists who introduced their foreign practice of buying and selling slaves as if they were chattel.

OUTCASTING OF KOREAN FEMALE SHAMANS

Korean Confucianism also is a patrilineal and patriarchal system that records family genealogies through male lines. Traditionally, only males could enter outside political life, while females usually were relegated to taking care of male-headed households. Only males could attend and officiate at important ancestor rites, while females—who married out and were not considered to be part of the family—increased their value only after producing male heirs. Children were taught to respect elders, boys were positioned over girls, and females were expected to obey and be subservient to their husbands and mothers-in-law. Traditional society was hierarchically organized and occupationally stratified in terms of sex lines that divided the domestic and public domains. Practically, women had no options other than arranged marriage, except for becoming a shaman, medicine woman, courtesan, or palace woman.

Anthropologist Youngsook Kim Harvey explains the long tradition of female shamanism in Korea. Today as in the past, there are two types of shamans: family priestesses who inherit their roles and professional shamans who work for a fee.[29] Professional shamans acquire their roles through the experience of four spirit possessions and rites of initiation conducted by a qualified shaman. Professionals enter a trance state and possess powers to perform services. Shaman séances are dominated, attended, and controlled almost exclusively by females, although there are some male shamans. This preoccupation of women with shamanism is understandable, considering that only males are named and honored in Confucian ancestor worship ceremonies held in ancestral villages and the home space. Who will remember deceased female relatives by name, if not shamans? Shamanism offers a way to recollect and appease otherwise restless and discontented spirits of the afterworld, among other services.

Shamanism predates the Yi Dynasty (1392–1910), when neo-Confucian government scholars and officials implemented a program of total social reform. They tried to eradicate shamanism because it appeared to be irrational in their scheme of the so-called rational society. At first, they criminalized shamans, banning them from practicing their profession in cities and towns. But shamans continued to carry on their work underground. Shamanism, not neo-Confucianism, met people's emotional and religious needs, which is why it flourished even in the face of adversity. Being unable to wipe it out, government officials imposed harsh restrictions on the practice of shamanism. Ever since, shamans have to be licensed for tax purposes. The position of shaman is a proscribed and outcaste status, which effectively restricts shamans from using their power and influence for family mobility. While today some shamans may become successful capitalist entrepreneurs, they cannot aspire to achieve any notable status in the hierarchical context of South Korean society.

After the fall of the Yi Dynasty (1910), subsequent governments continued the same persecution policy against shamanism. Even today, despite its popularity with the people, shamanism is rumored to be a base and low-class occupation. Today, Korean shamans continue to serve as religious functionaries and ethnopsychiatrists, explains Harvey. Clients call them to find out whether an ancestral spirit is comfortable, arrange reunions between dead ancestors and living descendants, pick auspicious days for weddings and burials, reveal causes of marital and family strife and advise resolution, find out about the situation of their children studying abroad, and heal the broken soul and body.

Interestingly, a woman is called to be a shaman through spirit possession sickness. Typically, those who are called to become shamans have endured dire economic circumstances and/or harsh treatment at the hands of their families for long periods of time. Until the point at which they fall ill, they may live with an overly demanding mother-in-law who expects too much of them or be married to an abusive husband who drinks and philanders all their money away. The family will bring in a Western doctor and use herbal remedies to help the sick woman recover, but to no avail. Then, they will bring in a shaman who diagnoses that the woman is suffering from spirit possession sickness. The sick woman and her family typically resist such a diagnosis because of the accompanying social stigma. Spirit possession sickness also indicates that something is amiss in the household, which is embarrassing. But unless the sick woman answers the call to become a shaman, she will continue to fall ill until she reaches the point of no recovery. Only by accepting the call can she get well. Acceptance brings some relief, as the family no longer has to spend its valuable resources on her medical care. It also causes some frustration and role reversals as the shaman, who now controls powerful ancestor spirits, becomes the new breadwinner and household head.

WITCHLORE IN SOUTH AND SOUTHEAST ASIA

Predominantly females but also transvestites played the role of shaman priestesses, mediums, and healers in the ancient Philippines. They participated in rituals and feasting ceremonies, and officiated in giving offerings of food and drink to the ancestors and nature spirits. As mediums, they could interpret people's dreams and signs in nature to predict the future. They were the keepers of sacred historical knowledge who were called upon during important rituals to chant epic myths that influenced local values and mores.[30]

However, Spanish colonization (1521–1896) of the Philippines brought an intolerant form of Christianity that was opposed to anyone who did not kneel to the cross and crown. Friars slandered and maligned the priestesses and shamans in an effort to negate the power of these women and institute a religious conversion of the population. The friars transposed shamans into witches to discredit them. Folklorist Hermina Menez explains that the colonizers attempted to instill fear in the people by calling shamans witches in consort with the devil.[31] She argues that this was one of the probable reasons witchlore of the flying half-headed female viscera sucker, a local variant of a witch, is found only in the Christian lowlands, especially the Visayan and Bicol regions, and not in the non-Hispanized uplands of Northern Luzon and Mindanao. Anthropologist Cristina Blanc-Szanton further discusses the changing status of women in relation to the Spanish colonization processes.[32] William Henry Scott provides detailed examples of precolonial women who enjoyed a politically and economically more balanced relationship with men than did their European counterparts.[33] Jesuit historian H. de la Costa wrote between the lines that women played more vital social roles as healers, warrior priestesses, and merchants before the colonial period.[34] He documents that female merchants swam out to meet the galleon ships when they first arrived. Female shamans performed the role of midwives and healers. They rallied forth together with men in rebellion against the colonial overlords.[35] Menez explains that the Spanish Catholics, with their dark and repressed attitudes toward sexuality, were shocked by the Filipinos' easy-going manners when it came to sexual behavior.[36] Colonial clerics zealously indoctrinated boys and men to take more control over women, put in place high standards for women's chastity, and allowed only male elites to take on roles of political significance.[37]

Spanish colonization changed everything about early society. They so vilified female shamans that they called them witches, colloquially referred to as aswangs. Cutting them in half to remove them from their sexual organs, the viscera sucker concept emerged from women's midwifery work because they are always around this material. Shaman priestesses, with their large followings, were perceived by the Spaniards to be powerful competitors. The Spaniards demonized the shamans and reinterpreted aswang lore into one based on the degradation of women healers and shamans in Europe. Yet even a cursory look at the aswang complex in the Philippines and nearby Malaysia and Indonesia reveals some significant cultural differences that include consideration of sex and gender, in comparison to Europe.

The aswang displays a particular set of characteristics that resemble some of the traits of Spanish and Portuguese witchlore. The aswang is a normal woman of considerable beauty by day. However, at night, she is able to transform herself into a horrible flying half-bodied female monster that takes flight. She then preys on the unsuspecting, sleeping population as a food source, focusing on infants and pregnant women. Through a long tongue she sucks out blood, viscera, and even fetuses. When compared to the early Spaniards' images of witches, the similarities found include the aspect of flying, feasting on children and/or drinking blood, being horrible to see, operating primarily in the dark of night, and being unsuspected by day.

"Bruja" is the Spanish name for witch, and they are often represented as being a living vampire, usually a female, who can transform themselves into various kinds of animals. They are generally reported as attacking primarily children. Another creature, found in Portugal, is much more like the aswang. The Portuguese bruxa, who is also female, is represented as being human by day and a bird by night. They suck the blood of children.[38] However, these examples represent the limit of similarities.

A Spanish witch is not viewed as beautiful at any specific time. On the contrary, she is most often represented as an ugly hag. She flies but only through the use of a magic broom or through the application of a magical ointment and usually, aside from bruxa, she cannot fly at all as a result of some special anatomical peculiarity. She goes undetected not so much through the use of disguise, as with the aswang, but through the image of being a helpless old lady. This suggests that the aswang myth is probably derived from the precolonial context of Southeast Asia, rather than Spain. At the same time, the Spanish demonization of shamans as aswangs, corroborates Menez's argument that the Spanish friars manipulated and used local myths to undermine the power and prestige of Philippine priestesses.

In the Philippines, different ethnic groups have different names for creatures like the aswang. That is, the word "aswang" is a general category that everyone seems to understand, even when they use a different term to describe their type of creature. For example, Cebuanos use the word "ungu" for ghost witches who ride through the streets at night looking for children, which are their favorite prey.[39] The Tagalogs describe the manananggal as an older beautiful woman capable of severing her upper torso in order to fly into the night with huge bat wings to prey on unsuspecting pregnant women in their homes. Using an elongated proboscis-like tongue, she sucks the hearts of fetuses or blood of unsuspecting victims. And there are other variants.

In Malaysia, the myth of the penanggalan is similar to that of the aswang. This female monster consists of a head that dangles entrails behind as she flies. The penanggalan actually separates from her whole, similar to the separation process of the aswang, leaving her motionless and gutless body hidden while the flying head goes about its gruesome business. She seeks out the blood of children or the blood of remaining childbirth. Another type of Malaysian vampire is the pontianak. The pontianak is usually a beautiful woman who died in childbirth and becomes undead, seeking revenge and terrorizing villages. She often appears as a beautiful woman, and there is a strong scent of frangipani (a local flower), which also is what happens when an aswang appears on the island of Cebu in the Philippines. Men who are not careful will be killed when she changes into a vampire. She also will eat babies and harm pregnant women. People believe that having a sharp object like a nail helps them fend off potential attacks by pontianaks, the nail being used to plug a hole in the back of a pontianak's neck. The Javanese vampire, the hannya, is likewise believed to have been formerly a beautiful woman. However, she was unfortunate enough to go insane. She feeds upon infants. Sundal bolong, also from Java, is yet another vampire-like creature that drinks blood primarily from men.[40]

There are some significant cultural differences that separate the Southeast Asian vampire myths from those of Spain and Portugal. There are distinct differences in terms of the way gender relations have been, historically, constructed in regional Southeast Asia in comparison to those of Spain, and by extension, Western Europe. From the perspective of the colonizers, a woman's place was in the home. She was seen as the natural caregiver for children. The common theme of Spanish vampire folklore implies that female revenants, in particular those who have died as a result of childbirth, return to prey on children. In some ways, this might seem to imply that men feel powerless over the product of their own ancestral line and/or over the birthing process that represents a threat to the continued relationship with their wives.

Upon examining European vampire lore in general, male vampires are common and are frequently represented as omnivorous as well as hypersexual. They are able to prey on whomever they choose, yet oddly enough, female vampires are restricted to feeding on children. As a result, it would appear that such gruesome folklore might be viewed as highly reflective of the originating culture's gender roles. In the European context, the female domain is centered on childbirth and childcare, and the masculine role might be viewed as the rational governor of a woman's actions. This is in contrast to the gender roles of the cultures of Southeast Asia, especially in traditional Indonesia and the Philippines, where men and women's roles are sometimes not rigidly applied, and women have long enjoyed greater equality with men as compared to their early counterparts in the patrilineal societies of Europe (e.g., in Spain). The female undead of the Philippines, Malaysia, Indonesia, and other areas of this region are represented as using sexual appeal primarily as a means of disguise, but the creatures' goals and functions do not indicate that hypersexuality is an innate part of their character nor a required means of attack. While male vampires exist in Southeast Asia, they are rare and do not play the same roles as their European counterparts do. For example, the male bajang of Malaysia appears as a cat, but unlike the European vampires, it seeks out specifically children, much like the female vampires do. This seems to imply that in addition to greater gender equality in real life, there is some corresponding equality in folklore.

Europeans' real fear may be uncontrollable women. In contrast, the fear in regional Southeast Asia may be of something or someone who may represent a danger to their children. A dangerous person from a Southeast Asian perspective may be someone who not only represents a physical threat, but who has succumbed to this-worldly vices and thereby can mislead children. Thus the two mythical traditions coming out of Southeast Asia and Europe are set on distinctly contrasting theoretical bases. The pertinent origins of the various European witch tales trace back to the hysterical witch hunts and inquisitions of medieval times, whereas the Southeast Asian tales may have something to do with the use of metaphors as a way of teaching children how to resist this-worldly vices such as selfishness, greed, jealousy, and lust for power, thereby transforming themselves into nurturing human beings.

Anthropologist Stephen Lansing describes the Balinese Calonarang dance-and musical performance, an exorcism of witches and demons that takes place in Bali, Indonesia. Indonesia was colonized by the Dutch, whose only interest was in the extraction of local resources for purposes of their own economic gain, not in changing people's religion.[41] This is why the ancient Calonarang ritual dance performance continues to be remembered. Lansing documents this ritual battle between the Barong, or village protector, and Rangda, the flying half-headed witch, as follows:

> The Barong, to the Balinese, is the arch foe of Rangda, the witch who controls black magic and delights in feeding on corpses and the entrails of young children. They are the main characters in a number of religious dramas. The dramas consist of the encounter of the two figures, from which ensues a battle that neither wins. In the course of the drama, the spiritual power (sakti) or "soul" (roh) of Barong and Rangda may enter their human impersonators, and spectators are often driven into trance by the mere sight of Rangda.[42]

This takes us closer to understanding the "hidden" meaning of this ritual combat between "good" and "evil" because we see it relates to the "inner" and "outer" worlds of the Balinese. The playful, gentle, and robust Barong represents the guardian of the village and all those who inhabit it. At the outer village level, he is the culmination of the four spirit guards, totem poles, who stand watch over the community. Each posted in one of the four cardinal directions, north, south, east, and west, and to whom ritual offerings of rice are made. At the inner level of the individual, Barong is the culmination of four spirit children who accompany each child at birth. These spirit children of the inner world of the child are unseen by the naked eye, but the Balinese believe that they influence the child all through her lifetime. They are the recipients of ritual offerings and gifts given to the child, during rites of passage as when the baby's feet first touch the ground, her first haircut, her first and subsequent birthdays, and at each of the major turning points over the course of her lifetime. It is believed by the Balinese that if the growing child is neglected and not honored that her spirit siblings will grow rambunctious, causing her to act out her problems as an adult. Hence the gentle and fun-loving but strong and able Barong guardian of the human is the beloved spirit protector of the Balinese, who controls all vices in the world.

In opposition, Rangda is the queen or culmination of approximately 100 witches that may correspond to known vices like anger, jealousy, and thievery. She stirs up trouble. Lansing explains that the Balinese have names for more vices than outsiders usually are aware of. Rangda is the daughter of Durga, one of the fiercest devi forms of Hinduism. "Devi" is the Sanskrit term for goddess.[43] Ancient Hindu scripture indicates that all goddesses are ultimately the same goddess, or devi, and it is interesting to note that unlike the Christian vision of a solely male god who is untouched by sin, Hindu gods and goddesses contain within themselves emanations of both good and evil. A well-known example is when Krishna philosophically encouraged Arjuna to take up arms against his "flesh and blood" cousins

who otherwise would forever wreck havoc on the world. That is, at its deep-
est root, there is only one god of which all others are emanations in
Hinduism. Monaghan explains that Durga was the eldest female devi in
the primordial war between gods and antigods.[44] Her daughter, Rangda,
is the one who sets loose the chaotic whirl of vices that tempt and torment
the human spirit. She represents the unappeased, unfulfilled, and restless
spirits who hover and cause havoc for the living. Asian studies professor
Lynette Parker tells the story of Rangda:

> The widow had a beautiful daughter who was of marriageable age, but because
> of the widow's reputation for knowledge of sorcery, there were no suitors for
> her daughter's hand. Furious, the widow took up her book, a palm leaf manu-
> script of magic invocations, which had been granted her as a boon by the
> Goddess of Destruction, Durgha, and went to a graveyard with her entourage
> of half a dozen young women. Dancing with her entourage of trainee witches,
> Rangda asked the Goddess Durgha for permission and power to ruin the
> country and its people. Durgha agreed but requested moderation. Rangda
> and her entourage danced at the crossroads at midnight and shortly after-
> wards people everywhere fell victim to contagious illness. Many died. The king
> sent soldiers to kill her, but she spewed forth fire from her eyes, nostrils, ears,
> and mouth, killing the soldiers. The widow was incensed at the king's actions,
> and, with her book and followers, she went to the graveyard again.
> Foreswearing moderation, she danced upon and desecrated the interred
> bodies, thus pleasing Durgha. Widespread destruction followed. The king
> then called upon the assistance of his priest, Mpu Bharada, who devised a
> strategy. The only way that the priest could counter the disaster was to obtain
> and read the widow-witch's palm leaf book. The priest's pupil, Mpu Bahula,
> would ask for the widow's hand in marriage. This was successful. After some
> time, this son-in-law managed to get his wife to give him Rangda's book of
> magic invocations. He gave the book to his guru priest, Mpu Bharada, who
> then had the power to control life and death. He found the manuscript con-
> tained only the teachings of good conduct and religion, but that Rangda sub-
> verted these by "going to the left, towards defilement." He managed to
> resurrect the victims of the widow who had not yet decomposed, and he con-
> quered the widow and then revived her, exorcizing and liberating her soul.[45]

Following anthropologist Mary Douglas's idea of pollution, Parker argues
that women through their bodily functions have greater access to the means
of sorcery.[46] Women "as daughters, wives, mothers, and widows are more
likely than men to be rendered ritually impure—hence to be vulnerable to
bewitchment, and to wield ambiguous power."[47] Women have access to the
placenta and aftereffects of childbirth, which, in many traditional villages in
South and Southeast Asia, as in Bali, are believed to be the tools of sorcerers.

Parker implies that men traditionally served as midwives because the Balinese believe that men are more powerful than women in warding off sorcery.[48]

For purposes of comparison, another way of looking at the role men play in childbirth is to see how they fit into the more egalitarian structure of parenting in Bali. Both parents contribute to fulfilling the physical, emotional, and spiritual needs of the newborn, that is, these are not considered exclusively female tasks. The parental pair participates in all of the rites of passage for their child. These rituals are geared toward giving offerings to the four spirit siblings who accompany the child at birth and "who will help to decide the fate of the child as it grows into adulthood."[49] During the first three months of life, the child is most susceptible to witchcraft. If a witch can find a way to steal the placenta, she can use it to create an invisible vampire spirit to attack her enemies. She grows the invisible vampire by feeding into the malicious aspects of each of the spirit siblings. However, the spirit siblings have a preponderance of positive qualities, which are nurtured and developed through the rituals surrounding childhood.

In short, witches from a traditional South and Southeast Asian perspective may represent the many forces of vice in the world. In the case of Hindu Bali, rituals continue to be performed to transform these potentially dangerous and chaotic forces into virtuous individual and social actions. The Barong represents the culmination of the four spirit children who accompany a human child throughout his or her lifetime. It is to the inner spirit children, associated with the four cardinal directions in the physical realm of the world, that the Balinese make offerings over the course of the child's development and into adulthood. Southeast Asian witches may represent the spirits unbound. Witches are simply the culmination of worldly vices, while the spirit siblings once ritually honored are reflective of what it means to become a good human being.

SHAMANIC HEALERS AND CONCEPTS OF BEAUTY IN THE PHILIPPINES

In Asia, local people have interlinking ethnic diversities and regional affiliations that form a national heritage and self-identity. They have unique cultures, steeped in tradition, that are passed down from generation to generation. Nothing is constant except for change; even as traditional cultural values and behaviors may change in response to outside forces such as top-down colonization and globalization, they often continue to persist in modern guise. To take a modern example, in Bicol, Philippines, anthropologist Fanella Cannell compared the key concepts of "power and intimacy" with "reluctance, pity, and shame."[50] She found that the power Filipino parents have over their children in arranging marriages to strangers is tantamount to the power spirit beings hold over the living. Reluctance to accept this power is effectively shown through a twofold lens: the bride's reluctance to accept her spouse is analogous to a novice healer's reluctance to accept a spirit being as her companion and co-healer.

Regarding shame and intimacy, the former is what one feels when one is forced into an intimate relation with a stranger, whether it is a spouse or spirit guide. Shame is the local equivalent to being shy, or modest and respectful of others' feelings, and not wanting to bring shame on oneself or one's family. Intimacy becomes comfortable and less shameful on both sides as the husband/wife and spirit/person become accustomed to each other's characteristics. That is, healers do not freely choose to become healers; rather, the spirit chooses them. The spirit is attracted to the person by feeling pity for the person's difficult life.[51] The person generally feels shame and reluctance to accept this relationship because it, and especially the spirit possession, scares and shames them.[52] The person can feel oppressed because of having the spirit guide with him or her. The spirit guardian wants to control the person, so an uneasy alliance is formed until each can become accustomed to the other's character. However, the guardian spirit can be seen as a rival to a living companion and therefore can also cause hard feelings.[53] The spirit generally cannot be tolerated when the living person is becoming used to a new spouse or a new child.[54]

The idea of travelling together with a companion is ancient in the Philippines. Nobody goes anywhere alone or meets someone new for the first time unless accompanied by another. It is never "When will you be back?" but instead "Who will go with you?" Many organizational concepts are found in the form of mediators and go-betweens. This is the case of the spirit possessor who, in taking pity on someone, allows that the healer can cure the sick person.

When the Spanish brought Catholicism to the Philippines, they introduced saints, the persona of Christ, and the concept of heaven and hell. They may also have introduced a different way of perceiving death as being opposite of life, rather than death being birth into the next life. The indigenous peoples incorporated the new beliefs into their own traditional belief systems. This is well exemplified by their use of the persona of Christ in the form of a life-size statue to celebrate the crucifixion and resurrection and also in calling upon spirits to help the local community.[55]

Fanella Cannell explains that Philippine beauty pageants are molded on U.S. tradition, although they have roots in Spanish colonial Catholicism, for example, religious processions such as the crowning of Queen Mary. Beauty from a Bicolano Filipino perspective is a sort of protective layer that also can elevate status in those who may be marginalized by society. An example is that the gay members of the community find they are most accepted during beauty contests, when they are at their loveliest. Gay men have somewhat ambiguous status with Bicol culture. They consider themselves men but with women's hearts. The occupations they take—for example, beauticians, hairdressers, and seamstresses—reflect their status.

Currently, however, many gay men can be found at work in professional leadership fields as teachers, nurses, and administrators. Gay men provide a fundamental service for nongay residents, especially when it comes to beauty contests. While the local people overwhelmingly accept the gay community, there is a lot of teasing. Elders mock gay greetings and teach their children to do so. Highly prized in the life of the gay community is beauty, for themselves and their clients. The pageants give them an opportunity to show off to the community just how beautiful they are. Accordingly, the male judges often find themselves uncomfortable when assessing such beautiful contestants. Cannell suggests that underlying these festivities is the U.S. ideal of a beauty pageant. English songs are sung, and beauty contests follow the U.S. pattern. In contrast, however, Filipino gays, lesbians, and transgendered people since time immemorial have been regarded as cherished members of their society.

ASIAN CHRISTIAN LIBERATION THEOLOGY

Late twentieth-century Asian liberation theology movements successfully overthrew dictatorships such as that of Philippine president Ferdinand Marcos (1965–1986), Indonesian president Suharto (1967–1998), and Korean president Chun Doo-Hwan (1981–1988). These movements were partially influenced by creative and nondogmatic Marxism, which has an open-ended perspective malleable enough to include local considerations of religion and culture. These revolutionary religious movements were reacting against the kind of capitalist modernization and development theory that was associated with patriarchal structures of globalization and authoritarian dictatorships. They transcended working-class unions and hierarchical organizations to organize grassroots people's power movements, coming up from below. Asian ecumenical liberation theology aimed to transform top-down development models and dictatorial regimes by experimenting with bottom-up approaches to social change.

Asian liberation theology also incorporates an obvert eco-feminist approach to social change that encourages men and women to become environmentally concerned feminists and parents to raise children to establish caring bonds with one another and the natural world of stars, plants, insects, animals, and all living things. The focus of what now is called eco-feminist liberation theology aims to (1) improve poor people's lives, (2) put citified people back in touch with nature, (3) further develop and push for organic farming in rural and urban gardens, and (4) fight for women's rights and indigenous people's rights, the latter of whose natural environments are under threat, if not already being destroyed, as a result of the impact of top-down development projects such as mining and logging operations. We provide a more detailed discussion on Buddhist and Hindu eco-feminism in the next section of this chapter. Christian liberation theology is most widely practiced in the predominantly Christian country of the Philippines but also is widespread in South Korea, where it is called minjung theology. The Philippine theologian Brother Karl Gaspar explains that it strives to promote cultural and ecological diversity in tangible ways that can be felt and experienced by the individual and society.[56] A Philippine application of this approach can be seen in the work of Sister Mary John Dumaug of the Good Shepherd Sisters.[57] Having lived and worked with the indigenous people of Mindanao for 30 years, she brought back to Manila a passion for caring for the earth and tilling the soil. She transformed her community's backyard, which used to be mound of junk, into a beautiful organic garden replete with tropical vegetables as a showcase for developing such gardens elsewhere in the city. Her community, located adjacent to a soot-covered bridge in one of the most congested parts of Manila, also is actively involved in counseling and retraining victims of sex trafficking for healthy reintegration into society. There is a small piggery in the garden. Unlike most piggeries, it does not emit a bad odor. The swine feed on a vegetable soup medley and, in between mealtimes, special leafy treats from the garden. Sister Mary John uses an indigenous, environmentally friendly way to dispose of their wastes that yields compost and organic fertilizers.

Philippine ecological liberation theology movements concentrate their training programs on providing support for people whose fundamental human rights have been violated, as well as increasing peoples' awareness about their rich cultural heritages and the inequitable roots of their own poverty in the present as a way to move them to action. Their training programs, at best, aim to transform the present direction of globalization by developing a new way of life that is concerned with promoting organic farming, mutuality and respect for one another in terms of gender equality, and the promotion and care of the natural world.

For example, in the early 1990s, anthropologist Kathleen Nadeau conducted fieldwork for one year on a Basic Ecclesial Community (BEC) movement that was doing liberation theology in an upland farm community located in the central Philippines.[58] Her primary research methods were formal and informal interviews as well as participant observation. This community had an engaged, comprehensive program, which included activities ranging from social analysis and creative theater to health care and sustainable agricultural development.

In the late 1980s, when community organizers and church workers first arrived in the area, they found the farmers were impoverished and struggling to survive. Many had forgotten traditional farming techniques that were practiced by their predecessors such as contour farming and the use of organic fertilizers. Instead, they had grown dependent on using expensive artificial inputs to grow their crops. The soil they cultivated was rocky and eroded. Also, they were growing a costly new hybrid variety of yellow corn

that attracted a lot of insects and required chemical fertilizers as well as artificial pesticides. In 1991, the organizers challenged the farmers to solve their
problems by using resources available in their immediate environment. They
introduced a traditional white variety of corn and organic farming techniques that were used by the farmers' forbearers. The farmers quickly
adopted the organizers' organic farming program because the traditional
white corn could be stored and used longer than the yellow hybrid variety.
It also was more pest resistant and did not require costly artificial inputs.
The decision of the male and female farmers (who worked together on task,
without having defined gender roles) to adopt the program and maintain
their livelihood in terms of "use value" as opposed to "exchange value" can
be seen as a form resistance based on cultural differences. As elsewhere in
Asia, traditional Filipino farmers differ from capitalist agriculturalists in
regard to land, food, gender relations, and the economy.

The farmers also used to think that being religious meant attending Mass
regularly and keeping the sacraments. Those who were perceived to be devout
Catholics practiced outward forms of religious behavior. However, the BEC
organizers introduced the farmers to a new way of practicing their religion by
reading and applying lessons learned from the Bible to their own life experiences. To explain what Jesus taught, they used local metaphors and real-life
examples from their own bottom-up perspectives. Whereas the farmers used
to rely exclusively on priests and religious teachers to read and interpret the
Bible for them, the organizers now empowered them to discern the meaning
of the scriptures for themselves and in conjunction with the clergy. This new
way of practicing their religious faith was derived mainly from liberation theology and post–Vatican II social teachings.

Philippine basic ecclesial communities also intersect with indigenous struggles for the right of tribal societies to live in their natural habitats. Tribal communities, for example, the Hindagaon tribe of Mindanao, largely seek to
protect their environments from being irreparably damaged by the influx of
unwanted forms of development such as mining operations and logging concessions that pollute and denude forested areas. Holden and Jacobsen document some of the most detrimental effects of modern mining practices on
the surrounding natural environment and communities in the Philippines.[59]
These comprehensively engaged communities are participating in the ecological village movement being organized by eco-feminist liberation theology practitioners. Tribal people are cultural bearers of indigenous knowledge systems
that offer important models for sustainable forestry and agro-forestry practices.
The 1993 United Nations Vienna Declaration recognizes:

> . . . the inherent dignity and the unique contribution of indigenous peoples to
> the development and plurality of society and strongly reaffirms the commit-
> ment of the international community to their economic, social, and cultural

well-being and their enjoyment of the fruits of sustainable development. States should ensure the full and free participation of indigenous people in all aspects of society, in particular, in matters of concern to them.[60]

In Asia more broadly, interreligious communities practicing liberation theology often look back at precolonial traditional ways, extant in the present, of taking care of the environment, animals, and mother earth. Philippine communities so engaged find some inspiration by reflecting on their precolonial animist, Hindu, and Buddhist influences that encouraged children to form a relationship with nature so as to grow into adults who live in harmony with the natural world. Basic ecclesial communities spend a lot of time talking about creation spirituality and a concept of God that is embodied and expressed through nature and people. The post–Vatican II way of being in the world professes to experience one's body, mind, and spirit as being integrated and interconnected. This stands in stark contrast to pre–Vatican II notions that divided soul and body, or church and society, into two separate planes of existence: the spiritual world as opposed to the material world. The earlier hierarchical church considered itself responsible only for ministering to the spiritual needs of its parishioners, while society, not the church, cared for people's material needs and personal, physical situations. However, the post–Vatican II church of today, despite being for human, animal, and environmental rights, continues to be based on a domineering and patriarchal system that has yet to allow women to be ordained as priests.

As Sharon Welch explains, contemporary liberation theology is not based on some abstract theory that stands apart from women's concerns.[61] Rather, it is based on a real and tangible relationship with a God who lives in women's history. Liberation theology is reflected theologically as it is lived in practice. It emerges from organized communities in the various Asian cultural and religious contexts that strategically and politically side with the poor and oppressed. Welch cautions, however, that liberation theologies are not variant strains of thought existing within a traditional theology, for example, progressive theologies versus conservative theologies, within traditional Catholic theology. Rather, they represent a disruptive break, a new paradigmatic shift, from traditional theology. They are continuous with one tradition, within all world religions, that is critical of social injustices. Hindu epics are replete with stories of virtuous characters who triumph over evildoers. In Christianity, Jesus is critical of hypocrites who feign to be public servants but really are in office for their personal benefit.[62]

Leonardo Boff sums up the basic approach of Christian liberation theology as being tantamount to an unfolding inductive methodology, or praxis, that combines theory and practice. It discerns God's presence in the world by also taking into consideration women's aspirations and then looking to see what the Bible has to say about that. It is biased for women and children, the poor, and the oppressed because the God of the Bible is on the side of women and poor people, and comes down to earth to live with them. Liberation theology does not begin through the entry point of some universal, male-centric idea of organized religion that is applicable cross-culturally; rather, like engaged Buddhism or engaged anthropological fieldwork, it goes back to the people to think and reflect upon their different and gendered experiences in relation to the earth and each other to better understand and identify their problems in solidarity with the people concerned.

Philippine basic ecclesial communities engage in a variety of livelihood projects designed to improve their members' quality of life. They are involved in income-generating activities such as handicraft production, food processing, garment making, soap making, cooperative stores, communal farming, and livestock dispersal programs. They typically use a participatory approach that partners with local people who are interactively given an education on how to do research to determine what types of livelihood programs they would like to implement. In accordance with the Philippine's Local Government Code, they often help to monitor internal revenue allotments to local governments and the election process to make sure there is no corruption, but, as Evita Jimminez of the Center for People Empowerment explains, computerized voting technology makes this difficult because they have no way to make sure the requirements for transparency and integrity of the software have been complied with.[63]

Women working with the basic communities are producing more varieties of vegetables and herbal medicines. Pharmaceutical drugs often are beyond the means of poor people unless they find medicines through groups that poor people do not always know about such as nonprofit, nongovernmental organizations or church clinics funded by outside and local donations. While public hospitals offer free social and medical care for the poor, they regularly are understaffed and lack essential medical supplies. Patients have to bring their own sheets, towels, and beddings as well as any surgical instruments and medicines to be used. Sometimes, out of compassion and pity, doctors and nurses go into their own pockets to help the needy. Given the excessive cost of Western pharmaceuticals and health care, one important component of the basic community movement is to make traditional health care available to poor people by provisioning them with free herbal medicines, especially if they help produce them, and selling them at inexpensive prices that local people can afford.

The Philippine ecclesial communities engage in so many programs for women and the poor, for example, organic farming, solid waste management, and tree planting, the latter of which significantly helps reduce global warming in the Philippines. They contribute to community-based justice and education programs that increase their awareness about women's equal rights being human rights. Another interesting program of the Philippine liberation theology movement is its work in the peace zones. According to Rufa Guiam of the Institute for Peace and Development at Mindanao State University in General Santos City, "decades of conflict have wrought substantial changes in women's lives, as well as male and female relationships."[64] Only when women participate in negotiations for peace and justice can a truly sustainable peace be attained. Women have long been at the forefront of negotiations between the Philippine government and the Moro Liberation Front, the Muslim wing of the Communist Party of the Philippines. On the recent signing of the Framework Agreement for Bangsamoro, in Mindanao, Philippines, 150 soldiers and Filipino Christian men and women from the BECs in the Peace Zone came together for the "Hijab Run for Peace: Religious Understanding Now" that was organized by the young Muslim professional network.[65]

The Philippines has experienced armed insurgent groups defying the authority of the state. The most widespread of these is the New Peoples Army (NPA), the armed wing of the Communist Party of the Philippines (CPP). Since 1969, the conflict between the NPA and the Armed Forces of the Philippines (AFP) has taken over 40,000 lives and it is one of the longest-running Maoist insurgencies in the world.[66] In a peace zone, BEC members make it clear that they are autonomous from both the AFP and the NPA and then refuse to give assistance to either side. Two of the earliest peace zones were in Candonia, on the island of Negros, and in Tulunan, on the island of Mindanao.[67]

What is interesting about peace zones is that both the AFP and the NPA decry them, claiming that their own group obeys them while the other side does not and, consequently, the other side gains an advantage. The fact that both the AFP and the NPA are so opposed to the zones of peace could well be a sign that they are disrupting the activities of both sides and ultimately making it more difficult for both sides to engage in hostilities.

Lieutenant Colonel Cesar Idio, commander of the Twenty-Fifth Infantry Battalion, held a press conference in May 2006 and declared that the NPA was using Tulunan, North Cotabato, as a refuge area and as a base for recruitment.[68] Major Randolph Cabangbang, the spokesperson for AFP Eastern Mindanao Command, stated that the zones of peace make it harder for the AFP to engage in counterinsurgency warfare but they "do not keep out the NPA because the NPA are outlaws."[69]

Professor Jose Maria Sison, the founder of both the Communist Party of the Philippines and the New Peoples Army, stated that the NPA is excluded from the "zone of peace," but the police and AFP troops as well as intelligence operatives in civilian clothes are not excluded, not to mention the local bureaucratic organs of the reactionary government and the line people from the presidential management staff. To Sison, the term "zone of peace" was "developed by clerico-fascists who have an agenda against the NPA." Furthermore, he contends, zones of peace actually fail to achieve their pacification objective because the armed personnel of both sides of the armed conflict can move in and out of the zones in civilian clothes. According to Sison, the best way to realize a just peace is to address the roots of the civil war with basic economic, social, and political reforms that are satisfactory to the exploited and oppressed people.[70]

In summary, the Philippine liberation theology program tries to lessen the gap between rich and poor, men and women by involving women and poor people in their own development process. Asia's problems of poverty and environmental degradation, for example, often are caused by top-down neoliberal development projects. Neoliberalism refers to a set of economic polices that emphasize free trade, privatization, deregulation, and the retreat of the state from matters of wealth redistribution and social service provision.[71] The Philippines has long been reputed to be among the most accommodating countries in Asia to the prescriptions of neoliberalism.[72] During the presidency of Gloria Macapagal-Arroyo (2001–2010), the government consolidated its commitment to neoliberalism by aggressively encouraging foreign investment in various economic sectors and by entering into free trade agreements with other countries.[73] Neoliberalism is widely regarded as a set of polices that prioritize efficiency over equity and growth over poverty alleviation. Therefore, the basic community movement, with its commitment to the poor, often finds itself opposed to the government's neoliberal agenda. Perhaps the most tangible sign of the basic Christian community movement's opposition to neoliberalism is its involvement in environmental activism and peace and justice programs.

In some cases, the basic communities have been instrumental in causing the flow of information to move upward through the hierarchy and thereby have helped to change the direction of the church's activism. An excellent example of this occurred in Sultan Kudarat, Mindanao, in 1995 and 1996, when communities became concerned about the mining's entry into their communities. Members commenced a vigorous antimining activism that then spread up to the level of the diocese. As Father Romeo Catedral, the social action director of the diocese of Marbel stated, "The church, through its BECs, has its eyes and ears opened to the wishes of the people on the ground."[74]

However, there are certain limitations to the efficacy of the BECs. They often depend on the support of the parish priest, which is understandable; without such support, they typically get bogged down at the liturgical level. As Brother Karl Gaspar explains, only a small percentage of all BECs are involved in what he termed "comprehensive engagement," which moves them past the liturgical level toward the developmental and transformative levels. To Gaspar, of all the thousands of BECs in the Philippines, "one can only expect a fraction of these to have the audacity to claim that they are the truly authentic ones, foreshadowed by the Acts of the Apostles."[75] That is, comprehensively engaged communities, unlike bible study groups, attempt to provide what political scientist Robin Broad calls "genuine development" as they strive to provide a development process that is not so dependent on the world economy and wherein "people participate in making decisions and planning projects that affect their lives and where inhabitants of an area decide what kind of projects they want and what kinds they can afford."[76]

ENGAGED BUDDHISM IN SOUTH AND SOUTHEAST ASIA

Buddhist ecology movements in South and Southeast Asia similarly engage in learning and teaching about gender equality and environmental stewardship through practice. They aim to help alleviate suffering, especially of women and poor people, who experience commodification, displacement, environmental pollution, and water pollution in homes and communities, from industrialization, and from global capitalism. Buddhist nuns and monks politically and strategically involved in this movement are criticized by those who wish to profit from the destruction of the natural environment. Despite being subject to threats of violence and sometimes even murder, these religious leaders continue their antiglobalization activism with the goal of helping people everywhere to live harmoniously with nature.

Tibetan nun standing amid prayer flags, Sichuan Province, China, 2005. (Remi Benali/Corbis)

An example is the Tibetan Buddhist nuns who struggle for cultural autonomy and independence from Chinese colonialism. While the Chinese government insists that Tibet is part of China and is being treated fairly, Chinese administrative officials and educators in Tibet refuse Tibetans the freedom to practice their own cultural and religious way of life, for example, the Chinese insistence in Tibetan schools that children speak only Chinese. Tibetan nuns and monks, who are single and at least in theory unaffected by family concerns, lead the Free Tibet movement. Today, they continue to organize mass protests against the Chinese occupation, despite risk of being arrested, tortured, and imprisoned. Many have given witness to undergoing gruesome torture in the Chinese jails.[77]

Father Aloysious Pieris, a Jesuit theologian and Buddhist practioner from Sri Lanka, explains that engaged Buddhists and Christians gain courage in the face of danger by identifying with the poverty and ethics of their religious founders, Buddha and Christ.[78] Adept role models, like the Free Tibet activist nuns, voluntarily take a vow of poverty, which serves a double purpose as a powerful spiritual and political weapon against religious and secular elites who act in a greedy and selfish manner. Accordingly, the antireligious roots of capitalism hinder such leaders from seeing into the religious depths of human nature.[79] Pieris has written extensively about traditional knowledge systems in Christianity and Buddhism that have produced methods for liberating the mind from selfish desires and ideological projections such as renouncing the world by practicing meditation techniques to clarify thinking. Evidence also indicates that world religions have been challenged from within by theologians who call for gender equality by allowing women to be fully ordained as monks or priests. These liberation theologians encourage women to think clearly and confront their problems collectively as exemplified in the culturally different Asian women's movements that point to ethical considerations coming out of their cultural philosophies and religions to promote gender equality and equal rights between the sexes.

Anthropologist Susan Darlington explains that the reinterpretation of Buddhism for equal rights and environmental justice movements is "an effort to put the basic ideas of religion in terms that meet the needs of the modern world."[80] Buddhist ethical values and principles include loving kindness, respect, and compassion for one another. Another precept refers to the environment and all living things, for "every form of sentient life participates in a karmic continuum."[81] Buddhism seeks to end human suffering, and some of the strongest causes of human suffering are directly connected with inequitable and unjust social and economic relations, including gender inequities and the destruction of the environment wrought by male-centric capitalist development processes. For example, "the rate of deforestation in Thailand is higher than anywhere else in Asia, except Nepal, and possibly Borneo," states Darlington.[82] This deforestation and destruction is caused by human vices such as selfishness, greed, and desire, which, ironically, are values apparent in capitalism. The most toxic environmental problems result from the practice of capitalist globalization. For example, corporatization and consumerism are largely responsible for the commodification of women, increasing economic inequality, environmental degradation, and war.[83] In her book *Altering Eden, The Feminization of Nature*, Deborah Cadbury documents male species of fish and alligators undergoing sexual reversal as a result of their habitats being saturated with noxious toxins from capitalist industrial wastes being dumped into rivers, lakes, and oceans. Since engaged Buddhist women and men perceive the causes of human suffering to be fundamentally derived from capitalist development that degrades nature, they feel bound by duty to oppose it.

Many villagers around South and Southeast Asia, and beyond, have lost access to needed land and resources for sustainable livelihoods. Instead, they are being encouraged by capitalist development processes to clear forests and participate in the market economy by increasing cash crop production and building roads to make the forests more accessible for clearing.[84] As part of an alternate vision, Buddhist monks have focused on "planting for subsistence, rather than for sale," which poses serious difficulties in practice because much of the cash earnings villagers stand to gain comes from the forest products. A Buddhist way of living, however, focuses on encouraging males and females to work together as partners, instead of males competing by dominating females. Villagers can thrive in this way of living by mutually building communal rice paddies and animal husbandry projects, irrigation projects, and other mutual self-help industries, such as the provisioning of alternative herbal medicines, health care, and social welfare programs.[85]

Engaged Buddhist activists show villagers by role modeling how to view the land, like their bodies, as sacred. They symbolically ordain the trees and forests, and offer protection for the environment by ritually sanctifying it, all the while encouraging local people to be spiritually committed to conserving the forests. Darlington documents examples of prominent nuns and monks such as Phra Prajak, Phra Khamkian, and Phrakhru Pitak Nanthakhum, who conduct these ceremonies on trees and forests. Monk Phrakhru Manas of Phayao province has been credited for being the first to ordain a tree for ecological purposes.[86] In actual social life, ordination ceremonies are reserved only for human beings, but "the ceremonies are used, symbolically, to remind people that nature should be treated as equal with humans, deserving of respect and vital for human as well as all life."[87] During the ritual ceremony, the tree is wrapped in orange robes, marking its sanctification. In Wang Pa Du village in northeastern Thailand, a whole mountain was so ordained by "wrapping a three kilometer strip of saffron cloth around its base" to prevent blasting and mining by a quarry company.[88]

For their reforestation and agricultural development work from 1970 to the present, some engaged Thai Buddhist activists have been falsely labeled communist insurgents by government officials and other elites with an interest in local logging concessions and associated industries. In 1991, for example, Phra Prajak, a Buddhist monk known for conducting ordination of trees, was jailed for his eco-feminist environmental activism. According to Walter, this was "the first time a robed Buddhist monk had been imprisoned in Thailand."[89] Phra Prajak had led villagers to oppose a eucalyptus plantation that was being developed on their land. He was accused of being a communist and underwent intimidation and harassment by local paramilitary and military forces prior to his arrest.[90] In another example, Phra Sopoj Suwagano was stabbed in 2005. His murderers have yet to be brought to justice but, at the time of his death, he was involved in conserving some 280 acres of forested land that was coveted by a group of local businessmen. Phra Pongsak, the abbot of Wat Palad near Chiang Mai in northern Thailand, is another example of a monk who has continued over the years to work with villagers to reforest and irrigate their rapidly desertifying land in the face of obstacles such as police raids.[91]

Another example of a Buddhist women's rights and ecology movement is the Tzu Chi Foundation, the largest humanitarian organization in the Chinese-speaking world, which was founded by Dharma Master Cheng Yen, a Buddhist nun, on May 14, 1966, in Taiwan. According to eco-feminist theologians Heather Eaton and Lois Ann Lorentzen, Cheng Yen was inspired by two life-changing events. The first occurred when she observed a poor indigenous Taiwanese woman having a miscarriage on the hospital floor due to hospital neglect related to her financial impoverishment. The other event occurred when two Catholic nuns pointed out to her that despite Buddhism being a compassionate religion, it had no social services for helping the poor in Taiwan. Emotionally and rationally moved, she founded Tzu Chi, which currently consists of some 40 million members, 80 percent of whom are women. Women have played a leading role in its household recycling programs that encourage thriftiness. Tzu Chi Foundation has been instrumental in establishing many hospitals and schools around the world and enjoys special consultative status at the UN Economic and Social Council.[92]

In the Theravada Buddhist countries of Sri Lanka, Thailand, and Burma, typically boys study to become monks in order to gain spiritual merit for their parents, while girls are culturally expected to work to provide for their family's material needs. Even though there is a long history of the initiation of nuns into the temple that stems back to the time of Buddha, their status is ambiguous. In Thailand, for example, according to secular law, women are not allowed to be fully ordained. They can be only quasi-ordained into the temple, although there are powerful nuns like Bhikkuni Dhammananda who was fully ordained on February 28, 2003, in Sri Lanka and now is the abbess of the only temple in Thailand with fully ordained nuns.[93] Thai parents typically dedicate at least one of their sons to study at temple colleges based in urban centers. As part of their degree program, they are expected to participate in development projects in rural communities. Many come from rural communities themselves and identify with the farmers. The earliest development projects were financed in the 1970s and 1980s by the Thai government in an effort to help counter communist insurgency efforts along the Kampuchean and Laos borders and to provide alternatives to opium production in the north. But many Buddhist monks and nuns remained in the villages long after graduation because they became increasingly immersed in the social, cultural, political, economic, environmental, and ecological aspects of sustainable rural development.[94]

Similarly, some Buddhist nuns in Sri Lanka have participated in a village self-help movement referred to as the Sarvodaya. The Sarvodaya movement emerged in 1958 under the guidance of Professor Ariyaratne when a group of Nalanda College students decided to get in touch with their cultural roots by living with and learning from local farmers. Their experiences were so rewarding that their ideas became popular with other students, who followed them to the villages. The movement spread rapidly. According to current estimates, the Sarvodaya movement has a network of about 15,000 ecologically concerned villages operating health care programs, educational programs, agricultural projects, and small industries.[95] These programs accomplished much not because organizers employed solutions coming from above, but because they were willing to listen and learn from the local people. They recognized that their greatest resources come from the spirituality and culture of local people. They also practiced Gandhi's teachings of active nonviolence as a revolutionary means to social change. This Gandhi-inspired development movement provides an indigenous alternative to the local government's top-down development program. Since 1958, the Sarvodaya movement has grown from a small group of pioneers working alongside the outcast poor to a people's self-help movement. Its program emphasizes the full range of human well-being; the needs of the whole person must be met—satisfying work, harmonious relationships, a safe and beautiful environment, a life of the mind and spirit, and food, clothing, and shelter.

In summary, ecological village movements discussed in this chapter are indicative of another kind of globalizing trend developing from the ground up that is paving the way for gender equality and new cultural alternatives to the dominant ideology of global capitalism. South and Southeast Asia, for example, are seeing numerous religious movements that are building networks with each other, locally and internationally, and in the process helping to build alternative forums for greater gender equality, environmental sustainability, reparation of nature, peace, and justice. Some lay and religious Buddhist women and men in Thailand are actively engaged in ecology and development activities that coincide with an emphasis on Buddhism's this-world teachings. Such is also the case for some Buddhist activists in Sri Lanka as well as Christian liberation theology practitioners in Korea and the Philippines. These movements seek to develop peripheral communities into self-reliant communities of interpretation and action by synthesizing social justice into a unifying theme with cultural tolerance, religious pluralism, and the practical concern for equity—without regard to matters of sex and gender. The various Asian liberation theology movements have emerged in reaction to the type of development ideology associated with male-centric and capitalist globalization processes. The justice-oriented and ecologically concerned characteristics of these religiously diverse movements, however, are ideologically closer to one another in the ecumenical movement than to religious fundamentalism as practiced in their own particular church organizations when viewed from the theological standpoint that creation is an open-ended process for which we share responsibility for the future.

AN ECO-FEMINIST APPROACH TO WOMEN'S LIBERATION

Traditional Asian religions share a common theoretical basis with eco-feminism. Eco-feminism looks to traditional Asian religions for ideas about providing tender care for and nurturing the environment, animals, and mother earth. Early Asian world religions such as Hinduism and Buddhism strove to create societies that lived in harmony with all living things. Eco-feminism considers humans and every other living species as interconnected with each other and the environment. Eco-feminism generally sees the exploitation of the natural world as being linked with the subordination of women. As eco-feminism theorist Ungrid Shafter explains, the ecological impact of human practices such as the cruel treatment of animals by Western science for the food and pharmaceutical industries along with the use of pesticides on farms negatively affects women's bodies and the bodies of their children.[96] Women experience spontaneous abortions and still-births, and are most often the ones who take care of children born with birth defects that often are caused by artificial and genetically engineered inputs in the food chain.

Ancient Asian religions have local conceptions of sacred geographical and cosmological space that were perceived to be part of the reproduction of their own societal bodies. Ancient Chinese and Indic cities were built to elevate the human spirit to get in touch with the divine.[97] An idealized plan of a city is given in the "Code Book of Works" preserved in the *Book of Rites*: "The capital city is a rectangle of nine squares *li*. *Li* refers to the rational and the official version of what is proper behavior. The essence of *li* refers to social norms or etiquette, which means to humble oneself so as to honor others. The use of *li* is to ensure security, orderliness, or correct conduct. Li-lessness means danger. On each side of the wall of the capital city are three gates. The Altar of Ancestors is to the left (east), and that of Earth, right (West). The court is held in front, and marketing done in the rear," forming a "Chinese mandala of nine squares with the human being in the center."[98]

Confucianism is mainly concerned with creating harmony in human society. This is done in accordance with an ancient Chinese cosmology. From this perspective, the cosmos is a sacred place, and all aspects of it are interrelated. Thus the ancient Chinese aimed to uphold the sacredness of life by maintaining harmony among humans and between humanity and nature. The ancient understanding of how the cosmos works was based on a notion that everything that exists—the heavens and earth, men and women, ancestral spirits and deities—is composed of opposing and counterbalancing life forces called *ch'i*. Ch'i is manifested mainly in two opposite but complimentary forces, *yin* and *yang*. Yin refers to that which is dark, moist, inert, turbid, cold, soft, and feminine (womb), and yang corresponds to that which is bright, dry, growing, light, warm, hard, and masculine.

The yin and yang view of the cosmos works in conjunction with five elemental forces that are considered metaphysical. These elements are fire, wood, metal, water, and earth, each of which exerts a dominant influence at any one time. Everything in the universe is linked to its participation in the cycles of transformation and varying proportions of yin and yang. These are the primal and cosmic patterns that influence human relationships. The teachings of Confucianism are the way through which humans can achieve an enlightened social life by living in harmony with natural and cosmic forces. While some feminists find fault with such a yin-yang distinction (women-nature as men-culture) for being guilty of the flaw of associating the differences between men and women with some innate notion, eco-feminists tend to be more appreciative of this imagery of birth, though they do call for a yin-yang partnership in which each party respects the dignity and integrity of the other, without any preconceived notions of superiority and inferiority.

Confucius also taught that younger generations should respect and obey their elders, women should be subservient to men, and everyone should be obedient to the emperor, who was a parent figure. But even the emperor who violated the moral order of the universe could be overthrown, legally, and the legitimacy of the coup was determined by whether it was successful. Confucianism is based on five relationships: ruler-subject, father-son, husband-wife, older brother–younger brother, and friend-friend. Except for the last, all of these relationships are based on differences in status and exemplify different power relationships in Confucian societies. However, Confucius taught that those in superior positions were supposed to be benevolent and caring. Hence, explains Shafer, this ethical principle can be called upon by local women to promote gender equality by exposing and making men who exploit them accountable for their bad actions.[99]

Asian religions offer culturally sensitive approaches to liberate women who are being subordinated and oppressed by male-dominated societies and households. The epic stories and oral traditions of India and Indonesia teach children, by way of examples, that with human rights come responsibilities. The ancient Chinese conception of a middle kingdom consisting of a multiplicity of states bound together by an unwritten code of virtuous conduct is another form of the same teaching. In Buddhism there are Bodhisattvas who, like Jesus, upon living virtuous lives reach nirvana but opt, instead, to come down from the mountain to work in the world to guide others along the path to enlightenment. Similarly, we can look at Judaic-Christian parallels in the Old Testament: Psalms, Proverbs, and Ecclesiastics 14:31–35: "He that opposes the poor blasphemes his maker: but he that honors him is gracious to the poor." The Koran also provides a similar message in Surah 12168–242: "The Society thus organized must live under laws—based on eternal principles of righteousness and fair dealing."

Humans everywhere are called upon to participate in women's struggle for equal rights, without regard to sex or gender, and this is especially so in Asia. In Confucian-based societies (e.g., Korea and Japan), for example, women are addressed less respectfully in relation to men in the public and domestic spheres in terms of language usage, and there is also inordinate pressure on young couples to produce male heirs, which results in a greater preponderance of aborted female fetuses.[100] In Buddhist and Hindu societies (e.g., Sri Lanka and India) as well, females traditionally have been less valued than males.[101] While males and females are accorded a more equal and interchangeable status in many Southeast Asian contexts, women still have to struggle for equal rights under the law (e.g., there is no divorce in the Philippines, while Indonesian marriage law considers men the head of the household).[102] Males also can have more than one wife, according to Islamic law, which allows for divorce, but the Indonesian Family Code requires a wife's divorce be formally recognized in a civil court if she is to get the many benefits offered by the government to heads of households. There are countless other examples. Even so, men and women in Asia continue to participate in the international movement for women's empowerment by getting involved in eco-feminist liberation theology agendas.

NOTES

1. James Watson, "Transactions in People: The Chinese Market Slaves, Servants, and Heirs," in *Asian and African Systems of Slavery*, James L. Watson, ed. (Berkeley: University of California Press, 1980).

2. Watson, "Transactions in People," 10–11.

3. David Kinsley, *Hindu Goddesses, Visions of the Divine Feminine in the Hindu Religious Tradition* (Berkeley: University of California Press, 1988).

4. Kinsley, *Hindu Goddesses*, 7–8.

5. The following discussion derived in part from Kathleen Nadeau, "Linga" and "Yoni," in *Encyclopedia of Middle East and South Asia*, Gordon Newby and Patit Mishra, eds. (Armonk, NY: M. E. Sharpe, forthcoming). For related readings, see, W. Y. Evans-Wentz, *The Tibetan Book of the Great Liberation* (London: Oxford University Press, 1973); Liza Lowitz and Reema Datta, *Sacred Sanskrit Words for Yoga Chant and Meditation* (Berkeley, CA: Stonebridge Press, 2005); Nelson Wu, *Chinese and Indian Architecture* (New York: George Braziller, 1963).

6. Wu, *Chinese and Indian Architecture*, plate 4, Brahminical rite on the shore of Dhanushkodi.

7. Babita Tewari and Sanjay Tewari, "The History of Indian Women: Hinduism at Crossroads with Gender," *Politics and Religion* 3, no. 1 (2009), 25–47.

8. Rita Gross, *Buddhism after Patriarchy* (Albany: State University of New York Press, 1983), 9.

9. Urgyen Sangharakshita, *A Survey of Buddhism through the Ages: Its Doctrines and Methods through the Ages* (Glasgow, UK: Windhorse Publications, 1993), 10. Note that Sangharakshita is a British Buddhist teacher and writer whose birth name is Dennis Philip Edward Lingwood.

10. Francis Grant, *Oriental Philosophy: The Story of The Teachers of the Past* (New York: Dial Press, 1936).

11. Grant, *Oriental Philosophy, The Story of The Teachers of the Past.*

12. Joel Kupperman, "Feminism as Radical Confucianism: Self and Tradition," in *The Sage and the Second Sex*, Chenyang Li, ed. (Chicago: Open Court, 2000), 43–56.

13. Kupperman, "Feminism as Radical Confucianism," 48.

14. Grant, Oriental Philosophy, The Story of The Teachers of the Past, 106.

15. Ibid.

16. Grant, *Oriental Philosophy, The Story of The Teachers of the Past.*

17. Ibid.

18. Ibid.

19. Liza Lowetz and Reema Datta, *Sacred Sanskrit Words* (Berkeley, CA: Stonebridge Press, 2005).

20. Such as Kay Jordon, *From Sacred Servants to Profane Prostitute: A History of Changing Legal Status of the Devadasis in India 1857–1947* (Oxford: Oxford University Press, 2003), 28–29; Leslie Orr, *Donors, Devotees, and Daughters of God: Temple Women in Medieval Tamilnadu* (New York: Oxford University Press, 2000), 161; Rosa Maria Perez, "The Rhetoric of Empire: Gender Representations in Portuguese India," *Portuguese Studies*, January 1, 2005, 1–19; B. S. Upadhyaya, *Women in Rig Veda* (New Dehli: S. Chand & Co., 1974).

21. Jogan Shankar, *Devadasi Cult: A Sociological Analysis* (New Dehli: Ashish, 1994).

22. Philippa Levine, *Prostitution, Race, and Politics: Policing Venereal Disease in the British Empire* (New York: Routledge, 2003), 192.

23. Levine, *Prostitution, Race, and Politics*, 197.

24. Levine, *Prostitution, Race, and Politics*.

25. Luang Chamroon Netisastr and Adul Wichencharoen, "Some Main Features of Modernization of Ancient Family Law in Thailand" in *Family Law and Customary Law in Asia: A Contemporary Legal Perspective*, David C. Buxbaum ed. (The Hague: Martinus Nijhoff, 1968), 91–92; cited in Craig Reynolds, *Seditious Histories: Contesting Thai and Southeast Asian Pasts* (Seattle: University of Washington Press, 2006), 189.

26. Andrew Turton, "Thai Institutions of Slavery," in *Asian and African Systems of Slavery*, James Watson, ed. (Berkeley: University of California Press, 1980), 251–92.

27. Theresa Hesketh and Zhu Wei Xing, "The Effect of China's One-Child Family Planning Policy after 25 Years," *New England Journal of Medicine* 353 (September 15, 2005), 1171–76.

28. Watson, "Transactions in People," 24.

29. Youngsook Kim Harvey, *Six Korean Women: The Socialization of Shamans* (San Francisco: West Publishing, 1979).

30. Stuart Schlegel, *Wisdom from a Rainforest* (Quezon City: Ateneo de Manila Press, 1999), 131.

31. Hermina Menez, *Explorations in Philippine Folklore* (Quezon City: Ateneo de Manila Press, 1996).

32. Cristina Blanc-Szanton, "Collision of Cultures: Historical Reformulation of Gender in Lowland Visayas, Philippines," in *Power and Difference in Island Southeast Asia*, Jane Atkinson and Shelly Errington, eds. (Stanford, CA: Stanford University Press, 1990), 345–83.

33. William Henry Scott, *Slavery in the Spanish Philippines* (Manila: De La Salle University Press, 1982); William Henry Scott, *Prehistoric Source Materials for the Study of Philippine History* (Quezon City: New Day, 1984).

34. Horacio De la Costa, *The Jesuits in the Philippines, 1581–1768* (Cambridge, MA: Harvard University Press, 1961).

35. Del la Costa, *The Jesuits in the Philippines*, 314–15.

36. Menez, *Explorations in Philippine Folklore*, 93.

37. Karl Gaspar, *The Masses Are the Messiah: Contemplating the Filipino Soul* (Quezon City: Institute of Spirituality in Asia, 2010), 98.

38. Matthew Bunson, *The Vampire Encyclopedia* (New York: Gramercy Publishing, 2000); Gordon Melton, *The Vampire Book: The Encyclopedia of the Undead* (Canton, MI: Visible Ink Press, 1998).

39. Susan Go, "Mothers, Maids, and the Creatures of the Night: The Persistence of Philippine Folk Religion," *Philippine Quarterly of Culture and Society* 7 (1979): 186–203.

40. Brunson, *The Vampire Encyclopedia*; Melton, *The Vampire Book*.

41. Stephen Lansing, *The Balinese* (New York: Harcourt Brace, 1995).

42. Ibid., 43.

43. Ibid., 35.

44. Patricia Monaghan, *The Book of Goddesses and Heroines* (St. Paul, MN: Llewellyn Publications, 1993).

45. Lynette Parker, "The Power of Letters and the Female Body: Female Literacy in Bali," *Women Studies International Forum* 25, no. 1 (2002): 79–96.

46. Mary Douglas, *Purity and Danger: An Analysis of Pollution and Taboo* (Taylor and Francis, 1996).

47. Parker, "The Power of Letters and the Female Body," 90.

48. Ibid., 89.

49. Lansing, *The Balinese*, 34–35.

50. Fenella Cannell, *Power and Intimacy in the Christian Philippines* (Cambridge, Cambridge University Press, 1999).

51. Ibid., 89.

52. Ibid., 100.

53. Ibid., 99.

54. Ibid., 100.

55. Ibid., 127.

56. Karl Gaspar, *The Masses Are Messiah: Contemplating the Filipino Soul* (Quezon City: Institute of Spirituality in Asia, 2010).

57. Kathleen Nadeau interviewed Sister Mary John Damaug at the Good Shepherd Sisters Motherhouse in Manila, Philippines (Summer 2008).

58. Kathleen Nadeau, *Liberation Theology in the Philippines: Faith in a Revolution* (Westport, CT: Praeger Press, 2002).

59. William Holden and R. Daniel Jacobson, *Mining and Natural Hazard Vulnerability in the Philippines, Digging to Development or Digging to Diaster?* (New York: Anthem Press, 2012).

60. M. R. Ishay, *The Human Rights Reader: Major Political Essays, Speeches, and Documents from the Bible to Present* (New York: Routledge, 1997).

61. Sharon Welch, *Communities of Resistance and Solidarity: A Feminist Theology of Liberation* (New York: Orbis, 1985).

62. Ibid., 24, 34.

63. Evita L. Jimenez, "The Hegemony of the Culture of Traditional Politics in Philippine Elections," paper presented at the International Conference on Philippine Studies (Kellog Hotel and Conference Center, East Lansing, MI, October 28–30, 2012).

64. Rufa Guiam and Leslie Dwyer, *Gender Conflict in Mindano* (Manila, Philippines: Asia Foundation, 2012); Rufa Guiam quoted in Maribel Buenaobra, "With Framework Signed Women Walk the Road to Peace in Southern Mindanao," *In Asia: Weekly Insight and Analysis of the Asia Foundation* (October 31, 2012): 2.

65. Maribel Buenaobra, "With Framework Signed, Women Walk the Road to Peace in the Southern Philippines," 1.

66. Roseanne Rutten, "Introduction: Cadres in Action, Cadres in Context," in *Brokering a Revolution: Cadres in a Philippine Insurgency*, Roseanne Rutten, ed. (Quezon City: Ateneo de Manila Press, 2008), 1–34.

67. A. L. Picardal, "BECs in the Philippines: Renewing and Transforming," in *Small Christian Communities Today: Capturing the New Moment*, J. G. Healey and J. Hinton, eds. (Maryknoll, NY: Orbis, 2005), 117–22.

68. M. C. Manar, "Army Intensifies Patrol vs. NPA in Tulunan, Columbio," *Mindanews* (http://www.mindanews.com/2006/05/16nws–army.htm, May 16, 2006).

69. Interview conducted by William Holden in William Holden and Kathleen Nadeau, "Philippine Liberation Theology and Social Development in Anthropological Perspective," *Philippine Quarterly of Culture and Society* 38, no. 2 (2010): 89–129.

70. Interview conducted by William Holden in William Holden and Kathleen Nadeau, "Philippine Liberation Theology and Social Development," 29–89.

71. K. Ward and K. England, "Introduction: Reading Neoliberalization," in *Neoliberalization: States, Networks, Peoples*, K. Ward and K. England, eds. (Oxford: Blackwell, 2007), 1–22.

72. N. G. Quimpo, "The Philippines: Predatory Regime, Growing Authoritarian Features," *Pacific Review* 22, no. 3 (2009): 335–53.

73. William Holden and R. Jacobson, *Mining and Natural Hazard Vulnerability.*

74. Interview conducted by William Holden in William Holden and Kathleen Nadeau, "Philippine Liberation Theology and Social Development," 29–89.

75. Karl Gaspar, *To Be Poor and Obscure: The Spiritual Sojourn of a Mindanawon* (Manila: Center for Spirituality, 2004).

76. Robin Broad, *Unequal Alliance: The World Bank, International Monetary Fund, and the Philippines* (Berkeley: University of California Press, 1988), 233.

77. Ellen Bruno, *Satya, A Prayer for the Enemy: The Resistance of Tibetan Buddhist Nuns* (EllenBrunoFilms.com, 1995).

78. Aloysious Pieris, S. J., *An Asian Theology of Liberation* (New York: Orbis, 1988).

79. Pieris, *An Asian Theology of Liberation*, 32.

80. S. Darlington, "The Ordination of a Tree: The Buddhist Ecology Movement in Thailand," *Ethnology* 37, no. 1 (Winter 1998): 1–15.

81. Donald Swearer, "Principles and Poetry, Places and Stories: The Resources of Buddhist Ecology," *Daedalus* 130, no. 4 (2001): 225–42.

82. Darlington, "The Ordination of a Tree," 2.

83. Pierre Walter, "Activist Forest Monks: Adult Learning and the Buddhist Environmental Movement in Thailand," *International Journal of Lifelong Education* 26, no. 3 (2007): 329–45.

84. Darlington, "The Ordination of a Tree," 3.

85. Walter, "Activist Forest Monks," 334.

86. Darlington, "The Ordination of a Tree," 6–7.

87. Ibid., 9.

88. Walter, "Activist Forest Monks," 334.

89. Ibid., 339.

90. Ibid., 340.

91. K. Brown, "In the Water There Were Fish and the Fields Were Full of Rice," in *Buddhism and Ecology*, M. Batchelor and K. Brown, eds. (London: Cassell, 1992), 87–99.

92. Heather Eaton and Lois Ann Lorentzen, *Ecofeminism and Globalization: Exploring Religion, Culture, and Context* (Lanham, MD: Rowman and Littlefield, 2003).

93. Chatsumarn Kabilsingh, *Thai Women in Buddhism* (Berkeley, CA: Parallax Press, 1991).

94. D. Gosling, *Religion and Ecology in India and Southeast Asia* (London: Routledge, 2001), 105.

95. Pradbodh Kumar Rath, "Gandian Sarvodaya," in *Orissa Review* (Orissa, India: October 2010), 36–39.

96. Ungrid Shafer, "From Confucius through Ecofeminism to Partnership Ethics," in *The Sage and the Second Sex: Confucianism, Ethics, and Gender*, C. Li, ed. (Chicago: Open Court, 2000), 97–112.

97. Nelson Wu, *Chinese and Indian Architecture: The City of Man, the Mountain of God, and the Realm of the Immortals* (New York: G. Braziller, 1963).

98. Ibid., 37.

99. Shafer, "From Confucius through Ecofeminism to Partnership Ethics," 108.

100. William LaFleur, *Liquid Life: Abortions and Buddhism in Japan* (Princeton, NJ: Princeton University Press, 1994).

101. C. Risseeuw, *Gender Transformation, Power, and Resistance among Women in Sri Lanka: The Fish Don't Talk about the Water* (New York: E. J. Brill, 1988).

102. Jane Monnig Atkinson and Shelly Errington, *Power and Difference in Island Southeast Asia* (Stanford, CA: Stanford University Press, 1990).

2

—∞∞∞—

Women and Work

This chapter looks at the issue of the subordination and emancipation of women in relation to their position in society. In precolonial Asia, most women did agricultural tasks and household chores. They also bartered and traded in the marketplace. Their tasks generally were associated with their roles as daughters, mothers, and wives. They mainly engaged in subsistence gardening, producing a variety of healthy vegetables and medicinal herbs, and farming, especially cultivating rice and millet. Agricultural crops such as rice and millet, as well as a large number of legumes, were first developed around 7,000 years ago in Asia by people living in northeastern India, Burma, Thailand, China, and Korea. These crops later spread to parts of Indo-China—which is now known as Laos, Cambodia, and Vietnam—and then to Indonesia, Malaysia, the Philippines, Taiwan, and Japan. There are many different kinds of rice and ways to cook it that vary by region. It is considered the main staple of every family meal in most parts of Asia. A common local expression is that a meal is not complete without rice. Rice is so important in daily life that it is widely considered to be an important symbol of prosperity and fertility, and there are many sacred rituals that women perform when cultivating and milling rice that continue to be practiced into the twenty-first century, such as when Javanese and Balinese women use a finger blade to gently cut rice stocks so as not to frighten the spirit of the rice plant. Rice traditionally is the food for the gods and ancestors in Korean, Japanese, and Chinese funeral and mortuary ceremonies. The custom of throwing rice at weddings is another example of the significance of rice and its relationship to women's lives and roles in Asia.

Planting rice almost a century ago, as seen in this photograph (ca. 1890–1925), is still done the same way today in much of the Philippines. This kind of "wet" cultivation is the most common agricultural technique in Southeast Asia. (Library of Congress)

Rice is a good but incomplete source of protein because it lacks many essential amino acids and needs to be supplemented by other protein-rich foods. Women traditionally collected minnows, frogs, crustaceans, shellfish, and other edibles that were more plentifully available from the rich and ecologically diverse rice paddies, riverbeds, lakeshores, and sea coasts in ancient times, although women engaging in subsistence agriculture and organic farming still collect edibles from the environment today. Women traditionally also gathered wild plants, berries, and useful wares from the forests. Women usually prepared daily family meals and took care of children and elderly parents. Some worked as servants in the royal households and agricultural fields of local political leaders. In each of the culturally diverse societies and communities of Asia, women have been busy passing down local customs, traditions, and knowledge systems from generation to generation, down through the ages, which contain medicinal solutions to ailments, recipes for foods that can sustain local temperatures without needing refrigeration, methods of dying fabrics using local and cheaply available natural ingredients, and agricultural practices for better crops without using costly equipment and implements. Their work varies by region, and in relation to their rank and station, but generally, early Asian women—as daughters, wives, and mothers—were expected to do domestic household chores and agricultural tasks. The coming of foreign European colonizers, however, changed the delicate balance of power in the traditional constructions of male and female domains. The colonizers largely disempowered men from the political sphere that used to tie the traditional family into the social hierarchy, and relegated women into the narrow confines of the individual family household, which made it even more difficult for them to ascend the social hierarchy and achieve notoriety in public.

As contemporary women have become more educated, their educational training often influences the types of jobs that they can pursue. Asian women today are found at work in a wide range of occupations and professions, including positions traditionally held by males as doctors, engineers, lawyers, politicians, computer technicians and programmers, and business administrators. They are also found in traditionally female posts as nurses, teachers, and social workers, which, in the new millennia, are positions equally filled by men. Asian women also are responding to globalization and migrating to work in professional, semiprofessional, and occupational posts overseas such as registered nurses and physicians in countries such as the United States and Canada, which have a shortage of trained medical professionals. However, in financially strapped nations like the Philippines, Sri Lanka, and Nepal, college and high school educated women are leaving en masse to work in skilled and unskilled occupations for which they are often overqualified. Southern hemisphere countries in Asia suffer from a "brain drain," that is, the outmigration of gifted and bright young women, and men, who have left their homes for better paying jobs overseas in an effort to better provision the educational and material needs of siblings, spouses and children (if married), and parents. Today, many poor, often overqualified Asian women from nations that are less well off and are struggling from multiple financial and political crises continue to work on temporary overseas contract visas in unskilled jobs that are in high demand as nannies, housecleaners, entertainers, and service industry workers in places such as Japan, Korea, Taiwan, Singapore, the Middle East, Italy, and elsewhere in Europe and North America. Other college educated women, more recently, have found work in international call centers and transnational corporations that shift between countries that offer global companies competitive incentives to invest locally. Such incentives include tax breaks and a large pool of college educated English-speaking young women and men who are looking for work and willing to earn less than counterparts in richer countries. As this chapter will illustrate and discuss, globalization and migration offer new opportunities and challenges for modern women in the workplace.

The forms and origins of women's subordination to men are influenced by, and need to be examined, in relation to the dominant social and economic systems of class and caste in which they are situated and being reproduced. Women, often subliminally, participate in the construction of their own inequitable gender relationships and socialize their daughters into these hierarchical systems. This chapter begins by looking at some of the inequitable arrangements of sex and gender in colonial and postcolonial societies of Asia, and at some of the struggles and social movements that arose to break through these discriminatory arrangements. It ends by discussing some of the negative effects of contemporary globalization processes on local societies, as characterized by the feminization of assembly work for export, overseas contract work, call center work, and prostitution.

AGRARIAN CHANGE AND GENDER DYNAMICS

For much of the twentieth century, most of the societies and cultures of Asia were based on agriculture. While Asia as a whole is rapidly changing in the new millennium and societies such as China and India that were once largely rural are becoming highly citified and globalized, many of their citizens continue to work in agriculture. Most of Southeast Asia—for example, the Philippines, Indonesia, Thailand, Cambodia, Vietnam, Laos, and Burma (also called Myanmar)—is still largely inhabited by subsistence farmers, sharecroppers, and plantation economy workers. This section looks at rural change with a focus on women in the peasantry and their role in revolutionary movements.

After World War II, largely peasant-based movements for independence from colonialism that began before the war continued to proliferate around Asia. In Vietnam, revolutionary leader Ho Chi Min led a peasant movement for national independence in which women fought alongside men to oust the French colonizers, and then the Americans. The Chinese revolutionary leader Mao Tse Sung came to power as a result of a peasant revolution comprised of women who fought alongside men in the battlefields. The rest of the region also was fraught with internal rebellions and conflicts, mainly between landed elite male politicians and businessmen aspiring to keep the status quo and peasants who were struggling for genuine land reform. Though following World War II some countries—such Korea and Japan—redistributed land more equitably to small farmers, other countries—such as the Philippines, Thailand, and Indonesia—instead encouraged small farmers and tenant farmers to participate in the Green Revolution.[1] The Green Revolution emerged in the early 1970s when hybrid varieties of rice

North Vietnamese president Ho Chi Minh is surrounded by North Vietnamese children at his official residence in Hanoi on the occasion of International Children's Day, June 1, 1969. (AP/Wide World Photo)

and corn were developed in an effort to increase production for sale on the market. In the Philippines, for example, even today, the society is rift with agrarian unrest as elite landed politicians continue to intimidate small subsistence farmers, sharecroppers, plantation workers, and indigenous peoples in the name of globalization and development. The progressive Philippine Left, consisting of some nongovernmental organizations (NGOs) and social action workers, continues to organize the peasantries and indigenous peoples in an effort to protect their land and environmentally concerned interests into the new millennia. Revolutionary peasant movements for land reform around Asia have a long history.

In societies such as India, Indonesia, the Philippines, and Vietnam, until recently, the majority of work roles outside the home were between peasant families and their landlords. Peasant-to-landlord relationships generally were based not on money, but rather patron-client exchanges that had some checks and balances to keep the relationships intact. Traditional landlords typically gave some help to their peasant workers during times of need such as medical emergencies or bad harvests. However, when capitalist practices such as paying farm workers a daily wage entered traditional peasant communities, they began to impersonalize the earlier patron-to-client relations. Landlords no longer needed to provide their workers with job security or social security; farm workers were expendable because the unemployed stood ready to take their jobs. By contrast, farm workers would work over-time, even without pay, when called on by landlords for fear of losing their jobs—or in the case of tenant farmers, their rights to take a small portion of the harvest and live on a tiny plot of land.

Agricultural economist William Collier examined the impact of the Green Revolution on peasant women's changing roles in Indonesia.[2] By the late 1970s, farmers who had already adopted new hybrid varieties of rice and mechanized farming techniques began to limit the number of female gleaners in their fields and to reduce their wages.Gleaners tradition-ally were women and girls who came to the fields ready for harvesting early in the morning. In the traditional rice farming communities of Indonesia, they typically used finger scythes to cut and tie as many bundles of rice as possible. Collier stated, "as many as 500 to 1,000 women may join in the har-vest and a one hectare field can be harvested in one hour."[3] Traditionally, landlords allowed villagers to participate in the harvest as an expression of reciprocity. When the paddy was harvested, each woman would carry her bundles of rice to the landlord's house, and his wife would divide them into two bundles according to the traditional sharing custom, one for the gleaner and one for the landlord.

However, the elimination of gleaning, combined with the introduction of mechanized farming techniques and artificial inputs in agriculture, meant that peasant women were forced out of the fields to find other kinds of work for survival.[4] An unprecedented number of women got involved in trading products and goods with each other and at marketplaces, with little money exchanged. They did various odd jobs in the town centers such as house-cleaning and laundering other people's clothes. Farm households, unprece-dentedly, were forced to survive by engaging in different occupations and using a flexible division of labor among members without adherence to tra-ditional agrarian concepts of gender-related work roles. In an effort to make ends meet, each individual household became increasingly dependent on a variety of sources of outside income, not just farming alone, especially remit-tances sent back home by members who decided to migrate further away to work for wages in urban centers.

James Scott's *Weapons of the Weak*[5] and Ann Laura Stoler's *Capitalism and Confrontation in Sumatra's Plantation Belt, 1870–1979*[6] document how gender relations changed as a result of the introduction of capitalist relations of production in agriculture. The historian James Scott looked at the controversial issue of class and gender in a Malaysian farm community. Building upon his earlier thesis of a moral peasant economy, he investigated the question of how small farmers organize openly, or covertly, to express their class interests. Scott contends that the gendered composition of the moral economy becomes eroded by the infiltration of capitalism. He describes the objective effects of mechanized farming, double cropping, changes in demography, gender roles, land tenure, and rents by looking at how large-scale cultivators, small-scale cultivators, and landless and tenant farmer men and women interpret them. Scott argues that the Green Revolution, or the post–World War II introduction of new hybrid varieties of rice and artificial inputs together with mechanized farming, created a situation of increased inequalities between patrons and clients.[7] That is, the introduction of capitalist farming destroyed traditional patron-client ties.

Peasants—sometimes covertly—take revenge against landlords who do not abide by traditional codes of reciprocity. Scott documented Malaysian farm laborers who secretly destroyed property, tampered with machinery, stole, and killed livestock in the work fields.[8] He argued that their individual acts of resistance helped pave the way for other kinds of struggles and revolutions in Southeast Asia.[9] However, when a peasant machetes a cow, is he really doing it to retaliate against well-to-do households as Scott claims?[10] Or is he only trying to protect his own land from overgrazing by his neighbor? Are such secret acts of sabotage done by hired thugs who work for local warlords or patron bosses to control peasants in their domain? Peasants themselves, in relation to capitalism, may already be involved in manipulative, stratified, and inequitable subclasses with respect to matters of gender and economics at the local levels. Clandestine acts of peasant resistance may also be similar to passive forms of resistance committed by urban workers.

Historian James Scott has raised an old yet still contentious question: Do peasants form a class for themselves or are they merely a class in themselves? While he theorized that peasants had the potential to be a revolutionary class capable of organizing on their own behalf, nineteenth-century economic theorist Karl Marx argued to the contrary that peasants, without the help of outside revolutionary leaders, were incapable of organizing to promote their own best interests:

> In so far as there is only a local connection between small holding peasants, and the identity of their interests begets no community, no national unity, and no political organization, they do not form a class. They are consequently incapable of enforcing their class interests in their own name, whether through a parliament or through convention. They cannot represent themselves, so they must be represented. Their representatives must, at the same time, appear as their masters, as an authority over them.[11]

At the turn of the twentieth century, philosopher and social theorist Georg Lukacs defined class consciousness as being introduced to the peasantry by an outside revolutionary party.[12] In contrast, revolutionary feminist Rosa Luxemburg argued that leaders, especially leaders of women's emancipation and liberation movements, evolve out of the class struggle itself and that it is through such struggle that class consciousness is raised.[13] Vina

Lanzona, for example, writes about women who fought first against the Japanese during World War II and then against the Philippine Republic.[14] She explains this revolution would have been impossible without the strong leadership and encouragement of women and support of family, relatives, friends, and neighbors.[15] Women similarly took up arms and participated in educating villagers about the colonial roots of their poverty in the Vietnamese fight for independence (1959–1975) from colonialism and neo-colonialism. However, the argument also can be made that in so far as females exist in a relationship that is subordinate to dominant males who extract surplus labor from them, they form a class in themselves but, to the degree that they accept their subordinate status without struggling to change the systemic causes of their inequitable position, they are not a class for themselves.

Turning to Indonesia, Anne Laura Stoler investigated conditions that promote the formation of a class for itself and supraclass movements that unite peasant groups, and the women within them.[16] She critically examines the historical documents dealing with Sumatra's plantation belt from a bottom-up perspective. Before global capitalism, Indonesia came under the influence of the tributary mode of production in partnership with India, then China, and later the Middle Eastern Islamic empire, the latter of which over-rode India and China as a tutelary power. Muslim traders sought to win the allegiance of Indonesian princes who ruled the peasantry that supplied royal households with surplus wealth. Stoler suggests that it was through this background that the Dutch colonizers moved. They worked directly under the auspices of local male princes to extract the islands' rich natural re-sources for export to Europe but, she stipulates, the Dutch empowerment of preexisting hierarchical male figures and structures of authority, to the exclusion of that of females, was a process that was shaped not so much by colonial design as in reaction to local movements coming up from below.[17] In Indonesia, issues of contestation and change, not institutional stability and cohesion—as the hegemonic colonial discourse would have it—instigated the development of capitalism in addition to the capitalist plantation economy and society with its contingent division of labor along gender lines.

Take Java, for example, where peasants, due to their economic situation, had no other recourse than to produce crops for export while they lived in their villages in relation to a larger state apparatus held in place by a layer of indigenous civil servants. In other words, Java's culture was subtly sub-verted. In contrast, Deli was made up of labor settlements owned by the companies that ran them. In these settlements, mainly male masters and male workers left most of their cultural baggage behind as new relationships of hegemony were formed. Java and Deli illustrate two divergent conditions in the relations of production that gave rise to two distinctly different types of labor movements. In Java, collective resistance movements were organized under the umbrella of religious organizations. In Deli, to the contrary, largely individual acts of labor protest evolved out of the context of a plantation economy that enforced gender-specific policies of recruitment, wage payment, and job allocations that effectively worked against female empowerment and the formation of traditional family groups and collective action. On company-owned plantations, opportunities for mass organization and protest were negated mainly because male workers were intentionally and frequently moved from place to place to set them apart from one another. It is no wonder, states Stoler that "ties between workers were short-lived and not conducive to collectively planned and sustained action. Assaults, on the other hand, by individual or a handful of workers usually required little planning or long-term cooperation."[18] Hence labor protests on plantations did not emerge as a struggle between clearly defined classes, but rather as fragmented acts of resistance. Daily confrontations between laborers and their bosses represent some of the ways in which sublimated class interests were expressed along gender, ethnic, and racial lines.

The Japanese colonization of the islands, however, brought new conditions and possibilities for these male and female peasants to address felt wrongs. For example, the Japanese, largely because of the miserable circumstances of plantation workers and so that these workers could produce for the occupational forces, decided to allow men and women to live together as family units to cultivate small plots of land to feed themselves and reproduce. This started a new "squatter movement" in which peasant families began to settle down on small farms around the peripheries of large plantations. Stoler argues that this movement actually was a form of mass protest that had its own repercussions.[19] The Japanese took advantage of poor peasant men and women by taking their produce and forcing them to produce more than they would otherwise. After colonialism, the conditions on the plantations did not really change. For example, there was no real change in the working conditions or productive relations on the Deli estates.[20] There was not much difference between the quality of life of an indentured worker and a waged worker, and women, children, and older adults were generally left behind to work on the small farm plots at the social margins, which furnished men's needs for social security in times off from work or during periods of unemployment. In other words, there was no transition from a precapitalist system to a capitalist system. Stoler explains that it is through the loopholes in recruitment polices that precapitalist and feudalistic unpaid forms of labor exaction are continued and maintained.[21] Unlike in the past, however, when the plantation estates had to ensure their laborers' subsistence needs, today the availability of a large landless labor pool of temporary workers beyond the skeleton crew has freed companies from providing workers with social security. That is, farming communities at the margins of large plantations are not operating in terms of a production mode that is contrary to that of the plantation economy. These farmers are not part-time peasants and part-time proletariats; rather, they are an intricate part of the plantation estates. They are part of a preexisting economic and social system that has already been subsumed into the logic of the capitalist reproduction of the plantation economy.

By way of concluding this overarching section, the articulation of modes of production theory for the study of peasant societies came under wide-spread attack, after the fall of the Soviet Union in the early 1990s. Mode of production is an analytical way to approach the study of the relationship between precapitalist, semicapitalist, and capitalist economies in the context of different cultures and societies. Mode of production theory was faulted for being irrelevant and overly deterministic in terms of the end result of capitalism—socialism and then communism. Also, critics claimed that this general theory lacked a concept of individual agency. However, late twentieth-century theorists such as Anne Stoler used a mode of production approach that addressed newly emerging issues of class and gender in agrarian social change. Stoler conducted fieldwork and examined pertinent changes occurring in actual communities with unique configurations of gender and culture that were the result of local interactions that existed in relation to global capitalism. It is not that critics of mode of production theory were incorrect in calling for more progressive theories to account for questions of gender, culture, class, and individual agency; rather, they failed to also recognize the importance of looking at rural communities, historically and contextually, in relation to the changing modes of production and gender relations around which they are oriented.

GLOBALIZATION AND FEMALE EMPLOYMENT

Following World War II, there was widespread interest in modernization, which led to numerous development projects in Asia that included agrarian change, urbanization, industrialization, and bureaucratization focused mainly on changing local structures of employment in an effort to mitigate poverty and inequalities. Development encouraged rural to urban migration, initially by men who left women behind to take care of their children by farming small plots of land. Increased pressures from capitalist development caused these women to rely on both their own household production and a cash income. They increasingly participated in intensive cultivation agriculture that did not use expensive artificial fertilizers and chemical inputs, and that caused loss of soil fertility and low crop yields. They had to turn over an inordinate portion of the harvest to landlords, but in the equivalent form of cash, which added to the burden of these women. If they could not sell enough vegetables in the marketplace or find other supplementary means of support, their children's nutrition would suffer. As farms were commercializing and specializing and modern gadgets and TVs made their way into rural households, the family's work routines changed. To scrape by, the small subsistence agricultural family was forced to diversify by working part-time jobs for wages or on other people's fields as well as on their own and in other types of work. Pressures were also placed on schoolchildren to seek better incomes through educational training programs. However, rather than encouraging them to train for future occupations in agriculture and making agriculture a national priority, children were being prepared to study for jobs that were gender based and in high demand in the developed industrialized countries. For example, girls were taught to aspire to become teachers, nurses, or secretaries rather than agricultural specialists and engineers. When grown, they usually migrated alone or with part or all of their family in search of employment. If unskilled, these women often worked as domestic helpers or in other forms of casual labor.

By the late twentieth century, globalization successfully facilitated the mass movement of women into the labor market and largely reconstituted the gender composition of the national work forces of Asia. The growth of export-oriented industrialization and advances in telecommunications, transportation, and technology gave strong impetus to this development. Export-oriented processing zones, mainly based on keeping wages low and offering other kinds of economic incentives (such as tax breaks) to attract foreign investors to their shores became the leading strategy used by the developing countries in Asia. As capital was mobilized with the movement of transnational corporations, global assembly lines were made up of jobs that required little skill and short periods of training. Such jobs are flexible enough to be transferred anywhere, at any moment in time. For factory work, job announcements in the local media and press particularly targeted the young, so-called agile female workers who were quick and nimble fingered because young females often are considered by male bosses to be more malleable and suitable for working long hours at repetitive tasks, and easier to control than men, the latter of whom often are deemed to be more difficult to manage and less tolerant of the tedious and repetitive conditions of factory work. Finally, export-processing zones served to further increase the international division of labor between the rich and poor as Asia's economic giants (e.g., Taiwan, Japan, South Korea, and China) arose from the work of large numbers of women in free trade zones.

FEMINIZATION OF MIGRATION (CONTRACT WORKERS IN THE GULF STATES)

Until the 1970s, most people migrating out of Asia headed to developed countries (e.g., England, Canada, and the United States) that offered opportunities for them to gain permanent status. However, the first oil crisis of the 1970s correlated with an increasingly high unemployment rate in many of the developing countries of South and Southeast Asia.[22] At the same time, there occurred a burst of economic activities in the Gulf region, which attracted Indian, Nepali, Sri Lankan, and Filipino men, among others, who migrated there in large numbers for waged work. That is, the Asian economic crisis of the 1970s paralleled the growth of the oil industry in the Middle Eastern Gulf states. The Gulf governments collaborated among themselves to raise the selling price of oil on the international market, which resulted in a sudden influx of surplus funds. Profits were channeled back into the development of local infrastructures, which resulted in a huge construction boom that created many new job opportunities for foreign workers. Because the populations of Kuwait, Bahrain, and the United Arab Emirates (UAE) were young and still less then 1 million, these nations were unable to meet the new demands for labor.[23] Also, Middle Eastern females scarcely participated in the local work force, so to fill this gap, Asian women began to be recruited and migrated to these countries for work as well.[24]

At the same time, international labor opportunities and local economic insecurities and poverty created outmigration from the Third World, or developing, countries of Asia. The Philippine government was one of the first to implement a strategic plan of placing its own citizens in jobs abroad to shore up its economy, a plan that soon was replicated and used by other countries such as India and Thailand for the same purpose. The 1970s oil crisis, increasing militarization, and warfare, especially the United States' war against communist Vietnam, contributed to solidifying the structural conditions that compelled many to seek work abroad.

By the 1990s, another Asian economic debt crisis occurred. In exchange for restructuring debt repayments in Thailand, the Philippines, and Korea, International Monetary Fund (IMF) and World Bank policies continued to exert pressure over these nations to further liberalize and restructure their economies. In 1989, for example, the Philippine government was given a US$1.3 billion loan from the IMF on the condition that the liberalization (e.g., abolishing price control, oppressing labor unions, and export-oriented development) of the economy would be continued, as would privatization of government-owned industries and institutions. President Fidel Ramos (1992–1997) added another US$650 million loan from the United States to the Philippine foreign debt.[25] In such cases, worker remittances become a significant source for generating foreign currency and helping repayment of the national debt.

The outward migration flows of temporary contract workers from South and Southeast Asia to the Middle East and Europe became increasingly feminized beginning in the 1980s, when more women than men started migrating, mainly for jobs as nannies, maids, cooks, entertainers, and in other helping professions and service occupations.[26] This new type of feminized migration flow was patterned after and facilitated by expanding social support networks, including nongovernmental organizations, churches, and cultural organizations.[27] In another example, before Iraq invaded Kuwait in August 1990, approximately 500,000 Filipinos were reported to be working around the Middle East, although few worked in Iraq during this time period because ordinary Iraqis were too poor to hire them. However, explains *New York Times* journalist Arnold Wayne, this situation changed when the United States invaded Iraq in 2003. U.S. companies there preferentially hired Filipinos and other nationals with English-speaking skill, rather than local Iraqis who were looking for work.[28]

However, there are no available statistics about the gender and ethnic discrimination that women contract workers coming from Asia have been subjected to in the Gulf countries for decades.[29] Female migrant workers leaving for financially better off countries, for example, in the Middle East and East Asia, take certain risks with recruiters who charge high fees and are legally responsible for their safety. Desperate for jobs, many are tricked by illegal agents who send them overseas without any legal protection. The job search can be expensive, as female migrant workers are known to sell properties and incur debts to pay off high recruiter's fees and the costs of transportation. Once at the work place, they may face further hardships such as extremely poor working and living conditions. In the case of working inside the privacy of another's home, these temporary contract workers often work longer hours without extra pay: they are underpaid and may even get physically and/or sexually abused by their employers. Migrant workers have to learn new cultural ways of behavior. Far from their families and support networks, they are especially vulnerable during times of political instability and change. For example, according to environmental science professor and Philippine specialist Barbara Goldoftas, an estimated 40,000 to 60,000 Filipinos were stranded in Kuwait during the Iraqi invasion of 1990.[30] In the aftermath of the chaos, they received little assistance from the Philippine embassy. At first, the embassy was closed and when it reopened, the Filipinos were left to fend for themselves. Many took abandoned vehicles or paid Iraqi soldiers to lead them on a dangerous trip through the desert. They had to cross through many military checkpoints, and most had to sell their belongings for food and water. Once in refugee camps, some were stuck for weeks before they could get out. Goldoftas documented about 30,000 Filipinos who returned home this way.

In summer 2000 in the Philippines, anthropologist Kathleen Nadeau interviewed 10 returned female migrant workers from the Middle East, Singapore, and Japan. The story of Delia (a pseudonym) is presented here because it shares patterns with the stories of many, albeit not all, domestic workers.[31] Her saga uncovers unfair labor practices that commoditize and sell women to work as servants. These practices sometimes leave these women in almost slave-like conditions. It lends insight into the recruitment practices of fraudulent recruiters and some of the risks taken by female migrant workers. Delia's saga specifically chronicles a hidden world in which women are laid open to potential abuse and enslavement by employers in the global domestic worker industry that cuts across national boundaries. It also tells of poor Iraqi soldiers who—for a fee—risked their lives to help refugees across the desert into a safety zone in Iraq. Delia's tale shows the triumph of our common humanity during wartime. What is being retold here is also the reality of the dreams and sufferings of these women who migrate due to lack of local employment opportunities and send their hard earned remittances back home. The story also reveals the complexity of international migration; distinguishing regular migration from the irregular is not always straightforward.

In 1987 in the Philippines, Delia unwittingly applied for a passport at a fraudulent recruitment agency temporarily set up in her town's center. She believed in good faith that this was a legitimate agency. It cost her 25,000 pesos (US$5,000) to have her paperwork processed over a two-month period. To pay for her trip, her family had to sell a piece of land. Together with three other Filipinas, she was driven to the Aquino International Airport in Manila where, to her surprise, she was given passport with only a tourist visa for Hong Kong. The four women were instructed on what to say when going through immigration control and told by the recruiter escort not to "squeal" on the agency. Delia, by this point, had psychologically prepared herself to return home if immigration officials caught her with a fake passport. They all made it through customs. The recruiter exchanged their old passports for new ones with entry visas for Kuwait, then he left them on their own.

On arrival in Kuwait, Delia was met by two of her four female employers, who were sisters, who had never been married, living together in one compound: one was teacher, the second a businesswoman, the third a doctor, and the fourth a banker. Delia was interviewed by each of them and then made to do all of the housework alone. As she explained, while making a huge gesture with her hands, "They lived in a Big House." Not only did she have to do all of their housework, she was responsible for washing four cars every day. "Imagine four cars," Delia reiterated in exasperation. There was only one other helper, an Indian cook, and Delia "had to do all of the household chores alone." Each sister lived in a separate quarter, and there was a large inner quarter that they shared. Delia was given no days off. She was not allowed to use the phone, not even to receive calls. She had to contend with four masters, each with her own personality. The two elder sisters were harsh, while the two younger sisters behaved more kindly toward her. She was not allowed to go to sleep until midnight and could never sleep ahead of her masters. Delia's workday began at 4:00 in the morning. Otherwise, if she didn't get herself up there would be loud ringing bells. Mealtimes were a constant struggle for her at the beginning. She was unaccustomed to eating lamb and spicy foods, and she lost a lot of weight. In addition to adjusting to a new diet, she was not given her full month's salary. Although her contract explicitly stated that she was supposed to receive 8,000 pesos a month, on arriving in Kuwait, she was given only 4,000 pesos (US$80) per month, and that was what she remitted to her family.

Of all the many chores that Delia had to do, it was washing the cars and ironing that she found most difficult. The four sisters wore veils from head to foot, and their laundry was no less than a mountain of clothes that piled taller than Delia herself. She had to iron daily, but that was not the real problem. Rather, after ironing, they expected her to wash the cars. As Constable (1997) noted, Filipinas generally believe that washing cars is a male task.[32] They also believe that it is not healthy to take a bath until one has cooled down. Delia believed that she "shouldn't wet her hands anymore after ironing," but at the outset she could not complain. One day, though, she told the sisters that having already taken her morning bath, she found it hard to proceed from ironing to washing the cars, and if they persisted to force her to do so, she would go crazy. So they agreed to release her from having to wash the car.

There were other acts of cruelty, a few of which stand out. She did not know how to use the "clamp system" to turn the stove on and off, so they scolded her. She broke three glasses when washing the dishes, and she had to pay for them. One day, she was cleaning the tropical birdcage, and all of a sudden, the birds flew out. She was made to pay one month's salary to reimburse her employers for the loss of the birds. She was not allowed to go outside of the house except to throw out the garbage. She had no friends, no contact with anyone, as she was not even allowed to use the phone. Throughout this ordeal, Delia could not complain, even though she wished that she were back in the Philippines.

Iraq invaded Kuwait in August 1990, and the home in which Delia lived and worked was dangerously situated just three minutes from the airport. Suddenly, they heard explosions and bombings all around. Her employers forbid her and the cook from going out to their embassies. She pleaded with them to allow her to return home. They responded: "If you want to go, you will get killed." They scurried her and the cook to a ranch outside of the city just as Iraqi soldiers were about to ransack their home. During the war, everyone was frightened because there was a constant barrage of bombings. Delia repeatedly demanded that her employers return her to the Philippine embassy; after two weeks of constantly pleading with her employers to let her go, they relented. Arriving at the embassy, Delia recalled hearing that there were some 60,000 Filipinos already there, out of a total of around 100,000 Filipinos working in Kuwait. All other institutions were closed.

Her employers asked the embassy officials whether they had to pay Delia her salary that was due her.

The embassy personnel said that they did not, so she was made to sign release papers. She spent another week languishing at the embassy before learning that the Iraqis were offering Filipinos a way out of Kuwait. Iraqi soldiers had promised to escort them to Baghdad for a price of 10 dinars per head. From there, they could go to Jordan and then back home to the Philippines.

A group of 40 Filipino men and women banded together when confronted by the Iraqi soldiers, each saying, "He is my husband" or "She is my wife." They did this to avoid the possibility of anyone being raped by the soldiers. Delia decided to take her chances with the Iraqis when she realized that she was not going to get any real help from the Philippine embassy. Her group walked for a couple of days through the desert during the bombings. It took three weeks for them to reach a refugee camp in Iraq. The Filipinos survived by sharing whatever resources they had. When they finally arrived at the refugee camp, it was packed full with people from the Philippines, China, the United States, and many other nations. They stayed for three weeks without having even a bath. There were no public toilets or restroom facilities. It was not until two days before they were to be deported home that they received blankets from their Iraqi caretakers. Prior to that, they slept with their bags and were prepared to die. As Delia explained, "Even if you had money, you couldn't use it and whoever had savings used it to buy water." There was strong bonding between the Filipinos who shared everything. Also, there were many incidents of Filipinos having nervous breakdowns. Many suffered from depression and other sicknesses. Some died.

One day in September 1990, a Filipino senator visited the refugee camp and told the refugees that Saddam Hussein had made an agreement with the Philippine embassy that the Filipinos would not be harmed. Some of the Filipino refugees had Iraqi passports; others did not. Some had lost all of their papers. There was a bit of a commotion until a decision was reached that the Filipinos would leave in groups. The first group to go would be those who had their passports; the second and third groups would be comprised of those who had lost their papers. Delia boarded the plane to go home with no money, no shoes, and no luggage. All she had was her handbag. Her necklace had been stolen by an Iraqi guard, and even her shoes were stolen by someone in the camp. What she remembers most about her ordeal is that it was a time of "Filipinos helping fellow Filipinos." Even when she landed "penniless" in Manila, one of her fellows who had a place to stay in the city invited her over. The next morning, her friend brought her to the bus terminal and gave her some pocket money so that she could go home.

Delia's arrival home caused a big commotion in the town. As she explained with tears in her eyes, "I was thin, very dark, and my hair was in disarray." Her parents were so overjoyed to see her that they were crying, and the whole town came out to welcome her home. Delia's story does not end here. While "the Philippine government did not even bother to check" to see how she was doing, Delia heard on the radio that President George Bush Sr. had made an agreement with the Iraqi government to pay a certain amount of compensation to those affected by the war. So, she went to the Bureau of Immigration to process the necessary paperwork. Seven years later, in 1997, she received 170,000 pesos (US$3,400) in compensation from the Iraqi government. This made it possible for her to construct a house. Also, she is able to make ends meet by selling vegetables produced from her own farm. At 37 years of age (at the time of the interview), Delia seemed happily married and had three children. She ended her story by wondering how she survived such an ordeal without going crazy. She concluded that her "strength was heaven sent." She brought "a bible, rosary beads, and a prayer book" to Kuwait, and it was her faith in God, she exclaimed, that carried her home safely.

As in the case of Delia, it often is poor women who fall victim in times of economic and political crisis. The governmental policies of some (especially poor) Asian governments that siphon off overseas working women's remittances may help to build up their national economies in the short term by lessening unemployment, but—over the long duration of history—such stopgap measures will only further divide the rich from the poor, rather than promoting world unity and peace.

PROSTITUTION

Global processes today are commercializing sex and alienating labor as part of the economy and culture of capitalism. Sex tourism is promoted in countries such as Thailand and the Philippines with loans that the World Bank and International Monetary Fund offer as a strategy for economic development. While legalized brothels organized as part of the British colonial empire[33] and those organized during World War II by the Japanese imperial army[34] have been disbanded, today there is still room for comparison in terms of the way prostitution zones have developed around U.S. military bases in the region. Researchers Saundra Sturdevant and Brenda Stoltzfus argue that prostitution was promoted by the U.S. military in the Asia-Pacific region after World War II to provide soldiers with rest and recreational activities.[35] This servicing of the troops was intensified and increased during the Vietnam War period. However, after the war, U.S. military bases everywhere in the region were scaled down, and the United States pulled out of Thailand entirely. Sex tourism began to be promoted instead.

Young women, gay men, and even children are lured by often illicit recruiters to work in the teeming array of brothels, massage parlors, and

Sex workers wait for clients outside a bar in Bangkok, Thailand, in 2001. In Southeast Asia, the sex tourism industry is substantial, fueling the enslavement of women, young girls, and young boys. (Stephen Shaver/AFP/Getty Images)

sex bars that service mainly males from the United States, Europe, Australia, Japan, Korea, Malaysia, Singapore, and the Gulf states. Despite Thailand's international reputation as one of the modern sex capitals of the world, public discussions of the subject inside Thailand are not undertaken. However, anthropologist Ryan Bishop and feminist activist and professor Lillian Robinson state, "breaking this silence that pervades the local people's everyday lives can begin the process of liberating prostitutes from the oppressive and exploitative circumstances that afflict their lives."[36] While there are some nongovernmental organization workers, human rights activists, and Buddhist and Christian social action workers partnering with prostitutes in Thailand, the Philippines, and elsewhere to assist them in their recovery and to provide them with needed job training for potentially successful reintegration into the dominant society, more needs to be done.

As political scientist Mary Sullivan and feminist scholar and political activist Sheila Jeffreys explain, "prostitution is violence in and of itself."[37] As part of the everyday practices of the sex industry, women must engage in acts that are sexually and physically degrading. They are forced to disassociate emotionally and survive by using drugs or alcohol. The acts that men buy the right to perform on prostituted women include all forms of sexual violence that feminists are seeking to eliminate. Furthermore, in countries such as Japan, Australia, and the Netherlands, for example, where the sex industry can operate above ground and is given the full protection of the state, "the standard act of prostitution, coitus, is experienced as so violating by prostituted women in legal brothels that they have to disassociate emotionally and engage in complex diversionary tactics to restrict the harm they suffer."[38] In addition, there is no way for legislators to predict what new demands prostitutes' employers may make on them for purposes of making money. Sex businesses are often connected to the lucrative international sex trafficking industry, including illegal syndicates operating from Asia. There are many examples of women and children who fall prey to illegal recruiters who have hoodwinked them into believing they will be doing other work but, instead, find themselves being kidnapped and scurried away into legal brothels in Bangkok, Japan, Holland, and Australia—and to illegal brothels in the United States and elsewhere. Typically, these women are forced to service hundreds of men to pay off high recruitment fees (passport fees, the cost of airfare, and board and lodging) before receiving any money. Also, women and children are sometimes locked up in brothels. That is, they are treated like slaves as defined in accordance with capitalism's profit-oriented ideology wherein a human or any creature (e.g., consider the harm done to animals for food and science) can be treated like an object for sale.

Researcher and writer Anne Seagraves provides an example of how the influx of colonial capitalism in the form of the transpacific slave trade undid Chinese traditional and customary forms of behavior.[39] From the mid-1800s to the early 1900s, thousands of Chinese slaves were brought to California. Many were girls procured by Chinese recruiters seeking profit. Typically, they were packed in crates like animals and shipped to San Francisco. By the turn of the twentieth century, female babies as young as one year old began to arrive to be auctioned off for as little as $100 each. These girls were sold to brothel owners or the notorious crib owners in Chinatown. The girls who were placed in cribs wore only a shirt with nothing below and were forced to sing out to passing customers. They had an average lifespan of six years. Seagraves explains that "when they were no more use to the owners, they were placed in a small cell where they had a choice of committing suicide or being murdered."[40] Would this lawless behavior have occurred in the early histories of the spread of the wider Indic and Chinese civilizations? Not likely, for as we already have seen in Chapter 1, they lived in accordance with ancient ethical codes of conduct.

Jeremy Seabrook interviewed actors involved in the sex trade industry, from clients to nongovernmental organization workers who provide prostituted women with alternative employment opportunities and training for reintegration into society.[41] Cultural geographer Lisa Law gives voice to the prostitutes themselves, who speak about their own experiences, struggles, hopes, and dreams.[42] She interjects her own voice as a questioning subject who interrogates her position in the debate over how best to define prostitution as being either (1) a legitimate form of sex work or (2) an exploitative setup that victimizes women (who, arguably, can be shown to have no other choice). Law conducts her fieldwork in nightclubs around Cebu City, Philippines. She wins the trust of local prostitutes, one of whom she eventually moved in with. This allowed her to delve more deeply into the lives and experiences of local sex workers. In the process, she opened a window for sex workers to tell their own stories about their employment in the bars. Law found that these women's stories do not fit the stereotypical stories of sex workers as victims of colonialism, sex tourism, or the political economy.[43] She argues that prostitution is only one component of these women's complex lives. It is a job that they often work for short periods of time, and this cannot be equated with their individual personhood. In articulating the prostitute as victim or agent debate, her analysis reveals a story that grapples with not only her own role, but that of nongovernmental organization workers and advocates of women's liberation. Law contends that this is a debate that denies the ambiguity of the identification of nongovernmental organization workers and feminists with women in the sex industry, as well as the possibility that this debate can provide a new theoretical basis upon which new identities can be constituted.[44] But her contention that prostitution can be a form of work that women freely choose is highly contentious in the Philippines, where impoverishment forces many to do what they otherwise would not dream of doing, and where increasing numbers of children are being caught up in this profession.

It is not really through spelling out the differences between women involved in the sex trade industry in terms of whether they freely chose their jobs or were coerced into it by a globalizing capitalist system, but by joining forces with them on equal footing in the recognition that their daily struggles are our common human struggles that result not so much from within, but from the very real outside force of an inequitable and unjust world economic system.

That is, policymakers at international lending agencies and local governments rationalized and perpetuated the sex industry in Asia by saying that it always existed there. But the kind of sexuality that can be bought and sold as a commodity on the market is not the same kind of sexuality that was integral to the social reproduction of traditional Asian societies. As we have already discussed in Chapter 1, precolonial relations of bondage and slavery were an integral part of the social reproduction of the underlying economy and society. There were moral and legal codes governing social relations of power and dominance. However, this is not the same as asserting that there were no exploitative and abusive sexual relationships in precolonial Asia. To the contrary, for example, political scientist Katherine Moon documents that the Korean government has a long history of using women and their sexuality for political ends.[45]

Ever since the Koryo dynasty (918–1392), females have been trained as entertainers, *kisaeng*, to serve the royal court of exclusively male scholar-officials. The Choson dynasty's (1392–1910) adoption of Confucianism implemented strict legal and social measures to enforce women's chastity in the rest of the female population. Early Korean monarchs sent thousands of women as tribute to emperors in China. In Korea, there are legends of concubines who sacrificed their chastity and lives for national welfare (e.g., Nongae, the concubine of General Choe Kyonghoe, who seduced a Japanese commander during the invasion of Korea in 1592). It is against this particular history, argues Moon, that we must understand the current South Korean government's emphasis on state-building, national security, and economic development, and lack of concern for the social welfare of prostitutes (who service military troops, businessmen, and tourists) and the policies on prostitution as a form of tribute.[46]

However, the contemporary concept of prostitution entails a more complex way of exploiting women. Precolonial women in Asia were sold into concubinage and as wives, but they were familiar with what was expected of them, there were some legal codes to protect their rights, and they knew the places where they were prostituted. Today—in contrast—the situation for prostitutes who may be sent to strange parts of the world is much more complex, and this disjuncture from the past needs to be recognized. Many problems are associated with the transnational sex trade industry. Also, the impact of economic recession and neoliberalization on the health and social welfare of local populations needs to be examined. The AIDS epidemic, for example, calls for a commitment on the part of the international community for resolution. The spread of AIDS brings a host of new problems as sex recruiters are on the lookout for younger women and even girls to meet the demands of their older clients. In addition, most of the prostitutes from Asia have experienced poverty and socialization to such a degree that they are willing to sacrifice their own individual well-being for the sake of their families. Because local governments stand to gain, financially and politically, by working with international lenders to promote tourism, it is unlikely that indebted governments are going to be able to change this sex tourism trend. Hopefully, the day will come when dialogue between policymakers, government officials, religious leaders, and those who are most affected on the ground will take up these issues, which are socioeconomic issues with cultural and religious dimensions.

GLOBALIZATION: INFLUX OF THE CALL CENTERS

Globalization has brought new economic employment opportunities, especially for young college graduates, to work in the call center industry.

Hewlett-Packard employees work at the company's Business Process Outsourcing call center in Bangalore, India, August 7, 2007. (AP Photo/Aijaz Rahi)

While call centers in the countries of Singapore, Korea, Vietnam, and China specialize in serving local communities within their region and country, those in India and the Philippines cater mainly to countries in Europe and North America, using the English language. The influx of the international call center industry to India and the Philippines has generated significant income and employment, while providing women with equal access to employment opportunities. However, the industry often suffers from negative stigmatization because night shift work changes local family paradigms. Feminist geographer Reena Patel explains that global call centers remove traditional restrictions on women's mobility, bringing them into the public world of the night.[47] As young people get connected with the call center culture, the family changes as a result of globalization.

The Philippines has overtaken India as the number one destination for the call center industry, employing some 350,000 operators as compared with India's 330,000.[48] The Contact Center in the Philippines reports that call centers generated some US$6.3 billion in tax revenues in 2010.[49] As well, the government offers some scholarships to train workers and tax incentives to multinational corporations that bring jobs into the country. However, Indian and Filipino families are changing due to globalization and the incoming global services industry because young people connected with the call center culture think that call centers represent the global culture, yet the reality of everyday local life for them is very different.

Business economists Robert Keital and Ramon del Rosario explain that graveyard shift work is potentially dangerous, especially for women.[50] Night work increases women's risks of breast cancer because it disrupts one's usual sleep patterns, which interrupts the nocturnal production of the hormone melatonin. This hormone slows down the growth of breast tumors.[51] Other potential health risks for call center workers are urinary track infections and kidney problems due to limited breaks, eye strain, backaches, stiff necks, insomnia, migraines, colds, itchy throats, voice problems, hearing problems, and musculoskeletal disorders. Philippine human resource management specialist and writer Fristine de Gula refers to such health risks as "lifestyle diseases."[52] Call center operators also are prone to hypertension and strokes, ulcers and acid reflux, diabetes, and anemia because they work at night, sit at their stations for long hours without relieving themselves until their break times, and eat fast food because that is what is available and they do not have time to go outside to eat right. de Gula explains:

> They practically live on unhealthy diets of processed food, smokes, cups of coffee and severe lack of exercise: a significant number of them believe having drinks with colleagues, after work [at 7 a.m.] is somewhat necessary to build up their social relationships and rapport. These practices lead to a whole host of diseases that traditionally were seen in old people and may even lead to depression and family discord.
>
> The call centers are air conditioned to create the ambiance of being, for example, in America. But this gives the young people a distorted perception of what is happening and what kind of life they want for their future. Those who are married go home to sleep during the daytime hours when their children are awake. There is no communication between them. The parents want to preserve the family but how can they do that if their stomachs are empty?[53]

WOMEN AND WORK TODAY

Over the course of the last century, globalization and development have opened up new employment opportunities for women in Asia. They can be found at work in all professions, as doctors, lawyers, teachers, professors, politicians, computer programmers, scientists, and engineers. The greater majority, however, still cannot afford to pay for the education that is required before applying for work in the professional fields. Most women in Asia continue to look for work as domestic helpers, service industry workers, entertainers, street vendors, and petty entrepreneurs. Many women work in agricultural subsistence farming or have moved to cities in search of work in the informal sector, especially as vendors, domestic helpers, or petty entrepreneurs and, in the formal sector, as entry level clerks and service industry workers. According to a recent UN Interagency Task Force report on women, 48.2 percent of all women in South and Southeast Asia worked in the agricultural sector in 2009, compared to 38.9 percent of men.[54] Agriculture remained the most widespread employer of women in this region but not in the developed economies of Asia. An International Labor Organization and Asian Development Bank report finds that women are the primary producers of food, while men manage most of the commercial crops. Working conditions for female farm laborers tend to be harsher than for their male counterparts. Also, there is a disproportionate share of unpaid female family workers. Despite the hazardous risks of agriculture, it remains one of the least protected types of work by the government.[55] Gender gaps in economic activities are high, as indicated by the preponderance of women in agriculture and low paid informal jobs. Increasing numbers of Asian women are migrating to work away from home. They migrate from rural areas to urban centers and other countries. Female migrants, especially young female migrants, often face discrimination, disadvantages, marginalization, and vulnerability. They are much more susceptible than migrant men and local women to abuse. Lack of employment opportunities in rural areas, the pressure to help improve the family income, and the desire for better opportunities and more personal freedom often push women to search for jobs away from home. However, lacking professional networks, family connections, and letters of recommendation, rural to urban migrant women often find that the only jobs open to them are feminized positions such as domestic servants, housekeepers, and caregivers in other people's homes; cleaners and servers in hotels and restaurant industries; and salesworkers in department stores. These jobs pay little, yet the 2011 International Labor Organization and Asian Development reports in *Women Labor Markets* that compared with their male counterparts, these migrant women send more of their income home to families, who become increasingly dependent on their remittances.[56]

Even in the most prosperous East Asian countries of Korea and Japan, women still have a long way to go, as preferential hiring practices continue to favor males over females. Some Korean and Japanese women work in token positions of power and authority at the upper levels of governance, education, and business, but most continue to occupy traditionally female work roles as teachers, nurses, secretaries, bank tellers, and small business owners, or stay at home mothers. Young women who work as bank tellers in Korea, for example, often are let go by employers who encourage them to be stay at home mothers and wives when they marry. Such employers typically give hiring preference to single young attractive female representatives and customer service personnel. By contrast, South and Southeast Asian women may enjoy greater representation and more equality with men across the professional and occupational fields but often are not paid enough to make a living unless they work outside their own country or for a foreign company or international organization. With globalization comes the international concept of equality of employment opportunity as exemplified by young college educated women and men given equal opportunity at work in call centers. However, the local realities of women's participation in the labor market, today as yesterday, often remain contradictory and complex.

NOTES

1. James Putzel, *A Captive Land: The Politics of Agrarian Reform in the Philippines* (Quezon City, Philippines: Ateneo de Manila University Press, 1992). For details on post–World War II land reform in Taiwan, Japan, and Korea, see Chapter 3.

2. In Noeleen Heyzer, *Working Women in South-East Asia: Development, Subordination, and Emancipation* (Milton Keynes, and Philadelphia: Open University Press, 1986), 20.

3. William L. Collier, "Agricultural Evolution in Java," in G. E. Hansen, ed., *Agricultural and Rural Development in Indonesia* (Boulder, CO: Westview Press, 1981), 147–73, cited in Heyzer, *Working Women in South-East Asia*, 20.

4. Collier, "Agricultural Evolution in Java," cited in Heyzer, *Working Women in South-East Asia*, 21.

5. James Scott, *Weapons of the Weak: Everyday Forms of Resistance* (New Haven, CT: Yale University Press, 1985).

6. Ann Laura Stoler, *Capitalism and Confrontation in Sumatra's Plantation Belt, 1870–1979* (New Haven, CT: Yale University Press, 1985).

7. Scott, *Weapons of the Weak* 147.

8. Ibid., 271, 289–90.

9. Ibid., 273.

10. Ibid., 271.

11. Karl Marx, "Primitive Accumulation Reversed: Society Owes Initial Expenses to the Peasant Communes," in *Peasants and Peasant Society, Selected Readings*, T. Shanin, ed. (New York: Basil Blackwell, 1987).

12. Georg Lukacs, *History and Class Consciousness: Studies in Marxist Dialectics* (Cambridge, MA: Massachusetts Institute of Technology Press, 1971).

13. Norman Geras, "Rosa Luxemburg," in A *Dictionary of Marxist Thought*, Tom Bottomore, ed. (Cambridge, MA: Harvard University Press), 293–94.

14. Vina Lanzona, *Amazons of the Huk Rebellion: Gender, Sex, and Revolution in the Philippines* (Madison: University of Wisconsin Press, 2009).

15. Lanzona, *Amazons of the Huk Rebellion*, 49.

16. Stoler, *Capitalism and Confrontation in Sumatra's Plantation Belt*.

17. Ibid., 6.

18. Ibid., 14.

19. Ibid., 97.

20. Ibid., 45.

21. Ibid., 209.

22. Raymond Bonner, *Waltzing with a Dictator: The Marcoses and the Making of American Policy* (New York: Times Books, 1987).

23. S. Birks and C. Sinclair, "Migration for Employment in the Arab Countries," *Development Digest* 4 (October 17, 1979): 65–89. Cited in Jonathan Addelton, "The

Impact of the Gulf War on Migration and Remittances in Asia and the Middle East,"
International Migration 29, no. 4 (1991): 509–26.

24. Addleton, "The Impact of the Gulf War on Migration and Remittances"; Andrew
Gardner, *City of Strangers: The Transnational Indian Community in Manama, Bahrain*
(Tuscan, AZ: Dissertation presented to the University of Arizona's Graduate College,
2005); Icduygu Sirkeci and Ibrahim Sirkeci, "Changing Dynamics of the Migratory Regime
between Turkey and Arab Countries," *Turkish Journal of Population Studies* 20 (1998): 3–15.

25. Ligaya Lindio-McGovern, *Filipino Peasant Women: Exploitation and Resistance*
(Philadelphia: University of Pennsylvania Press, 1997).

26. Barbara Ehrenreich and Arlie Russell Hoschschild, *Global Women: Nannies,
Maids, and Sex Workers in the New Economy* (New York: Metropolitan Books, 2003).
R. Gopinathan Nair, "Return of Overseas Contract Workers and their Rehabilitation
and Development in Kerala (India): A Critical Account of Policies, Performance and
Prospects," *International Migration* 37, no. 1 (1999): 209–42; Kathryn Ward, *Women
Workers and Global Restructuring* (Ithaca, NY: School of Industrial and Labor
Relations, 1990).

27. Lisa Law and Kathleen Nadeau, "Globalization, Migration and Class Struggles:
NGO Mobilization for Filipino Domestic Workers," *Kasarinlan: Philippine Journal
of Third World Studies* 14, no. 1 and 2 (1999), 51–68.

28. Arnold Wayne, "Philippines Is Likely to Supply Many Workers to Rebuild Iraq,"
New York Times (April 9, 2003), 8–9.

29. Alcestis Abrera-Mangahas, "Violence against Women Migrant Workers: The
Philippine Experience," in *Filipino Workers on the Move: Trends, Dilemmas, and Policy
Options*, Benjamin Carino, ed. (Quezon City, Philippines: Philippine Migration
Research Network, 1998), 45–80.

30. Barbara Goldoftas, "Despite the Gulf Crisis, Migrant Workers Still Pin Hopes," in
Women in Action (Manila: Isis International, 1991), 12–14.

31. Excerpted from Kathleen Nadeau, "Out-Migration from the Philippines with a
Focus on the Middle East," *East Asian Pastoral Review* 45, no. 3 (2008), 261–71.

32. Nicole Constable, *Maid to Order in Hong Kong: An Ethnography of Filipino
Workers* (Ithaca, NY: Cornell University Press, 1997).

33. Philippa Levine, *Prostitution, Race, and Politics: Policing Venereal Disease in the
British Empire* (New York: Routledge, 2003).

34. Sarah Soh, "Centering the Korean Comfort Women Survivors" [video review],
Critical Asian Studies 33, no. 4 (2001): 603–8.

35. Saundra Sturdevant and Brenda Stoltzfus, *Let the Good Times Roll: Prostitution
and the U.S. Military Bases* (New York: New Press, 1992).

36. Ryan Bishop and Lillian Robinson, *Night Market: Sexual Cultures and the Thai
Economic Miracle* (New York and London: Routledge, 1998).

37. Mary Sullivan and Sheila Jeffreys, *Legalizing Prostitution Is Not the Answer: The
Example of Australia* (Victoria, Australia: Coalition against the Trafficking of Women, n.d.).

38. Ibid., 10.

39. Anne Seagraves, *Soiled Doves: Prostitution in the Early West* (Hayden, ID:
Wesanne Publications, 1994).

40. Ibid., 139.

41. Jeremy Seabrook, *Travels in the Skin Trade: Tourism and the Sex Industry*
(London: Pluto Press, 2001).

42. Lisa Law, *Sex Work in Southeast Asia: The Place of Desire in a Time of AIDS* (London and New York: Routledge, 2000).

43. Ibid., 63.

44. Ibid., 119.

45. Katherine H. S. Moon, *Sex Among Allies: Military Prostitution in U.S.-Korea Relations* (New York: Columbia University Press, 1997), 40–45.

46. Ibid., 41.

47. Reena Patel, *Working the Night Shift: Women in India's Call Center Industry* (Stanford, CA: Stanford University Press, 2010).

48. News release, "The Philippines Passes India in Call Cente Jobs" in *USA Today* (January 1, 2011).

49. "Philippine Country Overview, 2010–2012, on Call Centers," in ReportLinker (October 2011).

50. Robert Keitel and Ramon del Rosario Sr., "Night Work Prohibition of Women Workers in the Philippine Call Center Industry," presented at the Conference on Regulating for Decent Work: Innovative Labour Regulation in a Turbulent World (Geneva, July 8–10, 2009).

51. Harvard Medical School Survey in Ibid. 7.

52. Fristine Gizelle S. De Gulla, "Life after Dark: Lifestyle Diseases among Call Center Employees," *Philippine Online Chronicles* (November 6, 2010): 16–24.

53. Ibid.

54. Interagency Task Force on Rural Women, "Rural Women and the Millennium Development Goals Facts and Figures," in *Women Watch: Information on Resources for Gender Equality and Women's Empowerment* (New York: UN Interagency Task Force on Rural Women, 2010).

55. International Labor Organization and Asian Development Bank, *Women and Labor Markets in Asia: Rebalancing for Equity* (New York: International Labor Organization and Asian Development Bank, 2011).

56. International Labour Organization and Asian Development Bank, *Women and Labour Markets in Asia: Rebalancing for Gender Equality.* (Geneva, Switzerland: International Labour Organization and Asian Development Bank, 2011): 162.

3

❧❧❧

Women and Family

The rich and culturally diverse ancient Asian family regimes were geographically vast and socially complex systems that had no parallels in medieval Europe.[1] The family consisted of the incorporation of the couple into the social hierarchy. Kinship played an important role in the development of hierarchy.[2] However, while in East and South Asia, for example, imperial courts largely operated out of large bureaucratic state structures, this was not ordinarily the case around island Southeast Asia, where charismatic authority figures shifted and arose in response to local circumstances. There were many competing centers of power whose leaders strove not to colonize their neighbors, but rather to include them in kith and kin networks. Mostly males, but also females, served as political leaders. Archaeologist Barbara Andaya documents cases of Malay-Indonesian queens leading royal followings in their own right, although there is no evidence of their existence after the eighteenth century, which makes logical sense if the colonizers chose to negotiate primarily through the agency of male leaders.[3] Many Southeast Asian islander women enjoy a position that is more respectful of their innate human dignity in relation to men than did their counterparts in for example, China or Mongolia, although there were exceptions. Chinese historical records resound with male voices saying that women are only for pleasure and their ability to bear children.

HISTORICAL FAMILY KINSHIP

The boundaries marking ancient Southeast Asian societies fluctuated as new political alliances formed and histories merged. Archaeologist Laura Lee Junker explains that early lord-to-vassal relationships were structured and patterned after those of the family.[4]Andaya explains that the exchange of women strengthened and solidified lord-to-vassal ties for children conceived inand out of wedlock because they were visible signs of kinship.[5] She states that "elite intermarriages and the flow of women through hypergamous marriages to men, especially *datus*, of higher rank were tied to a prestige goods economy through bride wealth payments, which redistributed foreign porcelains and other accumulated status goods between 'wife-takers' and 'wife-givers.' "[6] That is, successful leaders were able to accumulate a large quantity of prestige goods and slaves in the wider maritime economy that contributed to the pool of wealth to be drawn from to contract political marriage alliances for the kinship group. As Junker expresses, "heirlooms and other status goods flowed to the women's kin groups, while it was primarily 'prestige' which flowed to the man's kin group."[7] A man's prestige was tied to the status of his wives-to-be and the extravagance of the public display of the bride wealth payment his family could offer.

If the man's kin could not afford to pay the bride price, the prospective husband could sell himself into slavery to his father-in-law in the form of bride price, much in the same way as Jacob did for the hand of Rachel and Leah, as told in the Christian Bible. Sociologist Adelamar Alcantara, in the case of the Philippines, explains that by so doing, a man demonstrated his sincerity and strong work ethic to his wife's family by effectively proving that he would be a good provider.[8] His services to her family could last for a few months or longer, until the women's family was sufficiently satisfied that he would become a worthy member of the family. However, later this practice would be largely outlawed as a result of Spanish colonial Catholicism in the sixteenth century.

Important genealogical claims were the fulcrum around which ancient family regimes operated. In early East and South Asian civilizations, for example, these variegated and hierarchically organized societies emerged out of an agricultural basis that made use of ploughs and animals for cultivating crops on permanent fields. Managing and running efficient households was a primary concern of the family. From this developed corporate family structures with clearly defined rules governing who can, and cannot, be a member, such as Chinese and Korean lineage associations with elaborate genealogical records that trace back to ancestral villages in ancient times. Or consider the case of Maharashtra in central India, where individual family members are clearly labeled as guests and owners, guests being those who married in with no inheritance rights.[9] The position of family head, in corporate families, is a role that comes with special privileges and specific duties. The role was transmitted down through the generations into perpetuity in pre-Maoist China and ancient India, as when an emperor dies and his son is ascended into the throne.

By contrast, the Javanese can be said to have a sort of corporate family system, in the sense of their owning property, but they do not have strict rules on who gets to succeed as family head. This is because the Javanese trace their family ties bilaterally, through both the male and female lines. Households may be set up more for economic convenience than for the preservation of the corporate family cycle of succession of family roles. It can be explained that when Javanese children marry, they often move in with the wife's side of the family until they are able to set up a separate household of their own.[10] Another example, according to Islamic law, is that sons should inherit twice as much as daughters, but this does not tally with the Javanese folk belief that sons and daughters should inherit equally; inheritance practices are rather flexible in Java.[11] This noncorporate structure of the family is widespread in Southeast Asia and can be found not only among the Muslim Javanese, but also among peninsular Malays and Christian Filipinos. In South Asia, though, lawful inheritance is often deemed to be arbitrary. Tradition has it that sons have the right to inherit, while daughters are given part of the property in cash and/or in kind in the form of dowry.

Before the Persian invasion of the Asian subcontinent, around 1192 CE, the region was predominantly Hindu. Women, particularly in South Asia, were essentially held in high esteem in ancient times. The caste system, a strong social hierarchical system, dates back to the time of the *Manusmriti*, a sacred document of the Hindus written between 200 BCE and 100 BCE that prevailed across the region.[12] The Hindu caste system is stratified into four *varnas*, or categories. The Brahmans (the priestly class) are at the top of the hierarchy, followed by the Kshatriyas (the warrior class); then are the Vaishyas (the class of traders) and at the bottom are the Shudras. Historically this latter group was known as the untouchables, *dalits*, or the low caste; today, they are known as the scheduled caste. The dictates in the religious texts defined the roles for men and women, and those dictates were directed by caste hierarchy, class, and age. As a consequence, the status of women was declared to be inferior to that of men. The subordination of women continued, and to a large extent still continues, based on these formulations. *Sati*, a ritualistic burning of widows on the funeral pyres of their husbands, is an example of a wife's devotion to her husband. Sati was practiced among upper-class Indians and the aristocracies of Nepal, and was legally abolished in India in 1829 and in Nepal in 1920. It is a stark example of women's subordination to their husbands. The archaic images of women were drawn from religious epics such as the *Ramayana* where Sita, the consort of Rama, was the embodiment of chastity, truth, devotion, and love.

Even today, these traditional values often are held up as a standard to measure the so-called good woman. However, while many modern Hindu women continue to value these family virtues, they also consider themselves to be strong and independently autonomous women. Several religions in Asia today—mainly Hinduism, Islam, Buddhism, Shikhism, Jainism, and Christianity are practiced in the region—in addition to many other diverse tribal and ethnic minorities who each practice different belief systems. Broadly speaking, no matter what the religious background of the family is, the image and expectation of what a woman should be is culturally directed, and in the patriarchal order that prevails in Asia, women are more often subordinates than equals.

In early China, Japan, and Korea, the roles of women were always seen to be inferior to those of men. In the fifth century BCE, Confucius advocated an ideology in China known as Confucianism, according to which peace could be maintained in the family, state, and world through moral efforts. In the consequential hierarchical stratification, women were considered much inferior to men. This difference was emphasized at every step in the formulation of societal values. This Confucian ideology entered Korea in the sixth century as Buddhism declined.[13] In the fourth and fifth centuries when Buddhism was a significant part of Korean life, women were equal to men, even though they did not have leading roles to play. But after the sixth century, society became very stratified, especially where women were concerned. They were relegated to the indoor spaces, and the roles they played in the exterior domain until the sixth century BCE were severely restricted. Like South Asian culture, in early Korea and China, men's responsibilities were outside the home, in the public sphere; women's responsibilities were within the home. The inferiority of women was accepted as natural, and all social practices were formulated based on this. Another notion prevalent in these East Asian countries and similar to the South Asian one was of how the role or status of a woman was viewed across the span of her life. As a daughter, a woman was subordinate to her father; after marriage, to her husband; and after she became a mother, to her son. This naturally meant that the domestic sphere was dominated by the public sphere. But in Korea and China, within the domestic sphere the women were still allowed to exercise their authority to some extent.

The Confucian ideology swept across Japan in the eighth century. Family laws were developed, all based on the Chinese family system, which considered women to be naturally inferior beings. This had an adverse impact on the women's rights to property, inheritance, marriage, and divorce, which endorsed the patrilineal inheritance system, further discriminating against women. But in Korea, in spite of the prevalence of the Confucian ideology, the inheritance system retained the Korean cultural practice of patrilineal as well as matrilineal inheritance so that women too had inheritance rights.[14]

GIRLS

Most Asian societies are predominantly patriarchal. Many of the patriarchal norms and practices are contingent on religion, cultural traditions, and superstitions. From the very birth of a child, discriminatory practices that privileges boys over girls are perpetrated. Young girls in the region are venerated, even worshipped in many instances, for they are considered to symbolize the feminine characteristics of innocence, chastity, and purity. But again, females are often strongly discriminated against from birth rituals to funeral rites. When she is married and becomes a daughter-in-law, it is often the most difficult time in her life. But once she moves into the role of mother-in-law, her status is enhanced. In any case in this region, women—in all phases of their lives—are expected to embody the traditional role.

In China, girls were considered a drain on their family because eventually they would have to be married off and relocated with the husband's family. The practice still continues in traditional Chinese families as well as in many families in India, Nepal, and Pakistan. In parts of South Asia where the dowry system is prevalent, a daughter is considered a burden on the family. Both unmarried and married girls (and daughters-in-law) do not have power or status in the family unless and until they become mothers. For example, when a boy is born, the very occasion is celebrated with much zest and fanfare, singing, dancing, and feasting. Even poor families tend to celebrate in their own ways. But a girl is often a disappointment to the family. In Nepal, there is a common saying: "If a boy is born cut a goat, if a daughter is born cut a squash." The conventional thinking is that girls are born to be fed throughout their lives, and boys are born to earn and support the whole family.[15]Therefore, sex selection during pregnancy, which is achieved mainly via abortion of female fetuses, is common in many parts of India. It is very often much against the desire of the woman who carries the fetus. Inmany instances in Pakistan, women are forced by their elders, especially mothers-in-law, to keep on giving birth until a son is born. In the process, a woman may end up giving birth to five or six girls before a boy is born.

In rural and lower–middle-class families in South Asia, parents do not invest much in their daughters, for example, on education or other amenities. Among more affluent families, a certain amount of wealth is set aside either as the daughter's dowry or her wedding expenses. She is also given good education at the same level as the sons in the family. But in families where money is an issue, normally discrimination is unbounded. Sons are sent to better schools, are fed better, and are encouraged to participate in extra-curricular activities. It is considered very taxing for parents to do the same for daughters. Some families readily pay several hundred thousand rupees for their sons to go to a medical or an engineering school. But they provide no similar support for their daughters. In recent years, however, with all the awareness building and campaigns going on in developing countries related to free education for girls at the primary level, and in many countries up to high school level, parents are increasingly allowing their daughters to complete high school. But girls in rural areas and from families in lower income brackets still are frequently made to drop out at the age of 10 or 11 because they are considered at that age to be physically ready to work at home or in the fields with their mothers. Many times girls from poorer families are sent to work as domestic help in towns or cities, either in private homes or industries. This is because rather than spending money on daughters for education, parents consider themselves better off with the added income from a working daughter.

At an early age, children are encouraged by the parents, especially mothers where daughters are concerned, to discipline the body in a way that naturally differentiates girls from boys.[16]Mothers teach their daughters to "walk like a lady," not laugh too loud in public places, and pull their skirts down and put their knees together while sitting with elders and guests. Mothers become extra watchful when their daughters reach puberty. It is a markedly significant rite of passage in an adolescent woman's life and in Asia, a woman who has reached puberty begins to be closely scrutinized by her mother, family members, and society at large. Thus the transition to womanhood can be difficult. Young girls in Asia are trained to do household chores such as cooking, cleaning, mending, and sewing in addition to their school education. Instead of being allowed to participate in outdoor activities, girls are encouraged to learn practical household arts that would train them to become good wives. This compulsion for the girls to do household chores even among the quite well-to-do families is also so that they do not suffer at the hands of their in-laws once they are married.

Traditionally, only males acquired education, which also meant learning the holy scriptures. Among Hindus, Brahmins were the ones who were learned, and Kshatriyas and Vaishyas were given less formal education but were taught other practical skills. Shudras and women were not taught any sacred literature, though the latter were permitted to do a little reading of the scriptures. Muslim girls were also not allowed to attend schools, especially girls from upper-class families. They learned the Quran at home and also acquired some skills in keeping accounts. Sometimes among the wealthy families, tutors taught the little girls at home.[17]

India

Formal education of girls was almost unheard of until the eighteenth century on the Indian subcontinent. Education for girls was limited to learning only practical matters of the household. Girls from the upper-class wealthy families were taught classical literature, and those from propertied families were taught to maintain accounts. In the early nineteenth century, female literacy was very low compared to males. In 1816, the Hindu College and soon after that the Calcutta School Society were founded to promote girls' education, but they were limited to teaching practical matters that would be useful within the house. By 1854, several schools throughout India promoted girls' education. There were approximately 626 schools for girls:288 in Bengal, 256 in Madras, 65 in Bombay, and 17 in the North West Frontier Province (NWFP) and Oudh. But these schools were very small, and the total number of girls receiving education was insignificant compared to the total population of India at that time. Still, a marked shift had taken place.[18]

China

It was around the same time in China that missionaries founded two schools, one in 1844 by Miss Aldersley of the Church of England and the other in 1847by a Presbyterian mission.[19] After this, more schools for girls were started across the country. But initially, upper-class families did not send their daughters to these schools. Traditionally, education for girls was limited due to the relegation of women to the inner sanctuaries of the house. The girls were taught ways to carry out domestic chores and also rules of social etiquette. When the missionaries arrived, they picked up poor girls from the roadside or bribed very poor families into sending their girls to school. This was not only part of the missionaries' plans to proselytize, but also a campaign against foot-binding, a practice that was first started among the wealthy upper class and abolished in 1912, and other practices of female subjugation that were prevalent at the time. These schools were looked down upon by society and in 1877, such educational establishments were also condemned by the government. But by 1919, schools for girls had increased in numbers. At this point, many girls (and boys) also went to Japan to study because education policies that included both men and women were being implemented at that time for the advancement of the country.[20]

Korea

In Korea, as in India and China, foreign missionaries introduced education for girls. The goal of the missionaries was also to spread Christianity, so they focused on women who were repressed by the Confucian norms of subordination. In this process, many women converted to Christianity and became missionaries. But the country was against this practice and in 1839, many Catholics were massacred, out of which almost two thirds were women. In 1885, the missionaries were active again, and their primary goal was once more to educate females. Women's traditional roles were being shed, and they started attending church programs with men. In the 1920s, the necessity for female education was felt more than ever before, and schools for girls increased at a rapid rate so that by 1930, there were 105,000 elementary girls' schools. By 1931, there were 5,800 secondary schools.[21]

Japan

In Japan by 1870, the missionaries who were already active started schools for girls. A school to train primary teachers—known as the Tokyo Women's Normal School—was started in 1876. By 1910, primary education for children, both boys and girls, was fully achieved. The main objective behind educating girls was to prepare them to be good wives and mothers. Providing education to young girls beyond the primary level met with certain obstacles, so an ordinance had to be declared for their higher education. In 1900, a girls college and a medical college were started, both by Japanese women, and in 1901, the Japan Women's University was founded. The education of women by then was exemplary.[22] Though there were many issues pertaining to the style and topics being taught to women, the education initiated employment opportunities for women as teachers, doctors, nurses, and bank and office workers.

TWENTIETH-CENTURY EDUCATION

By the early twentieth century, the number of schools for girls as well as the number of girls attending schools and colleges had markedly increased in India. The girls had an almost equal choice as the boys in the selection of institutions and courses so that they no longer had to be relegated to learning only practical skills and vocational training. Around the mid-nineteenth century, there was a general feeling among the social reformists that only if women were given formal education could a proper social reform take place. In South India, especially in Madras (Chennai), the Theosophical Society encouraged the education of women. Anne Besant (1847–1933), a London-born and -educated woman who later became the second president of the International Theosophical Society, settled in India from 1893 and involved herself in social work to transform the roles of women in India. In 1898, she founded the Central Hindu School and College in Benares (Varanasi), and a few years later started the Central Hindu School for girls. In North India, it was the Arya Samaj, a reformist Hindu sect, that encouraged female education. By the end of the nineteenth century, these reformists had recognized the importance of educating females and involving them in their reform efforts.[23]

It is important to note that in advancing female education in India, certain women were pioneers. Pandita Ramabai Sarswati founded the Shraddha

Sadan in Bombay (Mumbai) and Poona (Pune) in 1889; Mataji Tapaswini started Mahakali Pathshala in Calcultta (Kolkata) in 1893; and D.K. Kavre started a school for widows in Poona in 1896. The first Muslim woman to start an educational institution for Muslim girls was Begum Rokeya Sakhawat Hossain, in Bhagalpur, Bihar, for which she was ostracized by her family and driven out of her home. She then moved to Calcutta (Kolkata) and started another school, Sakhawat Memorial Girls' School in 1911. She was encouraged by her husband and brother, and started the school mainly for Muslim girls who observed *purdah*, or the seclusion of women. For these young women, the language of instruction was Urdu.[24]

In Nepal, the royal families and the aristocrats did not send their daughters to school. Private tutors provided them with an education at home. Even other urban elites did not provide formal education to their girls. It was mainly in the 1950s with the start of the missionary school (St. Mary's High School, a convent run by Jesuit nuns) that girls from royal families, aristocracies, and the urban elite began sending their daughters outside the home for an education. Then much later another school, Mahendra Bhavan, was founded exclusively for girls. Education in Nepal for girls was a slow process and still is in the rural areas. Even today, sending daughters to good schools is considered a luxury.

Various factors such as scattered population, poor safety, and linguistic differences in low-income countries such as Afghanistan, parts of India, Nepal, and Pakistan, do not help to create a positive atmosphere for the education of girls. In Afghanistan and Pakistan, the enrollment of girls in primary schools is low even today because discrimination of girls versus boys in households is still high. Another factor that precludes girls from being sent to school is the distance between home and school. Parents are reluctant to send girls to school if it is far away, but this does not make a difference for boys. For example, in Pakistan, only about half a kilometer of increase in the distance compels girls to stop going to school. In rural Afghanistan, if girls have to cross any boundaries, outside their own community, the parents, again for reasons of safety, stop sending their daughters to schools.[25] After India secured its independence in 1947, education opportunities for women increased significantly. Yet according to the 2001census of India, only 54.16 percent of women are literates.[26] As of 2011, however, the UNICEF Afganistan November Factsheet reports that the literacy rate for females who are 15 years old and above has fallen since the wars to 13 percent.

Education today has brought about many changes in the lives of women. Looking at Malaysian women and their education scenario, besides preparing these women for their roles as wives and educators of their own children, higher education gives them greater access to professions other than homemaking and also increases the likelihood of economic independence. But women, wherever they are, have to face barriers that may hinder them from obtaining higher-level degrees. As in some countries of East Asia and South Asia and in Malaysia too, educating girls is not considered economical to the families, as these girls have to be married off sooner or later.[27]

MARRIAGE

The question about the status of women continues to change with the times as scholars debate over women's rights. In China, the son had all the freedom to accept or reject a prospective bride, even though he was not expected to actively participate in the search with his parents. The son's first duty was to provide his parents with offspring. Marriage was also about establishing ties with new families. It was the parents who were most active in the task of finding the prospective bride or groom, while the son and the daughter could be unaware of all the machinations. The wedding often was more of a social occasion than anything else. But the poorer families married their daughters off to anyone who offered a good bride-price. On the other hand, the parents of boys also looked for girls for their son whose family could cater to their needs first and then to those of their son.[28] Once the girl was married, she was always at her mother-in-law's beck and call. Getting a divorce was easy for men. Not only could a man get a divorce at will, he could also marry more than one woman. For women, this was not possible. In Korean society, the same Confucian values were practiced as well. In Korea and China, as in many other Asian countries, there were certain reasons for which a husband could file for a divorce, for example, if his wife was disobedient to her in-laws, was unable to give birth to a son, committed adultery, or suffered from any hereditary disease. There was also a manual in Korea that spelled out the rules for what was expected of a proper woman based on Confucian values.[29]

Korean authorities felt that the Buddhist influence had somehow loosened the tight grip on women's liberty that Confucianism had secured for a long time. In the fifteenth century, Confucianism was back in Korea with full effect, and once more women were forced back into their subordinate positions. A manual entitled *Samanghaengsil-to* (The Three Principles of Virtuous Conduct) published in 1432 set out rules for women to abide by. For a woman of noble birth, the rules were stricter. She could not go out alone, nor could she take part in any social activity without the consent of her husband. There was also an implicit policy in Japan that a woman had to be at least 40 years or older to be able to go out alone in public. The woman had no identity, either in Korea or Japan. She was not known by her name, but by her husband's or by the name of any other male family member. In both Japan and Korea, a wife was considered to exist for the sole purpose of procreation, that is, to provide an heir to the family. A woman

On the Gaye Holud, a Bengali wedding practice, the bride-to-be is traditionally smeared with turmeric by family and close friends to wish her a long life. Once separate events for the bride and groom, a sort of bachelor or bachelorette party, they are increasingly celebrated together. (Claudio Cambon 2013, all rights reserved)

had to consider family the most important part of her married life. In the Chinese tradition, the space within the home was where women were relegated. Men dominated the public sphere. This demarcation was also enforced to prevent women from being sexually promiscuous, which would consequently create a state of social disorder. In Korea, this differentiation was also manifested in house design, both inside and out. The outer part was for the men, where they could also receive guests, while the inner sanctuary was for the women, which they were not permitted to leave.[30]

Societal expectations in those days when Confucian values were practiced resonate even today in many parts of South Asia. In China and Korea, when marriages were arranged, girls had no say in the matter. Women of South Asia have always followed this practice, and it continues even today. Therefore, such arranged marriages endorsed by the parents unerringly took place within the caste hierarchy, or within their own class and ethnic community. In China, a married woman had to adhere to certain codes of honor. Chastity, moral integrity, and fidelity were the important virtues that had to be practiced where the husband was concerned. A married woman had to be very restrained while speaking. She had to remain attractive at all times and perform her household chores diligently.[31] The same values of chastity and domesticity were expected of South Asian women. As a daughter-in-law, she was, and still is, expected to be subservient to her husband and his entire family. She has to take up a managerial role in the family by managing serv-ants (if wealthy) or otherwise doing all the household chores necessary to ensure the smooth functioning of the family. At the same time, she has always been expected to dress well and look beautiful, especially in front of family guests. This practice continues to this day in many homes, urban and rural. As in China and South Asia too, once a girl is married, no matter how young she may be, she is not considered a girl or somebody's daughter but simply a daughter-in-law who is supposed to fulfill all the expectations of the family and society.

Among the royal families and aristocracies of India and Nepal, having simultaneous multiple wives was a common phenomenon. Normally, a man could have only one legally wedded wife while all the others, countless and still considered his wives, were not lawfully wedded. But all the wives enjoyed the same privileges as the legally wedded one. The wealthy feudal lords, who were plentiful in Nepal until the last decades of the twentieth cen-tury, also enjoyed maintaining several wives at one particular time. But there are new laws in place now that forbid the practice of multiple wives except if there is a strong credible reason and the wife is no longer able to continue with a healthy conjugal life. In the ancient royal culture of Thailand, too, polygamy was customary. Traditionally, the kings of Thailand had many wives, concubines, and children, and this went on until 1910 when the last polygamous king, Chulalonkorn, died. The social dynamics of having many wives was an important factor in Thai royal families. This also gave rise to a later culture in Thai society in which "men had relations with more than one woman at a time."[32]

Among the Muslim families, though the Sharia law—the sacred law of Islam—allows for polygamy, it at the same time regulates the conduct of the husband as far as the wife or wives are concerned and gives the women certain rights. Even though the man marries several wives, each wife is enti-tled to a fair and rightful share of his property, including food, clothes, living quarters, and conditions that he is able to provide. He should also be able to spend an equal amount of time with each wife so that the other wives do not feel unwanted or neglected. During the time of marriage or even later, a Muslim wife is able to make a contract with her husband stating certain marital rules, and if those rules are not against the law, a court can also enforce them. Thus the wife may even stipulate in the contract that her husband may not take a second wife. But if the husband breaks the contract and does take a second wife, the first wife is entitled to dissolve the marriage or exercise her right of *talaq*, or divorce. Then even after living apart, the husband would have to financially support her. But these conditions are often abused, with the man neglecting his other wives in favor of the desired one.[33]

Dowry

In almost the whole region of Asia, marriage has been considered an important part of a woman's life, irrespective of her religion, caste, or class. After marriage, as in traditional China, it is said that she is passed from her father's control on to the husband, and she becomes an inseparable part of the new family. Women are also valued on the basis of the wealth they bring in to the family. In India, Bangladesh, and some parts of Nepal (e.g., the southern plains bordering India), the dowry system has been common. When girls are married, they take with them a certain amount of wealth in cash and in kind to their new homes, depending on the status and inclination of their family. Therefore, the power relationship that exists between the woman and her husband as well as the family she is married into relates to this wealth, or dowry. Dowry is also one of the primary reasons for bride burning and domestic violence perpetrated by the in-laws of the bride. These violent acts, which are physical as well as nonphysical, are commonly termed "dowry deaths" or "dowry violence." Many times, bride burning is also the ramification of dowry violence. Once a woman is married, she is considered the property of not only her husband, but also her in-laws. When she marries and goes to live with her husband's family, her in-laws expect a steady flow of wealth into the family over the next few years. The abuse is institutionalized in many forms, for example, compelling a daughter-in-law to work for long hours doing household chores or working outside in the fields, denying her adequate food, refusing to give her medical treatments, or physically and verbally abusing her. Thus the violence perpetrated against girls is both physical and emotional.

Dowry violence is not the only form of violence perpetuated against married women in Asia. Wife beating is a common occurrence not just among lower- and working-class families, but also among the middle and upper classes. This demonstrates the power relationship that exists in the institution of marriage that relegates women to secondary status. Women are also subjected to a variety of types of violence in the home, primarily as daughters, sisters, and wives. Some of these violent acts include exchange marriages, marriage to the Quran, marriage to temples, karo-kari (honor killings), bride-price, dowry, female circumcision, child marriage, sex-selective abortion, and denial of widow marriages. Again in the Muslim community, a daughter is often forced to swear by the Quran that she would not covet the property of her brothers. Forced prostitution, mainly through the trafficking of girls and women, is also common in the region. In some rural areas of Sindh in Pakistan and Punjab in India, girls are deprived of marriage rights only so that the property remains within the family.[34] It is only after the woman becomes a mother-in-law that her status once again goes up. She is able to rule the household largely at will.

PREGNANCY AND DAUGHTERS

Pregnancy and raising children are important aspects of a married woman's role. In almost all wealthy families, the status of the woman is elevated. When a son is born, especially among into rural families, the mother's position within the family is secured because it is the son who is considered to carry on the family line. Unlike traditional rural families, in which women were made to give birth at home with the help of midwives, women usually, are taken to the hospital for pre- and postnatal care, throughout her pregnancy. But in rural areas, women are taken to a nearby hospital or health center only to give birth. Otherwise, they give birth at home with the help of a midwife. Among the royal families, the feudal class, and aristocrats, when a child was born, it was put into the complete care of a wet nurse to be fed and cared for, and was brought in to visit the mother only at intervals.

A young mother and her child with the child's aunt in Bandarban, one of the hill tracks in Chittagong, Bangladesh. (Sharon Panackal, all rights reserved)

The mother, meanwhile, was given all care possible for at least six months, which in many ways restricted her physical mobility. It was the norm in all wealthy families, and a welcome and much appreciated practice. But among poor families, women continued to work even as early as a few hours after the child was born.

The number of children a married couple should have was traditionally never an issue of contestation. The use of birth control technologies was never justified in any class or caste hierarchy. It was common for wives to give birth throughout their reproductive years. Therefore, earlier generations boast of large families, with the average numbers being anywhere between four and 12 children. In Asia, family planning measures were frowned upon because the birth of babies was considered to be a gift from god. In the 1950s in China, during Mao Tse-tung's rule, birth control measures were not permitted because he wanted as many people as possible to provide maximum labor to the country. Consequently, each couple had at least five or six children. During the period of the Cultural Revolution (1966–1976), people were also not very interested in birth control measures, and therefore family planning was not extensively implemented. But toward the mid-1970s, control measures were implemented so that births could be widely spaced, which was to discourage childbearing. Finally in 1979, China implemented its one-child-per-couple policy so that—as the government said—the country could prosper economically with the population in check. With the one-child policy, women acquired greater time to work outside the home and contribute to the household economy, and they were better able to send their sons to good schools and provide them with housing. Because of the economic contribution of women, their decision-making power also increased. But women still do not inherit property and they do continue with the traditional practices of working for the family and children in the husband's home after marriage. These situations of women and the one-child policy, which still continues in many parts of China, have led—albeit unwillingly—to the preference of sons over daughters to a fairly large degree.[35]

In South Asia, motherhood has always been taken as a social and economic event where families are compelled to make the right choice about the sex of the infant. The eternal waiting for a male child is often punctuated by sex determination tests and termination of pregnancies. The technology is for those who can afford to carry out the tests and the subsequent abortions if required. But those who are practically under the poverty line get rid of their female children only after birth. Feticide is one example of the violence that occurs in India among the rich as well as poor and middle-class families. In recent years, stringent policies have been implemented to curb sex determination tests. In contrast, among Javanese families, having many children, both boys and girls, is still considered a mark of prestige.

This is especially true of wealthy families who do not have to rely on their son's economic contribution to the household, which is why they have more children than even peasant families. It is also considered socially correct to address in formal terms men who have many children.[36]

Toward the latter half of the twentieth century, around the 1970s, with the help of international financial donors and family planning establishments and their campaigning, fertility checks started, first among the educated families. In Java, the success rate was higher in the rural areas than among the urban elites. In other parts of Asia, especially South Asia, women rarely had power over their own bodies, so it was the men who decided the number of children to be had. Slowly, with the increase in women's education and earning opportunities, they are now able to decide for themselves in urban areas. In rural areas, it is still a problem. People are still superstitious about family planning technologies and the use of contraceptives. Or again, the belief that the sons are more important than daughters, either according to religion or the social order that compels the families to wait for a son, even if it means giving birth to more and more daughters in the process. Among the Muslims too, birth control is not looked at favorably. But today, family planning efforts in Asia are curbing the high fertility rates even among Muslim families.

RAISING CHILDREN TODAY

At home, the mother is responsible for the upbringing of the children. If the mother is educated, she provides tutorials to her children and sees to it that the children, especially daughters, do not indulge in too much web surfing, unnecessary telephone calls, late night TV shows, or adult-rated movies. She monitors the types of friends her daughter has and may restrict her adolescent daughter's social evenings or any other social events with friends. She also makes sure that she gives enough time to the children, sees to it that her children are doing well in school, advises them, and helps them move along with the times. In educated families, it has always been the mothers who are the primary providers of informal education to their children. Because most women are stay at home mothers in the middle- and upper-class families, at least until the children are old enough to go to school, this is made easily possible.

In situations in which the mother is uneducated or illiterate, regardless of whether the family is rich or poor, she will neither be able to monitor her children's education nor give them proper advice. Her role will be that of a good mother in terms of providing them with food as well as clean and proper clothes. Also, very often, the uneducated rural mother may not see the necessity of her daughter getting a proper education and instead would like those extra pair of hands to help her around the house. Even in modern times, for women to pursue higher education, parental permission is highly valued, especially so among traditional and upper-class families. Thus unlike earlier times, in the modern period, it is both parents who decide the future of their children, including decisions about marriages. The primary aim of parents has always been to get their daughters married within the proper age limit, that is, before she crosses 24.

Married women in Asia have increasingly begun to occupy the workplace with their male counterparts. The common trend is that once the children reach school age, the educated mother begins to look for a job, managing home and work considerably well. In Malaysia, the past three decades have witnessed a significant change in the role of women within the family. At present, both men and women occupy the same workplace. The workforce is no longer male centered; rather, it is made up of both sexes, including single mothers and many other female workers. Both men and women are beginning to be aware of the better quality of life around them. But it is still the woman who is solely responsible for the home and the family, for example, the upbringing of the children, taking care of the household, and looking after the sick and elderly members of the extended family.[37]

In Japan in recent years, the number of women working outside the home has increased a great deal. In fact, the increase in numbers is higher for women than for men. By 1995, the number of working women had reached 20 million, which amounted to 40 percent of the total working population. Once out of school, girls immediately enter the job market. But as they reach their early twenties, they begin to fall out to get married and raise their families. After the children grow and are of school age, the mothers re-enter the job market in their early thirties and continue to work, but for a lesser salary because it is almost a mid-life re-entry into the workforce and a new job at that.[38]

It is common for women to acquire higher education and seek a job before they think of getting married and settling down. In India, Nepal, and Bangladesh, it is common for young girls to start working even while they are still in college. This is not because the family needs the economic contribution but because girls know they have to be independent. Often after they are married, they leave their jobs and become full-time housewives, looking after the family and raising children. But working wives are not uncommon. Marriage has become a matter of choice. A young woman may choose her husband, a choice that later on may be endorsed by the parents. In such instances, the young woman may not see caste, class, and religion as determining factors. Traditional forms of arranged marriages do exist—clearly to a large degree—especially in traditional homes. But unlike earlier times, the daughter is asked to give her consent or reject the parents' selection. If the daughter agrees to an arranged marriage of her parents' choice, she normally is allowed to get acquainted with the prospective husband several months prior to her wedding.

After the Cultural Revolution in China, and the rise of industrialization and market economy, the traditional family system based on Confucian values of hierarchical stratification and extended families began to change. The family today is no longer defined by Confucian values but by the legal system, which was established in 2001. Now the legally defined institution of marriage and family also defines the various roles of members of the family—the father, mother, wife, husband, and individual children. After marriage, a woman is able to legally retain her family name, and even the children are free to adopt either the mother or the father's family name. The husband and wife both share the responsibility of the household and family, including the adoption of birth control strategies. Divorce is also easily granted to the couple if both are willing. But if the wife is pregnant, the husband cannot file for divorce, and they have to wait until a year after the birth of the child, or six months if the wife miscarries or the fetus is aborted. It is also true that in many instances, the Chinese still give importance to traditional values and the continuation of the family lineage. The parents, both father and mother, consider themselves responsible for the education, marriage, and other welfare issues of their children. Children are obligated to look after their parents in old age. But with continuation of the one-child policy there has been a marked increase in abortion rates and a decrease in the number of girls because sons are still considered necessary to continue the family line.[39] With the increase in the female ratio of education and economic independence, divorces have become increasingly common in Asia. Prior to the last two decades, divorces were rare and considered socially stigmatizing. Couples would stay together even if there was marital disharmony, only for the well-being of the children and also to avoid social castigation. But this notion is changing today. A woman who seeks divorce is no longer considered a social pariah. In the countries of South Asia, a woman is able to file for a divorce and receive substantial alimony from her husband for her upkeep and for the child (or children) if she retains their custody.

WIDOWS

In Asia, the status of widows is demeaning. An extreme form of the ostracizing of widows was burning them on their husband's funeral pyres. Even though these forms of rejection have been done away with, other severe practices of prejudice still exist. As recently as the early twentieth century, widows were treated as household servants, carrying out all the works that a servant or maid would otherwise do, for example, washing clothes and dishes as well as tending the cows and buffaloes if in the rural areas.

Ferdous Ara Begum, a member of the UN Convention on the Elimination of Violence Against Women (CEDAW) committee, explains how in Asia, widowhood in fact represents a "social death to women."[40] No matter how

Several pairs of dye-stained red palmprints border a village archway. They were left as testaments by women on their way to perform suttee, the outlawed but ancient practice of suicide on the husband's funeral pyre. (Sheldan Collins/Corbis)

the husbands may have died, or whatever caste, class, or religion she may be, it is evident across the board that discriminatory social, religious, and customary laws and practices drive the widow into a state of misery and disgrace. In many cases among rural people and even among middle-class urban families of countries such as Bangladesh, Hindu widows are deprived of economic rights, suffer immense hardship and social injustice, and are forced to be completely dependent on their male relatives. In Nepal, the situation is almost the same or even worse. After a woman becomes a widow, she is not permitted to return to her maternal home. She is considered an ill omen and is not invited to any religious or social functions and festivals. Child marriage is still persistent in Nepal, and therefore, the girls are forced to drop out of school when they get married and remain uneducated or even illiterate. Thus once they become widows, they have to remain dependent on other members of the family because they lack appropriate education and are unable to get proper employment.[41]

In Pakistan, the story is different. Marriage is considered a civil contract between the man and the woman, so when the husband dies, the wife is neither blamed for her husband's death nor is she turned into an outcast. Traditionally, women have been encouraged to remarry. In Afghanistan, no matter how strong the patriarchal force is, after a woman becomes a widow, she becomes all-powerful because of the absence of the dominating male, and all decisions are made by the widow. They may not be rich, but they have more freedom within the household.[42] But with increasing women's activism and raised level of awareness, a single woman in Asia—whether unmarried, divorced, or widowed—is gradually gaining societal acceptance today, especially in educated urban societies. In the rural areas, these single women are still frowned upon, and marriages of divorcees and widows are still taboo.

Women's roles within the family are changing, especially among the urban educated families. However, in rural areas, it may still take a number of years before actual change can be documented. In the urban setting, nuclear families are becoming increasingly common as women acquire higher education and become economically independent. But these nuclear, or conjugal, families still maintain close contact with the rest of the family. Young educated wives often prefer to spend time and energy working outside the home to supplement the family income, rather than staying at home to look after the family. Women have started occupying the workplace with men. Business houses, banks, colleges and universities, nongovernmental sectors, and other informal sectors are the most popular work areas for urban women. In many parts of Asia, such as Korea, India, and Nepal, there is a popular tendency for young married men and women to fall back on their families, especially the husband's side, and live with them. This is not a continuation of the traditional family dynamics; rather, it is the result of negotiations and compromises within contemporary times, especially in terms of lack of reasonably priced, affordable housing for the young couple along with lack of reliable childcare and various other practical reasons. Many of those women—who are poor with very low family incomes—have opted to go to developed countries for employment rather than work in the agricultural fields or take up other menial occupation in their own countries. The Gulf countries and Japan are the favorite choices for the women of South Asia to go for employment. After a few years of working outside their country, they return with good remittance and consequently, the family economic status is raised. According to the World Development Report, when the greater part of the income is the men's contribution, it has an adverse effect upon the women's agency. When women begin to earn as much as men, or even more, their bargaining power increases.[43]

THE PERSISTENCE OF ASIAN FAMILY SYSTEMS

As educated women in East Asia, the Middle East, North America, and the European Union, have entered semiprofessional and professional fields outside the household in huge numbers, new employment opportunities have opened for poor Asian female migrants to do menial jobs that better-positioned women living urban centers and richer countries often no longer want to do. While Asian women who migrate to Canada and the United States usually can apply for permanent residency, those going to places such as Italy and Singapore are temporary workers who periodically must return to their home countries to renew three-year work visas. The outsourcing of migrant contract workers has become a major source of foreign currency for countries that are less well off—such as Sri Lanka, Nepal, and the Philippines—and helps raise the standard of living for thousands of families. But what happens when a daughter, mother, or wife migrates abroad to help to support her family back home? In Chapter 2, "Women and Work," interested readers can refer to the section on feminization of migration for a more detailed discussion of this issue in relation to changing household work roles within the family.

Despite the tumultuous and rapidly changing times in an age of globalization and migration, the resilience of Asian family systems living in the great diaspora becomes evident. While, as this chapter attests, the issue of adaptation of Asian family systems remains complex, and more research needs to be done, the persistence of the South, Southeast, and East Asian family systems is profound. Using a case study from Southeast Asia, sociologists Gelia Castillo, Abraham Weisblat, and Felicidad Villareal explain that the Filipino family is residentially nuclear but functionally extended.[44] In other words, it is common practice for young married couples living in a barrio to set up their own independent nuclear household, but their parents usually live across the way. That is, the household tends to be nuclear in form, but the family is extended in so far as relationships between members of the wider kin group are concerned. Members of the same kin group assist one another in times of need, and they participate together in joint family activities even if they do not live together in the same household or are living overseas. If the family living together in the same residential unit includes members other than a husband, wife, and their children, it is an extended family household. Many Filipino families living in the Philippines and abroad, such as in Canada or southern California, actually live in extended family households. It is practical and common for Filipino migrants looking for work in distant cities to be housed by relatives already in residence there, if they have them. Filipinos who have made it abroad are known to sincerely invite parents to stay as part of their filial obligations. The family household may include grandparents, an unmarried aunt, an uncle or a cousin, and a niece or nephew.

Today, the Filipino nuclear family household still is more commonly found in rural areas than in cities or abroad. To say it again, it is quite expensive for a typical family or single person starting a new life in the city to rent, build, or purchase a home right away. It is much easier for a family to construct a dwelling made of light materials such as bamboo and other natural plants that are freely available in a natural village or barrio setting. These simple homes are considered by many educated Filipinos to be elegant and attuned with nature. This appreciation for traditional dwellings was not the case under the influence of U.S. colonialism and Americanization, when concrete homes with corrugated steel roofs were introduced to replace them. Also, kin members can build their household dwellings close to each other in rural communities, which may not be an option in the city. Moreover, Filipinos who move away to study or work in cities, locally and abroad, tend to stay with their more affluent relatives, and this increases household size.

Sociologist Virginia Miralao examines the transformation of Philippine society in relation to modernization theories that were first introduced by Durkheim and Weber.[45] These evolutionary models posited that as societies modernize, social relationships become more impersonal and business-like. At the same time, modern societies were characterized as being less religiously oriented and more scientifically grounded. But Philippine society does not accord with this predictive model. While dehumanization processes caused by top-down globalization are all pervasive in Philippine society, popular religious and social movements for an alternative, holistic, and integral development paradigm are ascending. Moreover, family and family-like relationships are highly valued in the workplace.

Filipinos prefer to have smooth interpersonal relations and tend to create an atmosphere in which the people around them feel comfortable and accepted. There is a strong concept of face in the Philippines. This means that Filipinos are taught to be sensitive to other people's feelings and generally do not say words that may embarrass or shame a fellow human being, explains Miralao.[46] Parents also consider it their duty to provide for the material and educational needs of their children, if they can. Children are expected to obey and respect their parents, and to take care of them when they grow old. Decision making, traditionally and even today in Filipino America, is typically not done independently or arbitrarily on one's own; rather, decisions are made in consultation and by reaching a consensus. Older children, until they get married and have a family of their own, are expected to help younger siblings with school and to assist them in getting a job after graduation. While the traditional regime of the family system that ruled ancient society has been overturned and changed, its underlying structure continues into the twenty-first century.

Women's role within the family has always been ambivalent. Women have been revered as mothers, have embodied images of goddesses, and have been bandied about as objects of fascination. But no matter what, women have always carried half the sky. In Asia, the roles for women have been rescripted, and the activities and roles of women today, which perhaps even until 50 years ago were surmised to be unheard of are being fulfilled. But in spite of the progress in education and employment, women in Asia are in general still behind in terms of equal opportunities and positions of authority. With globalization and development, traditions have not crumbled; it is only that that the roles of women have been rewritten.

NOTES

1. Robert Baldick, *From the Medieval to the Modern Family* (New York: Alfred A. Knopf, 1962).

2. See especially Barbara Andaya, "Political Development between the Sixteenth and Eighteenth Centuries," in *The Cambridge History of Southeast Asia, Vol. 1: From Early Times to c. 1800*, N. Tarling, ed., 402–59 (Cambridge: Cambridge University Press, 1992); Vincent Rafael, *Contracting Colonialism: Translation and Christian Conversion in Tagalog Society under Early Spanish Rule* (Ithaca, NY: Cornell University Press, 1988); Willem Wolters, *History, Culture, and Religion in Southeast Asian Perspectives* (Singapore: Institute of Southeast Asian Studies, 1982).

3. Barbara Watson-Andaya, *The Flaming Womb: Repositioning Women in Early Modern Southeast Asia* (Honolulu: University of Hawaii Press, 2006), 169.

4. Laura Lee Junker, "Networks of Power and Political Trajectories in Early Southeast Asian Complex Societies," *Philippine Quarterly of Culture and Society* 27, nos. 1–2 (1999): 59–104.

5. Watson-Andaya, *The Flaming Womb, Repositioning Women in Southeast Asian History*, 408.

6. Andaya, "Political Development between the Sixteenth and Eighteenth Centuries," 81.

7. Junker, "Networks of Power and Political Trajectories," 294–300.

8. Adelamar Alcantara, "Gender Roles, Fertility, and the Status of Married Men and Women," *Philippine Sociological Review* 42, nos. 1–4 (1994): 94–109.

9. Anthony Carter, "Household Histories," in *Households: Comparative and Historical Studies of Domestic Groups*, R. Netting, ed., 46 (Berkeley, CA: University of California Press, 1984).

10. Clark Sorenson, "Asian Families: Domestic Group Formation," in *Asia's Cultural Mosaic: An Anthropological Introduction*, Grant Evans, ed., 89–117, see 93 (New York: Prentice-Hall, 1993).

11. Clifford Geertz, *The Religion of Java* (Chicago: Chicago University Press, 1960).

12. Ruth Manorama, "Dalit Women: The Downtrodden among the Downtrodden," in *Women's Studies in India*, John E. Mary, ed., 445–52 (New Delhi, India: Penguin Books, 2008).

13. Kumari Jayawardena, *Feminism and Nationalism in the Third World* (London: Zed Books, 1986), 214.

14. Ibid., 229.

15. Niaz Unaiza and Sehar Hassan, "Culture and Mental Health of Women in South East Asia," *World Psychiatry* 5 (June 2006): 118–20.

16. Karin A. Martin, "Becoming a Gendered Body: Practices of Preschools," in *The Politics of Women's Bodies: Sexuality, Appearance and Behavior*, Rose Weitz, ed., 219–39 (New York: Oxford University Press, 1998).

17. Usha Chakraborty, *Conditions of Bengali Women around the Second Half of the Nineteenth Century* (Calcutta: Usha Chakraborty, 1963), 52.

18. Geraldine Forbes, *Women in Modern India* (Cambridge: Cambridge University Press 1996), 37–39.

19. Jayawardena, *Feminism and Nationalism in the Third World*, 177.

20. Ibid.

21. Jayawardena, *Feminism and Nationalism in the Third World*, 219.

22. Paulson, Joy, "Evolution of the Feminine Ideal," in *Women in Changing Japan*, Joyce Lebra et al. eds. (Stanford, CA: Stanford University Press, 1976), 1–24.

23. Kenneth W Jones, *Arya Dharma: Hindu Consciousness in Nineteenth Century Punjab* (Delhi: Manohar, 1976), 104–5.

24. Forbes, *Women in Modern India*, 55.

25. *World Development Report 2012* (Washington DC: World Bank, 2011).

26. Census of India, 2001, Government of India, Part III, NSS 61st Round Survey Report 2004–05, p. 24.

27. Novel Lyndon, Maimunah Ismail, et al., "The Differences between Educational Attainment and Employment Participation of Bidayuh Men and Women in Development," in *Women at Work: Perspective on Workplace and Family*, 43 (Penerbit: University of Malaysia Sabah, 2007).

28. Margery Wolf, "Marriage, Family and the State in Contemporary China," *Pacific Affairs* 57, no. 2 (Summer 1984): 213–36.

29. Yung-Chung Kim, ed., *Women of Korea: A History from Ancient Times to 1945* (Seoul: Ewha Women's University Press, 1976), 35.

30. Ibid., 85–86.

31. Elizabeth Croll, *Feminism and Socialism in China* (New York: Schocken Books, 1980), 13–14.

32. Lipi Ghosh, "Religion, Sex and Issues of Identity: Women in Thailand," in *Women Across Asia: Issues of Identities*, Lipi Ghosh, Ishita Mukhopadhyay, et al., eds., 232 (New Delhi: Gyan Publishing House, 2006).

33. Alamgir Muhammad Serajuddin, *Shari'a Law and Society: Tradition and Change in the Indian Subcontinent* (Bangladesh: Asiatic Society of Bangladesh, 1999), 168.

34. Niaz Unaiza and Sehar Hassan, "Culture and Mental Health of Women in South East Asia," *World Psychiatry* (June 2006): 118–20.

35. Karen Hardee, Zhenming Xie, and Baochang Gu, "Family Planning and Women's Lives in Rural China," *International Family Planning Perspectives* 30 (June 2004): 68–76.

36. Ratna Megawangi and Marian F. Zeitlin, "The Javanese Family," in *Strengthening the Family: Implications for International Development*, Marian F. Zeitlin, Ratna Megawangi, et al., eds., 110 (Tokyo: United Nations University, 1995).

37. Noraini M. Noor, "Work, Family, and Women's Well-Being: The Malaysian Scenario," in *Women at Work: Perspective on Workplace and Family*, Rosnah Ismail, Mahmood Nazar Mohamad, et al., eds., 65 (Penerbit: University of Malaysia, 2007).

38. Yuko Ogasawara, *Office Ladies and Salaried Men: Power, Gender and Work in Japanese Companies* (Los Angeles: University of California Press, 1998), 17.

39. Aubrey R Fowler, Jie Gao, and Les Carlson, "Public Policy and the Changing Chinese Family in Contemporary China: The Past and Present as Prologue for the Future," *Journal of Macromarketing* 30 (2010): 342–53.

40. Masuma Hasan, "Widows' Voices: Empowered," *International Conference on Widowhood* (Kathmandu: Women for Human Rights, 2010), 39.

41. Ibid., 64.

42. *World Bank Report 2012*, 163.

43. Ibid., 153.

44. Gelia Castillo, Abraham Veisblat, and Felicidad Villareal, "The Concepts of Nuclear and Extended Family: An Exploration of Empirical Results," *International Journal of Comparative Sociology* 9, no. 1 (1968): 116.

45. Virginia Miralao, "The Family, Traditional Values and Sociocultural Transformation of Philippine Society," *Philippine Sociological Review* 45, nos. 1–4 (1997): 189–215.

46. Ibid.

SUGGESTED READING

Bennet, Lynn. *Dangerous Wives and Sacred Sisters: Social and Symbolic Roles of High Caste Women in Nepal.* New York: Columbia University Press, 1983.

Chakravarti, Uma, and Preeti Gill, eds. *Shadow Lives: Writings on Widowhood.* New Delhi: Zubaan, 2001.

Karlekar, Malavika. "Domestic Violence." *Economic and Political Weekly* 33 (July 1998), 1741–51.

Patel, Rashida. *Woman versus Man: Socio-Legal Gender Inequality in Pakistan.* Karachi: Oxford University Press, 2003.

Rayamajhi, Sangita. *Can a Woman Rebel?* Kathmandu: Across Publications, 2003.

Sangari, Kumkum, and Uma Chakravarti, eds. *From Myths to Markets: Essays on Gender.* Shimla: Indian Institute of Advanced Study, 1999.

Saunders, Kriemild, ed. *Feminist Post Development Thought: Rethinking Modernity, Post–Colonialism and Representation.* New Delhi: Zubaan, 2004.

Seth, Mira. *Women and Development: The Indian Experience.* New Delhi: Sage Publications, 2001.

Yan, Yunxiang. "Girl Power and the Waning of Patriarchy in Rural North China." *Ethnology* 45 (Spring 2006): 105–23.

4

———∞∞∞———

Women and Politics

It is not easy for the women of Asia to be in politics. This is primarily because of the masculine model of political practices and work procedures. There is conflict between what is expected of a woman when she is involved in politics and the all-male characteristics of the political domain. Women in this field are expected to accommodate both family and community, and be ready to participate in public activities and ventures at all times. Until less than a century ago, politics was exclusively a male arena and therefore, by that understanding, women were exempted from participating. This tradition still lingers in many Asian societies. Therefore, the strong patriarchal structure that persists in Asia makes it next to impossible for women to step into this arena without thinking twice. That said, there have been women political leaders in Asia for a long time. In 1960, Sirimavo Bandaranaike of Sri Lanka became the female prime minister in the world. There have been many others since her, such as Indira Gandhi of India, Benazir Bhutto of Pakistan, Sheikh Hasina and Khalida Zia of Bangladesh, Corazon Aquino and Gloria Macapagal-Arroyo of the Philippines and Chandrika Kumaratunga of Sri Lanka, and Aung San Suu Kyi, the Nobel Peace laureate who has spent a major part of her life in political activism fighting for democratic rights in Myanmar. In China, Japan, and Korea, while there have been empresses and women have been involved in national struggles, there have been no female prime ministers or presidents.

In this 1997 photo, Etsuko Kawada looks through the bars of a prison cell. Kawada, a member of the Japanese House of Representatives, is an active campaigner against governmental injustices. (TWPhoto/ Corbis)

WOMEN'S MOVEMENTS AND PARTICIPATION IN POLITICS

The history of women's movements in Asia shows how they are inextricably tied to male-dominated organizations, political parties, and other institutions. There have been countries such as China and India in which women's activism was started by urban elites or middle-class urbanites. But there are many instances of women's activism being started by female workers in factories and other workplaces. Women have been involved in a wide range of struggles, from gender equality and women's liberation to national liberation, human rights, freedom from authoritarian rules, and democratization of the nation. There are also isolated cases of women-only movements that have endured and have been able to meet their objectives. In the Philippines, the women's movement played a major role in the overthrow of the dictator Ferdinand Marcos. Between 1975 and 1977 when the prime minister of India, Indira Gandhi, suspended parliament and declared a state of emergency, it was the women's organizations that formed the civil liberties movement and fought against the emergency acts. The movements just discussed emphasize that women were present in all of these activities, and their visions and perspectives for social and/or political change were being put to use.

Another aspect of women's movements is also the spread of women's writings and specifically feminist literature in journals and magazines, especially in the late nineteenth and early twentieth centuries. Many of the writings addressed women's roles in their respective societies, where in many instances the main topic under discussion was the subordination of women. Some of these journals were the *Chinese Women's Journal*—which started its publication in 1906—was revolutionary, and almost all its issues contained feminist views; *Yoja Chinam* (Women's Guide) in Korea was first published in 1908; and *Seito* (Bluestocking) was first published in 1911 in Japan. All of these were significant journals that had a great impact on the women of the respective countries of the time. These writings were platforms for women to express themselves and at the same time create awareness among others.[1]

Grassroots organizations and the activities of women in their respective communities and neighborhoods are also effective ways of exerting political pressure. Women working at the community level have opportunities that they would otherwise not get at the national level. Generally, these women's groups focus on immediate problems that are evident in their communities and neighborhoods such as housing, water supply, health care, and education. These poor or rural women who know they have much to say and can do a lot are hindered by poverty and therefore cannot commute or travel to other parts of the country for networking or political interactions. In many ways, these women are excluded from mainstream political organizations and other interest groups or even government-run institutions. They are active within and around their communities, working and raising their voices, and even staging demonstrations and other forms of protest. At the same time, in developing countries, it is increasingly evident that urban women working for nongovernmental organizations (NGOs) are bringing together these grassroots women, helping them speak up for their rights, creating political awareness, developing their confidence, and drawing them into greater participation in the political system.[2] It is evident that the beliefs and prejudices that have hindered the progress of women to achieve a social or economic position have also hindered their capacity to acquire position of power in the political domain.

In China, the China Women's Federation (ACWF), founded in 1949, leaned heavily on the women's associations that were established between 1937 and 1945, and worked with those women's movements and the Chinese communist party during the anti-Japanese war and other civil wars. ACWF saw to it that all patriarchal practices that oppressed women were addressed, focusing mainly on the feudal practices of forced marriage and bride-price.[3] It also raised women's awareness of the oppressive practice of feudalism and at the same time showed them a vision that the new society would certainly bring about gender equality and fair practice. But with time, women's interests were somehow linked to the interest of the state so much so that women's interests were subordinated to those of the state. In 1957, the state finally pronounced that with the transition to socialism, women too had transitioned into a state of equality with men. But this was only a state rhetoric—it was far from the truth.

India

In India, the Indian National Congress (INC) was founded in 1889. Four years later, its annual meeting was attended by 10 women. From 1890 onward after the novelist Swarnakumari Ghosal and Kadambini Ganguly (the first woman in the British Empire to receive a BA and one of India's first female medical doctors) first participated as delegates, every meeting of INC was attended by women delegates. Even though these women did not contribute much in terms of intellectual or ideological input, their presence was a symbolic act of achievement.[4] While it was male Hindus who started the social movements in India, fighting for the rights of Hindu women, Muslim men and women also started to get involved in social movements. The issues of Hindu and Muslim women were not the same. Hindu social reformists were concerned about property rights for women, divorce, and widow marriage. Muslims were concerned about the *purdah* system, polygamy, and female education. Amina Tyabji and Begum Abdullah, started schools for girls and colleges in the first decade of the twentieth century. Then Muslim women from elite families formed an association of women and in 1916, the first All-India Muslim Women's Conference was held in Bhopal, India. They even passed a resolution that polygamy be abolished. As the political struggle started in India, Muslim women actively got involved. Orthodox Muslims were not happy about the resolution on polygamy or about increasing female education. They were not so much concerned about Muslim women's participation in the political struggle of the country, however.[5]

In spite of the participation of Muslim women in political activities, it was clear from the overall picture of Islamic countries such as Bangladesh,

Pakistan, Malaysia, and Indonesia that Islamic fundamentalists were less than happy to see the rise of women leaders. They felt that this was against Islamic principles and tried to block women's involvement. Yet the predominant Muslim countries of South and Southeast Asia have had women leaders, either sitting in government or as part of the opposition.[6]

In 1905, the British partitioned the province of Bengal. Women joined the men in protesting this division, boycotting foreign goods and buying only *swadeshi* (of one's own country) goods. Thus started the *swadeshi* movement (1905–1908). Many women took part in the movement in their own ways. Some joined revolutionary organizations, while others simply boycotted the use of foreign goods. Women helped to hide fugitive revolutionaries and the weapons they were to use. The women of the INC were seen to be on par with the men, even if they did nothing but attend the meetings, whereas during the *swadeshi* movement, women actively participated in political activities while maintaining and retaining their domestic sphere. It was a struggle against British imperialism. And in the process, the issues of social practices that troubled women—for example, the dowry system, child marriage, and widow marriage—were sidelined. One particular issue that was of interest to the middle class was the question of suffrage. In 1921, women acquired the right to vote and in 1926, they were given permission to enter the legislature. The first woman legislative councilor was Dr. S. Muthulakshmi Reddy. She immediately wanted to introduce a law called the *Devdasi* Bill that would have prevented the prostitution of young girls in the temple. But she was not successful.

China

In the first decades of the twentieth century, similar political activism was going on in China. The first modern women's movement unfolded side by side with China's other political movements carried out by other political activists. Women's problems, and in particular the issues of bound feet and the exclusion of women from education were brought to the forefront during the reform movement of the mid-1890s. Such movements told of a country that was faltering under the traditional rule of the now weak Quing Dynasty. Even though the elite women's organization had actually emerged at the turn of the century, it was not until 1919 that women's movements really flourished. During the May Fourth movement, large-scale women's organizations attacked the traditional culture, Confucian ideology, and "oppressive family and marital institutions."[7] Like the *swadeshi* movement in India, this movement in China was also anti-imperialistic and very patriotic, and it heralded the upward climb of the socialist movement.

An urban uprising of women occurred in the 1920s. Women from every field of life—industrialists, students, professionals, leftist social activists—got together to campaign for the inclusion of their respective organizations in the First National Congress held by the political party Guomindang (GMD) and its alliance, the Communist Party of China (CCP). The Guomindang is often referred to as Kuomintang (KMT) in English. It was the political party of Sun Yat-sen and later of Chiang Kai-shek, and is still one of the main political parties in Taiwan today. This party also had a women's wing, led by Soong Ching Ling and He Xiangning. In 1924, at the first congress of Guomindang, several resolutions were passed in favor of women—education and labor laws, equal rights, and employment.[8] There was also a rising peasant movement at this time, and rural women got together with them to defy the traditional culture and conventional practices that oppressed women—foot-binding and child marriages.

In 1930, there was another uprising by urban women activists. There was a regressive move to push women back into their domestic shells. Urban women fought back. At this time, there was also an anti-Japanese movement, which brought out urban women's organizations to support the cause. These movements encouraged women to participate in political activities as a collective whole rather than as individuals or individual organizations fighting for autonomy or individual freedom. But during the Great Leap Forward (1958–1960), the name given to a Chinese economic project, and the Cultural Revolution after that (1966–1976), women's liberation was tied to the state rhetoric of women's liberation and equality. In the 1960s, ACWF was abolished and there was no longer anyone, or any organization, to talk about or take women's issues forward.

Korea

If in China it was urban women who were involved in activism, in Korea around the second decade of the twentieth century, it was female workers who formed unions and called for strikes in their factories and other workplaces on issues that included low wages and the mistreatment of women workers. They formed an all-women union in Seoul in 1923 and became affiliated with the Communist Party, which was illegal at the time. They also carried out the first women's strike against an overseer for bad treatment of women workers in the factory. In 1931, however, this union was abolished.[9]

In Korea, there were sporadic resistance movements against the Japanese occupation, and women took part in these struggles. In the 1920s, a provisional government in exile was formed in China, and this government had a constitution that stipulated equality between men and women. Most of the participants who organized resistance activities and demonstrations were educated teachers and students, missionary workers, and nurses. From 1885, foreign missionaries started coming into Korea. They spread Christianity and founded schools for girls. Thus it was mainly after this that women became free to pursue activities outside the home. There were, of course, several outcries from men who held orthodox Confucian views about women's increasing freedom. But nothing stopped the women. Women's organizations were formed, such as Tongnip Sinmun in 1898, which included women of all classes and was led by upper-class widows. In 1906 with the success of women's schools, another organization, the Society for Women's Education, was formed. This organization also started the first women's journal, *Yoja Chinam*. Young women students participated in the resistance movement against the Japanese occupation in 1919. The Japanese closed down all the schools, yet from their hometowns the young Korean women and girls continued with their demonstrations. Korea was a very traditional society, with strong Confucian values and the subordination of women by men as the central feature. But with the influx of missionaries from the West and the start of schools for girls, the outlook toward women changed. Until World War II and the end of the Japanese occupation, women's movements continued to be active in one way or another.

Philippines

In the late nineteenth century, Manila, the capital of the Philippines, opened itself to world trade. Consequently, many factories were established and increasing numbers of men as well as women began to be absorbed into the industry. There were no workers' unions as such at the time, but bad living conditions led women to organize protests. Introduction of new technologies in the factories also led women to seek further skills and training. But the education system was completely biased toward males, and lack of education and skills compelled women to protest for reform in the education system.[10]

In the sixteenth century when the Spanish colonized the Philippines, the country was introduced to Western culture. These Spanish rulers also introduced the civil code, which adversely impacted the women. Like other parts of South Asia and East Asia, the women of the Philippines found themselves relegated to a subsidiary status in the society. Their freedom was limited by traditional patriarchal norms. But even in the midst of this subjugated situation, women got together to struggle against the Spanish rule in 1890. The nationalist struggle brought them success. There were quite a number of strong-willed women like Trinidad Tecson, who organized groups of women nurses and also fought in battles between 1896 and 1899. Agueda Kahabagan led a group of revolutionary fighters against the Spanish. Tandang Sera, was known as the Mother of the Revolution "for organizing food and shelter for the revolutionary fighters."[11]

It was in the 1900s that the first two women's organizations were formed in the Philippines. They were known as *feministas*. The president of the

Asociacion Feminista Filipina (Feminist Association of the Philippines) was Concepcion Felix Rodriguez, who campaigned openly for women's rights. It was as early as 1904 that women started struggling to gain gender equality. The association campaigned for women to be appointed at municipal- and provincial-level electorates and committees. Initiatives were taken to attain equality in political spaces and public governance. They also worked for social welfare as well as improvement of working standards in the factories, prisons, schools, and other workplaces. Slowly, other organizations working for similar causes started to grow. In 1912, two suffragists visited the Philippines. One was Carrie Chapman Catt, a reformer and leader of the women's suffrage movement in the United States, and the other was Dr. Aleta Jacobs from Holland. Soon after, the Society for the Advancement of Women (SAW) was formed, and it joined the Asosacion Feminista Ilonga (Association of Ilonga Feminists). Together, these women campaigned to attain their primary objective, which was the women's right to vote. It took them almost 30 years to achieve their goal, which they did in 1937. The victory of this suffrage also meant political empowerment for these women. It was not only about the freedom to vote, but it also meant that women were now able to hold public offices and take up places in governance. At the same time, this movement also connected them with the international women's movements that had already begun outside of the Philippines.[12]

Japan

In the last decades of the nineteenth century, women in Japan were included in mixed labor unions of both men and women, including skilled and unskilled workers. In the 1870s women were enticed to work in factories and they constituted 60 percent of the workforce. But the working conditions were very poor, and they were forced to work for 15 hours a day. In 1886, the first women's labor movement took place when 100 women walked out of the silk mill in Kofu, after the owners decided to increase the working hours and decrease the wage. This lent impetus to the workers, both men and women, to carry out strikes in order to have their voices heard by the concerned authority.[13] Four more strikes took place in the same year and many more in the subsequent years. In the early twentieth century, when unions were formed, they were considered illegal and went unrecognized until the Trade Union Law of 1947 was ratified. But women workers were very involved in industrial issues long before this. It was in the latter half of the nineteenth century that women's movements actually started in Japan. Toward 1868, the country finally began to emerge from almost seven centuries of feudalism, but societal thinking toward women was still conservative. Women such as Kishida Toshiko, who were influenced by French socialists like Jean Jaures and who were aware of the suffrage movements in Western countries, fought for women's rights. For Kishida, the issues of the right to vote, property rights, and gender inequality became major areas for contestation. She was Japan's first suffragist, and she travelled all over Japan to appeal for democratic rights for women. The representation of women in the Liberal Party was strong and women, such as Kishida, gave speeches about women's subordinate position. She also initiated the Kyoto Women's Lecture Society. In one of her speeches, she attacked the family system in Japan, in which women were subordinate to men. The women's movement gradually became politically vibrant. Kishida resorted to journalism in order to voice the sentiments of women for popular rights, raise the consciousness of women, and articulate their demands. But in 1890, a law was passed prohibiting women from joining politics. The Reform Society from then on was the only forum through which women could get their issues heard. They brought forward the issues of prostitution and concubinage, which was political. But the country was not yet ready to hear or solve these issues. It was still in a conservative phase. The Social Reform organization gradually moved away from these political issues and began to focus on social welfare and more so "on natural disasters like earthquakes and typhoons."[14] In Japan, many revolutionary women became active during the first years of the twentieth century. As socialists, communists, and anarchists, they opposed the rule of the government on various fronts. These activities continued even well after World War I, when the dominant ideology was democracy and socialism. Japanese women were now in contact with women of the West, including suffragists from the United States. In 1922, the government suppressed all the communist factions, including the Communist Party. Even feminist organizations were suppressed. With the rise of totalitarianism in the 1930s, the government endorsed aggressive policies, and the power of Japanese military spread across Asia. This adversely impacted women's organizations and movements.

Yet in spite of all the political changes, in 1932, the Third Women's National Suffrage Conference was held, which condemned the government for its recent changes in political ideology. But things were not to be the same. Women's movements no longer remained independent, nor did they continue to oppose the government's acts and policies. In 1937, Japan was at war with China, and many women, even those who had fought for women's rights, sided with the government and its policies. This Third Women's Suffrage Conference turned out to be the last ever held. Later, its name was changed to the Provisional Women's Conference. Like dictatorial regimes of the West, the Japanese manipulated women into voicing state rhetoric. In 1942, all the women's organizations were brought under the state-directed umbrella of Greater Japanese Women's Association (Dai Nihon Fujinkai), directed to support the war efforts. A law had been passed in 1890, forbidding the participation of women in politics. After the U.S.

occupation of Japan in 1945, the ban on Japanese women's political prohibitions that they had been facing until then were removed. In 1946, Japanese women finally acquired their right to vote and stand for political office. By the 1960s, voting became a part of their redefined roles.

Besides women's organizations, which were formed as part of liberation movements against imperial occupation, many more women's movements elsewhere in Asia were also organized to gain political participation as well as social and economic rights. But everywhere in Asia, it is clear that these movements have always been directly or indirectly linked to men's organizations or political parties, or have been part of the state apparatus.

In 1947, after India was decolonized, political activities within the country increased. But for women, it was only after the Committee on the Status of Women in India (CSWI) was formed in 1971 that the demand for larger representation of women in political institutions was systematically taken up. India is the largest democracy in the Asia Pacific region. Even though the constitution of India (first framed in 1950) calls for equal political rights for both men and women, and it prohibits any kind of gender discrimination, women are still discriminated against, as in other social and cultural contexts.

In the context of the electoral system, women in India hold a better record than those of the other South Asian countries. This is because women have, for a long time in Indian history, been involved in social and cultural issues such as child marriage, the dowry system, the struggle for economic independence, and other issues. This has led women to participate in several social and political movements. In the electoral process, voters show no gender bias. For example, since 1984, approximately 32.43 percent of women have been elected from the significantly recognized political parties, while the percentage of men elected has been only 26.50 percent. The same is not true at the national level. Women's participation has either decreased, or else women have not been able to attain seats at par with their male counterparts. In 2007, women's participation in politics decreased. For example, the country has only 8.26 percent of women parliamentarians in the Lok Sabha, also known as the House of People, and 11.20 percent in the Rajya Sabha, or the Council of States.[15]

Sri Lanka

In Sri Lanka, women started voting in 1931. They have the distinction of having elected the world's first female prime minister. The literacy rate of women in the country is the highest in South Asia. But in spite of this, women's participation in politics has been very poor; in fact, it is the lowest in South Asia. Participation is only 4.44 percent in the national parliament. In the early twentieth century, education for girls had spread across the country, a class of professional women emerged, and these women grew to be aware of the political situation and culture. They formed women's organizations, and some even entered the political organization the Young Lanka League, which was formed in 1915. In 1919, when the Ceylon National Congress was formed, many women delegates attended the first sessions. In 1923, the suffrage movement started, with women's organizations (some men's too) fighting to attain women's right to vote. It was middle-class and professional women who formed organizations such as the Women's Franchise Union in 1927. The members of the organization also included wives of nationalist leaders. In 1931, adult franchise was won, and women above the age of 21 were given the right to vote. Three women filed for candidacy in the elections, and two women, a Tamil doctor, Naysum Saravanamuttu, and another woman from an aristocratic family, Adeline Molamure, won. They were elected as the first women legislators in the history of Sri Lanka. In the meantime, female workers were actively struggling for the right to equal wages, better work conditions, and material gains.[16]

Thailand

In Thailand, women first got the right to vote in 1932, at almost the same time as in Sri Lanka. This was also when the country transformed from absolute monarchy to constitutional monarchy. In spite of this, women did not take part in any electoral activities. It was only in 1949 that the first woman was elected to the parliament; in the 1952 elections, four women were elected. Women have made a lot of progress in other areas of development, and the ratio of women working outside the home is high compared to other countries in Asia. Yet in politics, the involvement of women is insignificant. In the years between 1949 and 2000, there was no significant increase in the number of women in the political arena. In 1960, there were only six women in the house of representatives, and a mere 2.8 percent in the full parliament, which increased to 4 percent in the 1980s and to 6 percent in 1992. In the 2005 general elections, the proportion of women in the lower house reached 10.6 percent.[17]

In 1995, women from around the world met in China for the Beijing Platform for Action Conference, where the whole discourse was about their respective governments and significant political institutions having to focus on certain institutional practices "setting gender balance as the goal, and demanding that governments and political parties commit themselves to affirmative action." This was a consequence of a consensual agreement that discriminatory attitudes and practices along with unequal power relations were the causes of women's underrepresentation in political decision-making domains.[18] The conference of women came up with a resolution stating that the responsibility for dealing with the underrepresentation of women lay with political institutions and that to remedy women's under-representation in politics, "electoral gender quotas for the recruitment and election of female candidates" was a necessity.[19] This resolution was implemented by reserving a certain number of seats for women in parliament. This system was seen to be more relevant to Arab and Muslim countries.[20]

Pakistan

In many parts of Pakistan, women's sociocultural conditions have prevented them from being actively involved in matters outside the home, let alone in politics. The constitution of Pakistan in 1956 formulated the quota system and set aside 10 seats for women in the national assembly. The quota system—or the "reservation," as it is often termed, is the prescribed number of seats allocated by the government for women and those marginalized in society to contest in elections or apply for state examinations and jobs. In 1999, a bill was introduced in the senate by the Pakistan People's Party (PPP) that proposed to set aside nine seats for women in the senate, 40 seats in the national assembly, and 20 percent in the provisional assembly. The quota system was introduced again in 2002, according to which 60 seats were set aside for women in Pakistan's national assembly. Seventy-one women have since then obtained representation at the national level, out of which 60 were from within the quota and 11 on the general seats. At present, women have been allocated 33 percent of the seats in the local government. With the reintroduction of the quota system, there was a significant increase in the number of women in the national assembly.[21] But there has been criticism about the quota system practiced in Asia, especially when women's involvement in the political arena is concerned. This institutional mechanism has been adopted in some of the countries "in local and national elections—raising many daunting, but important, questions about interest representation and accountability."[22] For example, in some countries, the quotas (or reserved seats) are not taken up by women elected by voters. Rather, the women are appointed to those seats by male-dominated institutions that are not even supported by women constituents. Once appointed by these male leaders, the women succumb to the whims of the male-dominated political institutions or parties and fail to support women's causes.[23]

In other ways, too, women have actively participated in political movements and other related activities. Awami League, a strong political party in Pakistan, began an agitation in 1966 to gain the autonomy of East Pakistan. There were protests, imprisonments without trials, and shootouts that grew worse in 1969 and 1970. It was at this point that a few women activists who were associated with the leftist parties sought the support of influential women, including members of the women's wing of the Awami League. To fight for the release of prisoners, these women, with the support of the prominent political women, formed a committee that later became known as the Mahila Parishad (Women's Council). By the 1980s, the membership of Mahila Parishad had exceeded 30,000. [24]

Afghanistan

In Afghanistan, women were very involved in politics starting with the uprising against the British in 1880. Their involvement continued for almost another 100 years until the communist movement in 1980. Though women from the royal families were involved in the country's politics and reforms, they were never an integral part, and they were never head of government or state. In the recent spate of political activities after 1992, women who were not involved with the muhjahidin camps were barred from politics. In 1996 with the rise of the Taliban, women were prohibited from taking part in any activity outside the home or taking up any profession. With Hamid Karzai as president, women's freedom and empowerment was promoted, but nothing much has come of that. Since 2007, with the onset of democracy in Afghanistan, women have been caught between answering the government's call to work together with men in building of the nation and the traditional mindset of the men who harass women and even perpetrate violence in order to hinder women's involvement in the public domain. Because of the religious fundamentalism in Afghanistan, "women have been kept strategically aloof from decision making." Often, women's political participation has been threatened and women leaders, media persons, and activists have been "victimized for their active involvement to promote women's issues including women's political participation."[25]

Nepal

In Nepal, it was only in 1990—after the introduction of multiparty democracy—that women entered politics. Prior to 1990, for 240 years, Nepal was under the rule of absolute monarchy. For 30 years prior to 1990, the country was under the one-party Panchayat system. During the one-party Panchayat system women's participation in politics was almost unheard of. Aristocratic women and those who were somehow related to the monarchy were nominated to the upper and lower houses of parliament. As in Afghanistan, women have never been head of state or government. Women found a voice in the elections held in 1991 and 1994. But even during these elections, less than 5 percent of the candidates were women. In 1999, the major political parties declared in their respective manifestoes that there had to be a minimum of 10 percent women in the electoral candidacy. But the actual numbers turned out to be 6.3 percent, and only 5.85 won seats. In 1995, the country had a new multiparty political system with a constitutional monarchy. During the 10-year insurgency from 1996 to 2006, thousands of lives were lost, and there was massive destruction of the country's physical infrastructure. Monarchy was abolished in 2007, and the country took a major political turn when in 2010 it became a democratic republic with a president as head of state. Now the country has made constitutional provisions for women. It has stipulated that women should have 33 percent of the seats in parliament. In other words, space has been provided for women in politics and other areas of governance. When the new constitution was being drafted, women sought more inclusion and identity-based politics. When the constituent assembly was formed, there were 25 major political parties with representation in the assembly, and each party had a women's wing. More than a third of the members of the constituent assembly were women. There is an increase in the political awareness among women and progress at multiple levels.

Bangladesh

In 1935, long before Bangladesh became an independent country, voting rights had already been handed to women. So the women of Bangladesh were already experienced in political activities of motivating women to vote. Violence against women was seen to be an accelerating problem in Bangladesh in the 1970s, soon after the Liberation War. It became evident, and women started being vocal and aware of what was going on around them, in their houses and communities. This was also due to the declaration of the UN Decade for Women (1976–1985), which occurred at the same time. Women's groups organized campaigns and pressure groups, which ultimately resulted in the Prohibition of Dowry Act of 1980 and then in 1983, the Cruelty to Women Ordinance (Deterrent Punishment). These government responses encouraged women to continue to exert pressure to change family laws and laws relating to inheritance where women were concerned. The women—students, lawyers, teachers, members of voluntary organizations, wives of businessmen took to the streets of Dhaka in 1985, shouting slogans and advocating for women's rights. But they were silenced by police intervention. Later, most of the women joined the larger political institutions, thus participating in the movement for democracy rather than simply focusing on women's issues.[26]

After the Liberation War of 1971, women realized how badly they were discriminated against. The government did not respond positively to the 30,000 females who became rape victims of the Pakistani military. The Five Year Plan of the government recognized women, but only as mothers. Despite the fact that women had been voting for such a long time, it was clear that they were being used only as vote banks. Women rarely hold positions of power, and when they do, as shown by the women in the centrist parties, their commitment to women's issues is vague or weak.[27]

The women of Bangladesh do involve themselves in grassroots politics, but they have never been able to attain positions of power and a voice at the top level. This was clear from the elections of 1991, which showed no commitment to women's issues. There is a quota of 30 seats for women in parliament. But these seats have always been taken by women who have been selected by the male members of the party and who consequently pledge to work by the rules set up by the male-dominated parties. After 1997, direct elections have been held at the local level. And in the same year (1997), 42,000 women contested the elections, out of which 14,000 won. This was a major shift in the political culture. But the staunch patriarchal order stifled women's enthusiasm and the ability to go outside the home and perform tasks on the same footing as men. Women form 50 percent of the population of Bangladesh, and they are the backbone of the country's economy. Through microcredit and the garment industry, they have become independent. Yet at the political level, they are still far behind.[28]

The country has had two women prime ministers, Khaleda Zia (now an opposition leader) and Sheikh Hasina, the current prime minister. But in spite of having two women as political leaders, there has not as yet been an increase in women's political participation in the country.

FEMALE POLITICAL LEADERS OF ASIA

In the context of history, Asia boasts of myths, legends, and even faraway times where women have ruled. They speak of matriarchal worlds in which women have led and men have followed, of queens who have ruled and led the male warriors into the battlefield to return victorious. But the status of women over the centuries has changed in Asia. One can take the example of Japan, where women ruled in the earlier years of the country's history. It is said there were civil wars from the years 147 to 190 CE and anarchy until Queen Pimiko brought back law and order. She was succeeded to the throne by a 13-year-old girl who was her relative. The chronicles say there were six empresses who ruled Japan in the two centuries after 592 CE. In the eighteenth century when Empress Koken ruled, she was not married and had no children. With her, women's rule eventually came to an end, and women were barred from being heirs to the throne, a practice still continued today.[29]

Exemplar of the million celebratory wooden pagodas commissioned by the Empress Koken, bearing a printing of Hyakumanto Darani, 764, Japan. Japanese Civilisation, Nara period, 8th century. (De Agostini/Getty Images)

In the Henian period (794–1185) in Japan, once again women had important roles to play. Even though they did not have much contact with the outside world, they were well educated. Some of the best literature of the time was written by these women of the royal court. Then in the eighth century, the Chinese family system was introduced in Japan, which immediately led to the adoption of the patrilineal family system along with Confucian beliefs that considered women as inferior beings. This naturally led to the oppression of women in terms of property rights, marriage, and divorce. Things changed a little for women in the Kamakura period (1185–1333)—they regained property rights and continued to hold an important place in society. But the Muromachi period (1338–1500) saw the rise of feudalism and the masculine samurai warriors. This completely changed men's outlook toward women. To a large degree, women lost their status and their rights. When feudalism flourished starting from 1600 to the late nineteenth century, women were forced to be increasingly subservient to men. Thus even visions of women political leaders who could possibly rule the country simply vanished.[30]

In the same way, Sri Lanka has chronicles of women rulers. The legend has it that around 25,000 years ago, the island nation was ruled by Kuveni, a demon queen. In later years, there were queens such as Anula Devi, Soma Devi, Lilavati, and Sugala, all of whom led their armies into battle.

The Pali chronicles, written by Buddhist monks, refer to Vihara Mahadevi, the strong and courageous woman who rescued her father from the rage of the seas and anger of the gods. Ultimately, she gave birth to a son who saved the country. But such queens and strong women were often also mothers, wives, and good daughters. These women are not a reflection of the position of women in the country.[31]

In Asia in the twentieth and twenty-first centuries, all the women who have become heads of state or leaders of the opposition have occupied spaces left vacant by either their fathers or husbands, who have always been by birth or marriage in privileged positions of power. This is not say that after they assumed their positions they did not strive to take the country forward with necessary reforms and good practices. But they did not rise from the grassroots level vying for a position, full of ideals and ideology, and fighting to lead the nation in the face of adversaries. All the women leaders who have led their countries as presidents, prime ministers, or opposition leaders inherited the legacy of a culturally rich dynasty. They did not become rulers out of personal choice, but because either their husbands or fathers had become martyrs. Nevertheless, all of them attained political legitimacy through elections or referendum.

India

Indira Gandhi, the first and the only elected female prime minister of India, was born into a well-educated and politically active family. She completed her higher education in Switzerland and at Oxford University in England. On her return to India from Switzerland in 1936, she became actively involved in the ongoing national movement against the British imperialists and also became a member of the Indian National Congress Party. In 1947, when India gained independence from the British, Indira Gandhi's father Jawarharlal Nehru was the first prime minister of India. Indira Gandhi, though married by then and the mother of two sons, moved to Delhi to support her father in his political pursuits and became one of his political advisors. In 1951 and 1952, during the parliamentary elections, Indira Gandhi campaigned for her husband, who was contesting from Uttar Pradesh (Northern State). She gained experience while working for her father as well as by supporting her husband in his political pursuits. In 1959, she was elected president of the Indian National Congress Party. When her father died in 1964, she decided to contest the elections and was elected to the parliament and given charge of the ministry of information and broadcasting.[32]

From 1966 to 1977, she was prime minister of India. During the struggle between East and West Pakistan in 1971, she supported East Pakistan. India at that time sent troops and provided logistical support to East

Pakistan (Bangladesh) to fight against West Pakistan (Pakistan). In 1975, Indira Gandhi was charged with violating the election procedures during the 1971 elections, and the high court ordered that she resign from her position. The common people were angry due to rising inflation and rampant corruption in the country. They turned against her. On June 26 of the same year, President Fakhruddin Ali Ahmed declared a state of emergency upon the advice of Indira Gandhi. With this, democracy in India came to a complete halt, and panic spread in the country especially among the working-class people. The slumdwellers were evicted from their homes with no alternative spaces allocated to them, forced sterilization programs were introduced to curb the growing population, press censorship was imposed, and brutal police forces went into action to suppress the protesters and arrest the opposition leaders. After 21 months of such authoritarian rule, Indira Gandhi set the imprisoned opposition leaders free and called for elections. On March 23, 1977, the emergency was lifted. But Indira Gandhi lost the elections of 1977.

In 1980, she assumed power once again as prime minister (1980–1984) after winning the elections. In 1984, she brought herself trouble when she used military force against Sikh militants within the premises of the Golden Temple of the Sikhs. Thousands of civilians were killed in the process. On October 31, 1984, she was assassinated by two of her own bodyguards.

The Philippines

In the Philippines, Corazon Aquino finally stood up to regain democracy for the people after the assassination of her husband on August 21, 1983. Aquino was from a wealthy family, graduated from Mount St. Vincent College in New York City, and married Benigno Aquino, who later became a prominent opposition politician. He was imprisoned by President Ferdinand Marcos for eight years. In 1980, Corazon accompanied him to the United States when he was again exiled by Marcos. They returned to the Philippines in 1983. After her husband's death, Corazon joined politics, a space that until then had always been male dominated. After 1983, the Philippines became a hothouse for political intrigues. President Marcos was seriously ill, his wife Imelda Marcos was vying for power, the economy had fallen apart, press freedom was curtailed, and the opposition was completely divided. This was the state of affairs when Corazon ran for the presidency against Ferdinand Marcos. She united the opposition and used the story of the assassination of her husband as a weapon against Marcos. At every campaign speech, she told the public how her husband Benigno had been shot as he stepped foot on the tarmac while returning from a three-year exile in the United States. She told the people that—like they were—she too was a victim of Marcos. But it was not until 1986 that she contested the elections against Marcos as the candidate of the unified opposition party. She was declared to have lost the elections. But the people were not satisfied. They rallied against Marcos's military force, declaring that the elections had been fraudulent because of Marcos's intrigues. The military soon declared Aquino the rightful president, and in February, both Aquino and Marcos were declared presidents by their respective parties. That same night, Marcos and his wife fled the Philippines. On March 8, International Women's Day, thousands of women marched the streets of Manila. It was a victory not only for Corazon, but for the women's movement in the Philippines.

Corazon Aquino received strong support from the women's movement, which was critical for her election. While she was in power, many women also took positions of power in public offices. Since a new democratic process was implemented with Corazon's presidency, reform measures were also initiated, such as the Philippine Development Plan for Women.[33]

The country was bent and struggling from being under the dictatorship of Marcos. Corazon Aquino brought back a semblance of stability to the tottering democracy. The constitution abolished by Marcos was revived. The economy made a steady upward climb. But in the long run, Corazon was unable to carry out appropriate social reforms or economic changes, and slowly her popularity began to decline. This situation was in turn marred by the continuous battle between the communist insurgents and the military, whose allegiance to Corazon was ambivalent. In 1992, she was succeeded by Fidel V. Ramos as president.

Pakistan

Benazir Bhutto, like Indira Gandhi, was educated at Oxford University in England. She returned to Pakistan in 1977. On April 4, 1979, her father, Prime Minister Zulfikar Ali Bhutto, was executed. In 1982, Benazir Bhutto became the first woman to head a political party when she became the chairperson of the People's Political Party, a position left vacant by the death of her father. In 1988, she became the first woman and the eleventh elected prime minister (1988–1990) of Pakistan. After she won the elections, her opponents did not want her to become the prime minister. As a woman, they said, she could not be head of state under the Sharia law (the sacred law of Islam). A religious pronouncement had to be made after that, declaring that it would be the president—who was male—who would be the head of state, and not the prime minister.[34] Two years into her premiership, she was dismissed by former president Gulam Ishaq Khan on charges of corruption. In 1993, she ran for office and was again elected prime minister (1993–1996). She faced constant charges of mismanagement, nepotism, and corruption, and also faced constant opposition from Islamic fundamentalists. She lost the next election in 1997 and went on a self-imposed exile to Dubai, United Arab Emirates in 1998. She returned to Pakistan in October 2007 and was preparing to run for the 2008 general elections when she was assassinated in December 2007.

Bangladesh

Sheikh Hasina is the daughter of Sheikh Mujibur Rehman, the country's first prime minister and one of the main leaders who carried out the separation of Bangladesh and Pakistan. He was killed in a coup in 1975. Sheikh Hasina was prime minister of Bangladesh from 1996 to 2001 and was reelected again in 2009. Even as a university student, Sheikh Hasina was active in politics and took part in the uprising during the War of Liberation, helping her father in many of his political works. A few months after her father became president of the country, the whole family was assassinated except for Sheikh Hasina, who at the time was away from the country and did not return for six years. When she returned, she became leader of Awami League, a party founded by her father. Her father had left vacant a political space that she had to fill. In 1991, a general election was held for which she stood as one of the candidates. Hasina failed to obtain a majority, and the power passed to Khaleda Zia, leader of the Bangladesh Nationalist Party (BNP). Khaleda Zia was the wife of Ziaur Rehman, a former president of Bangladesh who was assassinated in May 1981. He was also the founder of the Bangladesh Nationalist Party (BNP). Justice Abdul Sattar, the acting president and leader of the BNP, appointed Khaleda Zia as the vice chair of BNP. Later that same year, she was elected chair. In 1991, she became the country's first elected prime minister. She won a second term in February 1996. But the election was boycotted by many political parties, and the position was contested. Governance was handed over to a caretaker government. In June of the same year, Sheikh Hasina was elected as the prime minister and in 2001, she became the first prime minister after Partition to complete a full five-year term in office. In the ensuing elections, Khaleda Zia once more returned to power. She brought about several reforms, primarily in the education sector, including the introduction of free education at the primary level and free tuition for girls up to grade 10. The maximum age for people to enter government service was until then 27. She increased it by three years and made the age 30. During both female leaders' premiership, the country was steeped in problems. Fighting between the two main political parties and parliamentary obstructions became a common feature.

During Khaleda Zia's tenure, Sheikh Hasina continued working for her Awami League. During the 2007 parliamentary elections, there was so much trouble and violence that the interim government declared a state of emergency and cancelled the elections. Charges of extortion and corruption were filed against both female leaders, and they were subsequently imprisoned and released almost a year later. Hasina was released in June and Zia in September. Later the same year, in December, elections were held once more. Both women filed for candidacy. Hasina won and continues to be prime minister today. These two women of Bangladesh, Sheikh Hasina and Khaleda Zia, have become leaders because a father and a husband were martyred.

WOMEN LEADERS TODAY

In almost all Asian countries, women fought for suffrage rights. By the time they emerged victorious, the principles they had adopted to attain the rights had been accepted by their respective nations. For the women of the countries that had to fight for rights outside of suffrage, the struggle was more formidable. Women in many Asian countries gained rights not just because of their gradual struggle within their own countries, but also because of external forces, for example, in the contexts of colonial countries such as India and Malaysia; in the case of revolution in China, where they were guided by

Members of the Japanese Woman Suffrage League approaching the Imperial Diet with 20,000 signed petitions for the passage of the women's suffrage bill to be introduced into the Diet, Tokyo, Japan, ca. 1920. (Underwood & Underwood/Corbis)

Western ideologies; or due to Western influence in occupied Japan.[35] Therefore, even though rights were achieved in these countries, they lacked roots, so the process of redefining women's roles to include participation in politics has been difficult. The conflict between male and female political roles takes place at the point at which political activism starts. This point varies according to the various responses of the society to the role. Thus it is never a one-sided approach where the woman's role goes through the changing process. There has to be a simultaneous change in the perception of society as well. Otherwise, the country will be left with isolated examples of elite women who actively participate in political activities in all their forms.

Almost all the female leaders of Asia did not become political leaders out of personal choice, but because their fathers or husbands were martyrs. Except for Benazir Bhutto, all the other female leaders unwillingly assumed their power positions either because of pleas from political parties or because of public demand.[36] All of them share some common features regarding their political backgrounds and their personal developments. All of them have a dynastic descent and were educated in the best Western universities, where other top politicians of the world have acquired their education. They have socialized at the highest national and international political and social strata. But all of them, except for Gloria Macapagal-Arroyo of the Philippines and Chandrika Kumaratunga of Sri Lanka, who had at some point held formal political offices, had very low levels of political experience when they assumed office as political leaders.[37]

Women political leaders have had distinct handicaps as well. In the case of Pakistan, Bangladesh, and the Philippines, men supported the women during the antidictatorship struggles, and praises were forthcoming for the women politicians and their roles in the revolutions. But once they were elected to government, they were merely political symbols. Male rivals and male colleagues, including husbands, were unable to come to terms with a woman who had assumed such a position of power. They felt the political intrigues and the "realities of politics" were not suited to women. Many men felt that winning an election was one thing, but actually running the country was a job to be done by a man. For example, when Corazon Aquino assumed power in the Philippines in 1986 as president, the defense minister and her vice president—two male rivals—showed dissatisfaction at having to work under female leadership and demanded that there be an immediate presidential reelection.[38]

Gloria Macapagal-Arroyo, like many of the other well-known Asian women leaders, inherited her political legacy. Her father, Diosdado Macapagal, was the ninth president (1962–1965) of the Philippines. In 1998, she was elected to be the vice president, and in 2001, after the resignation of President Joseph Estrada on charges of corruption, she became president. She was the fourteenth president of the Philippines. Arroyo, like her Asian counterparts, was educated in the West. She got her graduate degree from the University of California–Berkeley, and her masters degree from Georgetown University. She was educated and rose to power. She was a professor of economics and later served as assistant undersecretary and undersecretary during Corazon Aquino's presidency in 1986. She was elected two times to the senate (1992–1998). In 1998, she was elected vice president, and the vote count showed she was more popular than Estrada, the presidential candidate.

Arroyo's presidency was fraught with problems and political unrest. Soon after she assumed office, Estrada supporters, thousands in numbers, stormed the presidential palace. A state of rebellion was declared. Again in 2003, many soldiers, unhappy with her regime, seized an apartment building and demanded Arroyo's resignation. In 2004, she was reelected after promises to reduce corruption and handle the state of affairs better. But she found herself in a whirlpool of accusations, corruption, and rigged elections. In 2006, she called a state of emergency after a military coup was foiled. The emergency was lifted in five days, but it left an unhappy public. She had to face many terrorist activities of bombings and killings in and around the islands. She was forced to cut ties with a political ally, a powerful clan in the Philippines, after they were accused of killing a political opponent. After she completed her six-year term as president in 2010, she ran for election to the house of representatives and won. Once more, however, she was accused of electoral fraud during the 2007 senate elections along with other crimes such as accepting bribes. She was investigated for accepting bribes and was not permitted to leave the country to seek medical help. In late July of 2012, she was released on bail.

In the 1990s in Sri Lanka, three widows entered the political arena. All three women's husbands were political leaders. Hema Premadasaa, the widow of President Ranasinghe Premadasa, did not file for candidacy at the elections, but she has been more active in politics than when her husband was alive. Srimao Dissanayake also stepped into the shoes of her assassinated husband to take up candidacy against Chandrika Kumaratunga, in 1994. The third widow, Srimani Athulathmudali, was elected as leader of her political party and became a member of parliament.

In India, the women of the Gandhi family, with the banner of the Gandhi legacy, entered a political arena left vacant to some degree by their husbands and fathers. In 1998, after the assassination of her husband Rajiv Gandhi, Sonia Gandhi stepped in to take up the role of political leadership. Rajiv Gandhi was Indira Gandhi's son. Sonia has assumed the leadership of the male-dominated and significantly large Congress Party. Today, she stands at the forefront of political leadership. The young daughter of Rajiv and Sonia Gandhi, Priyanka Vadra, is actively involved in politics today. She is a member of the youth wing of the Congress Party. Maneka Gandhi, the widow of Sanjay Gandhi (another son of Indira Gandhi), entered politics in opposition to her mother-in-law, Indira Gandhi.

In 2004, elections were carried out in nine countries of Asia: Afghanistan, India, Indonesia, Malaysia, Hong Kong, Philippines, Sri Lanka, South Korea, and Taiwan. In the majority of these countries, women were elected to leadership positions. Even today, in spite of legal policies, the roles of women in politics, such as voting, participating in political meetings, and discussing politics in open forums are curtailed by the prevalence of discriminatory sociocultural practices that include illiteracy, unemployment, unequal wages, having to look after the family, and above all, societal attitudes toward women. Therefore, women have had to go through many changes in the adoption of their roles in personal as well as social fronts. Society also undergoes similar changes as it accepts, resists, and adopts the changes made by women through their struggles.

NOTES

1. Kumari Jayawardena, *Feminism and Nationalism in the Third World* (London: Zed Books 1986), 17.
2. Howard Handleman, *The Challenge of Third World Development* (Boston: Longman, 2006), 143.
3. Amrita Basu, "Introduction," in *The Challenge of Local Feminisms: Women's Movements in Global Perspective*, Amrita Basu, ed. (Boulder, Colorado: Westview Press, 1995), 9–11.
4. Geraldine Forbes, *Women in Modern India* (Cambridge: Cambridge University Press, 1996), 122–23.
5. Jayawardena, *Feminism and Nationalism in the Third World*, 92–93.
6. Mark R. Thompson, "Female Leadership of Democratic Transitions in Asia," *Pacific Affairs* 75, no. 4 (Winter 2002–2003), 538.
7. Basu, *The Challenge of Local Feminisms*, 28.
8. Jayawardena, *Feminism and Nationalism in the Third World*, 190.
9. Kaye Broadbent and Michele Ford, eds., *Women and Labour Organizing in Asia: Diversity, Autonomy and Activism* (New York: Routledge, 2008), 137.
10. Lilia Quindoza Santiago, "Rebirthing Babaye: The Women's Movement in the Philippines," in *The Challenge of Local Feminisms: Women's Movements in Global Perspective*, Amrita Basu, ed. (Boulder, CO: Westview Press, 1995), 115.
11. Alzona, Encarnacion, *The Filipino Woman, Her Social, Economic and Political Status 1565–1933* (Manila: University of the Philippines Press, 1934), 161.
12. Santiago, "Rebirthing Babaye," 118–19.
13. Sharon L Sievers, *Flowers in Salt: The Beginning of Feminist Consciousness in Modern Japan* (Stanford, CA: Stanford University Press, 1983), 79.
14. Jayawardena, *Feminism and Nationalism in the Third World*, 240.
15. Rohit Kumar Nepali, Upendra Kumar Paudel, and Binisha Shrestha Ranjitkar, eds., *Invisible Faces of Violence on Women in Politics: Breaking the Silence* (Kathmandu: South Asia Partnership International, 2007), 114.
16. Jayawardena, *Feminism and Nationalism in the Third World*, 128.
17. Kazuki Iwanaga, *Women in Politics in Thailand* (Lund: Center for East and South East Asian Studies, Lund University, Sweden, 2005), 3–5.

18. Drude Dahlerup and Josefa "Gigi" Francesco, eds., "Gender, Governance, and Democracy: Women in Politics," *ISIS Monograph Series 2005*, 1, no. 1 (2005): 13, 15.

19. Dahlerup and Francesco, "Gender, Governance, and Democracy," 16.

20. Handleman, *The Challenge of Third World Development*, 150–51.

21. Nepali, Paudel, and Shrestha Ranjitkar, *Invisible Faces of Violence on Women in Politics*, 116

22. Shahra Razavi, "Women in Contemporary Democratization," *International Journal of Politics, Culture, and Society* (Fall 2001): 201–24.

23. Pamela Marie Paxton and Melanie M. Hughes, *Women, Politics and Power: A Global Perspective* (Los Angeles: Pine Forest Press, 2007), 161–62.

24. Basu, *The Challenge of Local Feminisms*, 92–93.

25. Nepali, Paudel, and Shrestha Ranjitkar, *Invisible Faces of Violence on Women in Politics*, 112.

26. Roushan Jahan, "Men in Seclusion, Women in Public: Rokeya's Dream and Women's Struggles in Bangladesh," in *The Challenge of Local Feminisms: Women's Movements in Global Perspective*, Amrita Basu, ed. (Boulder, CO: Westview Press, 1995), 100.

27. United Nations Development Program, *Human Development Report* (Dhaka: United Nations Development Program, 1994).

28. Jahan, "Men in Seclusion," 103–8.

29. Joy Paulson. "Evolution of the Feminine Ideal," in *Women in Changing Japan*, J. Lebra, Joy Paulson, et al., eds. (Stanford, CA. Stanford University Press, 1978), 2–3.

30. Paulson, "Evolution of the Feminine Ideal," 8–10.

31. Jayawardena, *Feminism and Nationalism in the Third World*, 109.

32. Forbes, *Women in Modern India*, 232.

33. Basu, *The Challenge of Local Feminisms*, 15.

34. Anita M. Weiss, "Benazir Bhutto and the future of Women in Pakistan," *Asian Survey* 5 (May 1990): 433–34.

35. Susan J. Pharr, *Political Women in Japan: The Search for a Place in Political Life* (Berkeley: University of California Press, 1981), 4.

36. Mark R. Thompson, "Female Leadership of Democratic Transitions in Asia," *Pacific Affairs* 75, no. 4 (Winter 2002–2003), 546.

37. Andrea Fleschenberg, "Asia's Women Politicians at the Top: Roaring Tigresses or Tame Kittens?" in *Women's Political Participation and Representation in Asia: Obstacles and Challenges*, Kazuki Iwanaga, ed. (Copenhagen: Denmark: Nordic Institution of Asian Studies [NIAS] Press, 2008), 40.

38. Thompson, "Female Leadership of Democratic Transitions in Asia," 550.

SUGGESTED READING

Bose, Sugata, and Ayesha Jalal. *Modern South Asia: History, Culture, Political Economy.* New Delhi: Oxford University Press, 2004.

Clements, Alan, *Aung San Suu Kyi: The Voice of Hope.* London: Penguin Books, 1997.

Howe, Brenden, Vesselin Popovski, et al. *Democracy in the South: Participation, the State and the People.* Tokyo: United Nations University Press, 2010.

Jeffery, Patricia, and Amrita Basu, eds. *Appropriating Gender: Women's Activism and Politicized Religion in South Asia.* New York: Routledge, 1998.

Sanbonmatsu, Kira. "Gender-Related Political Knowledge and the Representation of Women." *Political Behavior*, Vol. 25, No. 4, December 2003.

Political Behavior

Mann, Susan, and Yu-Yin Cheng, eds. *Under Confucian Eyes: Writings on Gender in Chinese History*. Los Angeles: University of California Press, 2001.

Siu, Helen F. ed. *Merchants' Daughters: Women, Commerce, and Regional Culture in South China*. Hong Kong: Hong Kong University Press, 2010.

5

—◦◦◦—

Women and Literature

The social structure of most Asian countries is strongly patriarchal even today. The art of literary writing has been predominantly very male-centered through the years, and that tradition has continued to the present times. In the literature written by men, women have occupied center stage but have embodied roles where they have been relegated to the kitchen, drawing room, or bedroom as passive receivers and not as active agents of change. When women first emerged into the literary arena as writers in their respective geographical locales, they sought an identity in self-expression and resistance. Women's writing, therefore, started off only as a growing subculture in every society. Elaine Showalter, an American feminist and a writer on cultural and social issues, talks about the three categories or phases that are common related to any minority writing anywhere in the world: "a phase of self discovery, a turning inward, freed from some of the dependency of opposition, and a search for identity."[1] These three phases typically describe Asian women who express themselves through literature.

The Southeast Asian region is in fact divided into two cultural parts: (1) Greater China, where Chinese influences predominate, and (2) Greater India, where Indian cultural experiences dominate. There are significant cultural similarities in this part of the region, including the climate as well as the flora and fauna. In most locations, the societies of "Greater China" and "Greater India" also share a common kinship system and community bonds. They "uphold East Confucian values. Together their common histories include Hindu, Buddhist, and Muslim, as well as Christian, influences and a syncretic approach to multiple cultural and racial crossings."[2] South Asia,

Illustration of Murasaki Shikibu at work by Suzuki Harunobu, 18th century. (Burstein Collection/Corbis)

on the other hand, is characterized by diverse people, religions, cultures, and languages. In many ways, India, Bangladesh, and Pakistan have a shared history of being colonized by Western powers. Even Sri Lanka shares the same colonial history. Thus the literature of this part of the world crosses and recrosses boundaries because themes of women's writings often are born out of patriarchal structures, colonial appropriations, or diasporic sensibilities.

MYTH AND LITERATURE

The literature of Asia evokes the myths of its cultural past, a history that was perhaps fabricated to lend legitimacy to certain power-filled actions, thoughts, and perceptions. When talking about myths, it is not possible to disown "the myth of one's culture," even though it may have a negative influence on people. The individual would feel "culturally impoverished" without that prehistorical burden of myth, "strangely weightless, and yet with them, one feels oppressed. Our myths can subjugate women as much as men can."[3] Looking at the myths that abound in Asia, recalled, remembered, and centralized through literature, one sees that the myths that relate to women are often oppressive to women, albeit in a subtle form, by denying "voice and visibility to women." For men, the myths themselves turn submissive,[4] Or, in other words, men are able to control myths.

Subjugation, or subversion, of myths is next to impossible, but at least the literature of women has many times attempted to successfully recast myths by giving voice to women, allowing them to be active agents narrating their own stories. In such literature, the burdens of the myths are unloaded and set aside, perhaps never to be picked up again. But again, myths are useful as well in that they help us understand the historical consciousness of both men and women. It is a platform from which literary writers are able to see and sense the historicity and thus build on that consciousness.

Myths about the faithful and virtuous woman are popular in Indian mythology, which has maintained its consistency since the time of the Hindu epic Ramayana. Sita, the consort of Rama, and Parvati, the consort of Shiva, are the two role models of women, "the epic heroines or goddesses," handed down by myth.[5] Sita is the embodiment of the ideal Hindu wife who gives up all the luxuries of the palace to spend 14 long years with her husband in the forest, in exile. During the exile, Sita is abducted by Ravana, the king of Lanka, and she spends her days worshipping and waiting for her husband to rescue *her*. Once she is rescued, she is compelled to go through *agni-pariksa* (the fire ordeal) to prove her fidelity. Unable to bear that her husband Rama should doubt her, she calls upon mother earth to take her into her womb. The earth opens up and takes her in. Sita is an example of ideal womanhood, selfless and passive.

As for Parvati, her only wish is to attain Siva as her husband. To achieve this, she performs austere fasts and penances for 60,000 years. Then her next wish is to have sons, after which she lives a happy life of devotion and self-sacrifice with her husband. Even today, a married woman will fast on a particular religious day so that she can be happy like Parvati, and an unmarried women will fast so that she can find a husband like Siva. Thus girls and women in the Hindu region are made to emulate these two goddess women. To be unfaithful is to be evil. In Asia, many women carry the burden of this myth.

In both South and East Asian regions, individuals, culture, and society are defined and directed by their myths. Even when Euro-Americans write about the Chinese culture and tradition, they repeat the myth about the Chinese women, "the myth of submission, oppression and the bound foot," whereas the myths about women outside of China are always about goddesses and female deities, ghosts "and their occasional this-worldly manifestations and appearances as character types often represented in puppet plays, folk tales and rituals and temple art or home decorations."[6]

The Javanese puppet theater known as *kethoprak* is very popular, especially among women. A female is always at the center of this show, where she is strong and articulate in opposition to the expected submissiveness of Javanese women. Such myths of womanhood are found woven into modern narratives as well; the eternal loving, chaste, and virtuous woman; images of the ideal widow; and the strong and powerful woman on the battlefield are all images that idealize women and at the same time speak of oppression.[7] In the folk arts and cultures of Asia, images of goddesses destroying demons are seen painted on walls or wall hangings. During Balinese festivals, the demonic goddess Durga is evoked. In the literature of the present time, one can see the popularity of myths invoked. Chitra Banerjee Divakaruni in *Mistress of Spices* evokes the myth of the Native American in the image of Raven, or the power of the old woman on the Spice Island. The same writer also takes Mahabharata and reinterprets this great epic by giving voice and visibility to the central female character, Draupadi, in *Palace of Illusions*. When in distress, Draupadi of Mahabharata calls upon Krishna to rescue her from the clutches of her husbands' enemies, their cousins the Kauravas. Another example is Mahasweta Devi, the contemporary writer who evokes the goddess *Ganga*, the bearer of water (river Ganges), through the narrative *Jal* (Water) of the marginalized class. One can see female suffering and male power reiterated in the twentieth century in the words of Gandhi from 1921: "To me female sex is not the weaker sex; it is the nobler of the two; for it is even today the embodiment of sacrifice, silent suffering, humility, faith and knowledge."[8]

In China, images of women stepping into the world of men are common in today's narratives. We find women eulogizing other legendary figures who stepped into a man's world to achieve great things, such as female historian Ban Zhao. Confucius's portrait was replaced by hers at a girls' school. Ban Zhao's biography was also published in 1940 in the *Women's Journal* (*Funu zazhi*), which reminded readers "of the courage and the vulnerability of highly educated Chinese women throughout history, who were forced to strategize as they maneuvered in political circles dominated by men."[9]

LITERATURE OF EAST ASIA

For women in China, a new era began with the end of the Qing Dynasty in 1911 and the start of the Chinese Republic. They had found a freedom that had been next to nonexistent for the previous 2,000 years. Chinese women, after having lived for more than 2,000 years in a state of near servitude, were now clamoring for freedom "from their status of serfdom within the family-clan complex." These women also wanted to dismantle the traditional notions of marriage, the selling of wives and children, and foot-binding, which had started in the tenth century. It was primarily after the founding of girls' schools that women were actually recognized as individuals rather than simply as prostitutes, concubines, or at best extensions of their husbands.[10]

Women did write during the Qing Dynasty. But novels—written by men—were very popular. Women did not write novels; they wrote only poetry. No female writer wrote novels before 1840. Novel writing by traditional women writers was considered "indecent," "anti-Confucian," and "evil by the feudal ruling class." Most enlightened literati and officialdom felt that only poetry writing was suited to the soft nature of women. Novel writing was considered unfit for women because themes were drawn from folk life and incorporated much sex, violence, and "street gossip."[11]

In Japan from 794 to 1192, with the economic and political collapse of imperial rule in Heian, women writers and artists were deprived of artistic ventures. During imperial times, courtly women such as Murasaki Shikibu, Sei Shônagon, and Izumi Shikibu were great literary writers who wrote poetry, essays, and waka poetry. This was around the year 1000. During the Tokugawa era, from 1000 to 1868, women had to abide by Confucian ideals, which taught them to be submissive to men. It was during this period that feudalism flourished and restrictions were placed on women. Their status in society declined, and their subservience to males went unquestioned. But the Meiji Restoration in 1868 brought about the beginning of a new era, during which women could finally get a taste of egalitarianism.[12]

The Taisho period (1912–1926) saw the evolution of literature by Japanese women with strong feminist consciousness. Murasaki Shikibu brought out a number of literary masterpieces, including *The Tale of Genji*. There was a huge gap between the two periods of the literary history of Japanese women. The staunch patriarchal sturcture of earlier Japanese society saw to it that women's creativity was surpressed. When the women of the Taisho period began to write, their main aim was to break the long silence, and they were in turn supported by the increasing activities of the feminist movement of the time. The writings of these Japanese women reflected a common desire to search for newer identities and shed the older stereotypical images of docility and obedience. Their works showed a sense of freedom and the need to assert themselves.[13]

In China too, in retaliation against the traditionalist notions of Chinese girls, women began to cut their hair short, join the army, and protest against several social and political policies and ideologies. Ding Ling, a pseudonym for Chiang Ping-chih, was born in 1906 and began to write by tracing her own political experience. Her main aim was to bring about political reform. In 1942, she joined the Communist Party, and even though she was actively involved in party politics, she gave continuity to her literary works. In 1942,

Japanese print by Hiroshige depicting a scene from a 19th-century edition of *The Tale of Genji*.
A masterpiece of Japanese literature, the work was written by the Heian court lady Murasaki
Shikibu in about 1010. (Library of Congress)

Mao Tse-Tung's *Yenan Forum Talks* was published with the aim to do away
with the criticism of government policies. But his anti-intellectual stand did
not change. With literary activism of women writers like Ding Ling, literature became more closely tied to politics and was used as a tactic during
the Cultural Revolution. Later, in 1957, Ding Ling and her second husband
were accused of rightist activities, and she was sent to a forced labor farm
for 12 years.[14]

Ding Ling wrote novels and short stories such as *Miss Sophie's Diary*
(1928), "Flood" (1932), "Mother" (1933), "When I Was in the Xia Village"
(1950), and several others. In 1951, her novel *The Sun Shines over the
Sanggan River* (1948) was awarded the Stalin Prize. Most of her stories
reflected the realities of her time, with characters that ranged from peasants
to landlords and union leaders, and they depicted struggles for land reform, a
struggle in which she herself was involved from 1946 to 1947. Since Ding
Ling's writing was politically motivated, though authentic, her novel *The
Sun Shines over the Sanggan River* is more theoretical and full of ideas rather
than an in-depth study of characters. It is an autobiographical novel, like
many other novels of the time, and it depicts the life of a woman from 1867
to 1937. It is a wonderfully written account of corruption, squalor, and difficulties a working mother faces, as well as the harrowing experiences with her
husband, other members of the family, her employer, and friends as she
trudges on in life.

The female literary writers of Japan were far more advanced, or rather less oppressed, than their Chinese counterparts. If at this time Chinese women writers were impacted by the political events and were strongly resisting political ideologies, then their Japanese counterparts were focusing on major themes of patriarchy, identity, and self-assertion.

In 1911, just a year before the Taisho era began, a young group of women started the nation's first feminist magazine, *Seito*. It was clear at this point that the impact of Western culture was strong on the cultural trend of the times, since the name *Seito* itself was "a translation of the eighteenth-century English expression *Bluestocking*."[15] The bluestocking movement was initiated in mid-eighteenth-century England by a literary women's group to establish their identity as literary and intellectual women as opposed to the nonintellectual, traditional women of the time. They founded a society of the same name in 1750. The primary objective of the magazine *Seito* (whose first editor was Hiratsuka Raicho, a recent graduate of Japan Women's College) was to bring forth the creativity of Japanese women. But slowly it also became a forum for women to discuss all matters pertaining to their lives, from marriage and sexuality to women's labor. It also covered issues on social reform, economic rights, rights of women to participate in politics, and of course the right to education.[16] For a few years, *Seito* became a source of inspiration to other young and aspiring women writers, but after Raicho's resignation as editor, the magazine slowly turned into a stage for political activism, so much so that it had to close down in 1916.

Toward the last decades of the nineteenth century, there were quite a few well-known female writers, including Yosana Akiko (1878–1942) and Tamura Toshiko (1884–1945). Akiko was closely associated with *Seito* and was considered a staunch feminist who revolutionized poetry. Her 1901 collection of poems *Tangled Hair* was an example. She analyzed patriarchy and the family system of the time. She was also very much involved in anti-militaristic and revolutionary political activities.[17] Toshiko contributed an article to the first issue of *Seito*, though she did not get involved in the political activism thriving around the magazine. Nevertheless, she produced all her best works during the lifetime of the magazine *Seito*. *Seigon, Onna Sakusha* (Woman Writer, 1913), *Miira no Kuchibeni* (The Painted Lips of a Mummy, 1914), "Ho raku no Kei" (1914), and "Eiga" (1916) are some of her popular works. Among these fine writings, *Miira no Kuchibeni* and *Horaku no Kei* can be considered the first examples of feminist literature by Japanese women writers.

The characters of Toshiko's works are mainly female protagonists searching for identity or fighting to gain autonomy of the self. They are smart, outspoken, and very revolutionary. Toshiko's women protagonists are completely opposite to the archetypal Meiji heroines of Higuchi Ichiyo, who was about 12 years senior to her. For example, Ichiyo's protagonist

Oseki of the story *Jusanya* (1895) lives within a family system where the norms and values are fundamentally Confucian. Like in the age-old patriarchal system, also depicted in the literature of South Asia, Ichiyo's female characters too are compelled to abide by the rules set by the father before marriage, by the husband after marriage, and of the son once she becomes older.

Another prolific writer of the Taisho era was Miyamoto Yuriko (1899–1951), whose life and works endured well into the Showa era. Yuriko's best work was *Fujin to Bungaku* (Women and Literature, 1948), and like Toshiko, her female protagonists defied male dominance. Yuriko was better known as a literary writer than Toshiko because she had a broader perspective of society at large and did not allow personal prejudices to enter her writings. She went through three stages during her writing career: humanitarian, feminist, and Marxist. A mixture of these three schools of thought can be seen in almost all of her writings. Unlike her predecessor Yuriko, she was influenced by the Shirakaba School. This school, or organization, was comprised of young men who were influenced by Western humanitarian thought and who read works of writers such as Tolstoy. Yuriko published *Mazushiki Hitobito no Mure* (The Flock of Poor People, 1916) when she was 17. It brought her instant fame.[18]

Twelve years after the founding of the women's magazine *Seito*, another journal, *Nyonin Geijutsu*, was founded in Japan, which like its predecessor focused on women's issues. But these two journals, though centered around women's issues, were different because *Seito*'s emphasis was on reclaiming women's rights, and *Nyonin Geijutsu*'s was on asserting women's rights in what continued to be a conservative society. In any case, these journals offered a space for women to express themselves. One such example is of the writer Hayashi Fumiko, whose *Horo-ki* (Diary of a Vagabond, 1930) was first published in installments in *Nyonin* and attained great fame.

During this period in China, there were other women writers such as Hsieh Ping-ying who began to write about women too, especially about the difficulties of girls growing up. In *Autobiography of a Chinese Girl* (1943), the narrator is forced to succumb to the dictates of tradition that said girls had to be groomed in preparation for their prospective husbands. For Hsieh Ping-ying, the life of this Chinese girl was her personal resistance to traditional norms and values, but eventually she herself had to give in to foot-binding, which led her to cut off ties with her own mother. In 1936, she completed *The Autobiography of a Girl Soldier*.

Another woman writer of the time, Dai Houying—unlike her contemporary writers who were impacted by the Cultural Revolution and the noted Gang of Four—goes beyond the political experience to portray the empirical realities of the times. Dai Houying wrote poems, several short stories, and works of fiction, but the most significant is *Stones of the Wall*. In this book, she adopted techniques used by the ancient Chinese theaters, for example, the thirteenth-century plays of Guan Hanqing. Her works are not simplistic, nor are they melodramatic like those of her contemporaries, and therefore, Dai Houying's works are considered more critcally acclaimed than theirs.

Zhang Jie, Zhang Xinxin, and Zhang Kangkang are a few other women writers who, after the 1970s, slowly began to mingle politics with love, music, and theatrical settings while carefully delving into contemporary Chinese life more in line with China's cultural renaissance of the 1980s.

After the mid-twentieth century, women's writings in China and Japan were increasingly visible and the themes turned subjective, while in Indonesia, especially between 1966 and 1998, during the period of the New Order,[19] the image of women was built along the national identity prescribed by the government. Women in Indonesia, like those of other Asian countries, embodied the traditions of their culture, in which marriage and family took center space. For example when rape charges were filed against alleged rapists, it was the women who were blamed because of the way they dressed or because of their body language. The media helped to further this notion by focusing on women's bodily expressions so that ultimately the blame would fall on the women for having enticed the alleged rapists.[20]

These types of representations were often reflected in literary texts as well as in the films of the New Order. In Indonesian literature, it was always men who were at the center, and even when women wrote, they scarcely discussed the female body. In sexual scenes, "good" women were always projected as being submissive and inexperienced, as if they were guarding the " 'innocence' of their body."[21]

A novel called *Saman* by Ayu Utami and another novel called *Jendela-Jendela* by Fira Basuki were published in 1998 and 2001, respectively. The blatant emphasis on women's sexuality surprised audiences. Though different in many ways, both books delineate the sexual escapades of women and promote discussions of female sexuality. Both books received wide acclaim but also criticism about the sexual exploitation of women's bodies. Some senior writers even considered the books close to pornography. *Saman* also critiqued the New Order so that the period came to be known as the start of a reformation in Indonesia. But after the fall of President Suharto in 1998, literature by women, which focused mainly on female sexuality, began to flourish without much resistance. The literature of this time was known as *Sastra Wangi* (Fragrant Literature). Such features had not been found in the earlier literature of Indonesia.[22]

In Japan too, a new generation of women writers was forming, and their works were slowly starting to be on par with the male literary writers of the time. The works of the writers of 1980s and 1990s, for example, Aoyama Nanae and Kawakami Mieko, reflect the collapse of the traditional value system, like that of marriage, family, and love. They could easily be said to be the successors of Yamada Eimi of the 1980s and those other women writers whose works was on the sexually explicit lives of women. In the literature of this part of the world, the focus was increasingly on women's bodies and sexuality, as women writers broke away from conventional themes. Kanehara Hitomi and Wataya Risa, both born in the 1980s, are still more articulate in their writings about the contemporary times because unlike their predecessors, they do not expect anything from their own society. Hitomi's *Snakes and Earrings* and Risa's *Kick Me* (or *The Back That I Want to Kick*) daringly opposed the norms of the contemporary concept of gender and sexuality, depicting lives of youth expressing their sexuality without restraint.[23]

In the developing countries, or for that matter, throughout almost all of Asia, sexuality is all about the "patriarchal control exerted over the female body" through the tradition of the obedient and docile woman or wife, the all-sacrificing mother and wife, in the "discrimination against girl children in terms of malnourishment, or in the last twenty five years, technology deployment of amniocentesis being used as an instrument of female feticide. All these have direct impact on women's bodies."[24] Women writers through the centuries therefore have wrestled with particular issues at particular times in women's literary history. Many times, they have succumbed to the stereotypical images presented by male literary artists; at other times, they have rebelled. Nevertheless, when women have written, it has always been a documentation of their achievements and initiatives, or forms of self-expression.

LITERATURE OF SOUTH ASIA

Looking at the history of South Asian women, we see that they are molded in a certain stereotypical fashion. They are presented or looked upon as being weak, meek, and docile. It is evident that woman were denied public spaces, a forum in which to make themselves heard. They had limited power within homes and society. Yet women left behind them the impression of their presence, especially in the form of poetry and oral folk tales, or what is today documented as folk literature. Women feature in folktales, ritual practices, folk dramas, folksongs, and folk ballads, and the central character in folklore is always a woman. The central character is often a princess who either lives in the palace or lives in a cursed state, such as a monkey girl— *Bandarni Maiya*[25]—living in the hollow of a tree. Sometimes, the character is depicted as an animal or bird waiting to be revived into its original human form with the magic stroke of a strong prince or a handsome young man turning up one day, driven by a desire for adventure, which only he is capable of, being a man and a prince at that.[26]

Rama and Lakshmana confer with Sugriva about the search for Sita on this page from a dispersed Ramayana series, ca. 1700–1710. Opaque watercolor and gold on paper. Made in Mankot or Nurpur, Punjab Hills Northern India. Brooklyn Museum, Brooklyn, New York. (Brooklyn Museum/Corbis)

The woman or girl is at the center of the story but somehow is not her own agent. She is "loved, rescued, looked at, liked, painted and made to dance to the music of the folk artists . . ."[27] but she is seldom the active agent. Understandably, these stories were kept alive by women as an oral tradition, and they handed the stories down as a family heirloom. Therefore, women are not seen as prime agents in political, economic, or other external matters, but they are visible in the domestic sphere. The folklore, folksongs, and poetry express this domestic aspect of women, which also includes singing while working outside in the fields and all possible issues of domesticity. These folksongs also include lullabies and puberty songs, which are sung only by women in Tamil Nadu in India and are "bold and often vulgar in their expression,"[28] The Tamil folksongs express two common beliefs about women: (1) that a woman who laughs loses her modesty in the same way a tobacco leaf loses its freshness once it unfolds and (2) that a woman who laughs often or walks boldly is a whore. Both beliefs delineate the patriarchal stance in the society.[29]

Nepal

Similarly, in the *Teej*[30] songs sung in Nepal, women express their emotions, suffering, and pain. At some point in a woman's song, which she sometimes creates at the spur of the moment, she may bring out the poignancy of her banishment from her maternal home to a life of drudgery in her husband's. At other times in the same event, standing by the roadside with her friends, she may sing of liberation from daily toil. In the oral folk traditions of Asia one can recognize the subaltern characters in the way they sing, dance, and play musical instruments. They are the main role players in these oral texts, who create and re-create to lend continuity to the oral heritage.

The first recorded poetry of India (greater India, which includes present-day Pakistan and Bangladesh) is by Buddhist nuns of sixth century BCE. Few of these poems from the first few centuries still exist today. Nevertheless, the poems that do remain are evidence that these women were happy because of the freedom they had achieved—freedom from domestic drudgery as well as social and spiritual freedom. The songs and poems are simple philosophical statements and promises of love for the ascetic life, and they provide a glimpse of the life of the women who entered the ascetic community from all walks of life, rich and poor, irrespective of caste and class.[31]

Then there are poems from the Sangam period (150 BCE–250 CE), almost 150 of them, all with themes of warrior ethics, for example, a poem of a mother preparing her child to grow up as a warrior or a wife preparing her husband to go out to the battlefield.[32] Later, there were poems in the period between the ninth and eighteenth centuries written with the theme of the goddess-woman equation, and almost all poems and songs were of the Buddhist, Jain, and Hindu faiths as Hinduism swept across the region. Some of the well-known women poets of the time are Antal in the ninth century from Tamil Nadu, Akka Mahadevi in the twelfth century, Jana Bai (a poet from Maharashtra) in the late thirteenth century, and Atukuri Mollain in the sixteenth century, who was a low caste woman from Andhra Pradesh.

Mirabai was another poet of the late fifteenth century (1498–1565) who carried on the tradition of the bhakti songs (religious hymns). She was a devout worshipper of Krishna, a god of the Hindu pantheon. Though she was from an aristocratic family and married into another, she left her husband's family and spent the rest of her life writing and singing devotional songs in the name of Krishna.

The bhakti (devotion) movement, which started in the eighth century in Tamil Nadu, South India, and spread northward until the seventeenth century, was initiated by those who believed that god was at the center of life. It was a movement of religious escapism. The women of this movement could express themselves freely, whether through spiritual songs devoted to the gods or erotic and romantic ones devoted to Lord Krishna and his consort Radha. Women of the bhakti movement, also known as the saint poets, freed themselves from the shackles of family, household, and marriage because they believed they could devote themselves to god only if they were unfettered by the material responsibilities of the world. The movement was comprised of women (and also men) of all classes and castes, from the upper class as well as from among the scheduled class, or untouchables. The last woman to join this movement was a Brahman woman Bahinabai (1628-1700). Her songs talk about oppression meted out to women related to learning the religious scriptures. But unlike the other women of the movement—for example Mirabai, whose ecstatic songs were only for Krishna—Bahinibai devoted her songs to her husband as well as the to the gods and saints.

In Nepal, documented records reveal that Nepali literature, primarily poetry written by women, started in the first decades of the nineteenth century. Bhakti songs were written and sung only as late as 1919. Most of the regional songs in both India and Nepal draw from the bhakti songs. Yogmaya was one such bhakti poet, an ascetic of the late nineteenth century. She was a child widow who went to India and returned to Nepal after 30 years with a daughter. She is considered the first female activist of Nepal. Lila Luitel explains how Yogmaya's feelings were depicted vividly in such songs but were only much later written and published in a book called *Sarvartha Yogbani* (Universal Voice of Yogmaya) by her daughter Nainkala in 1933.[33] Her themes were primarily about class and caste discrimination, the *sati* system, slavery, bribery, and other social perversions. She also spoke out against the administrative system prevalent at the time. Several editions of her books were burned. During this period, other poets, such as Lavanyamai Devi, Swarnakumari Birahini, and Nalini Devi, had their poems published in the newspaper *Rajbhakti*. In India, many of the bhakti songs made fun of the burden of suffering within the household. Normally, the bhakti songs did not have much to say about the political situation within the country, instead presenting the rich details of domestic responsibilities and the shared aspirations of women. These songs were also the basis for much of the folk literature that was being handed down through the generations.

Even though women started writing much earlier, it was only after 1950 that short stories, novels, poetry, and essays written by them began to be published and read in Nepal. Even then, women did not emerge as literary critics or playwrights until the late twentieth century. There has been no documentation of any research work conducted on Nepali literature. Many female writers' works were first published in daily or weekly newspapers. When Shashikala Sharma wrote a short story called *Cinejagat* (Film World), it was first published in the newspaper *Jagriti*. Similarly, Prema Shah's short story *Pratikriya* (Response) in 1963, and Gita Keshari's *Aparadhi Ko?* (Who is the Culprit?) in 1966, were first published in local newspapers, *Sharada* and *Arunodya* respectively. Gita Keshari's short stories are primarily about issues prevalent in society such as poverty, hunger, and family lives, that is, they are stories about social realism. Prema Shah focuses on female sexuality and eroticism. In her later works, she merges sex and intellectuality in a poetic manner, which has become a trademark of her writings. Bishnu Kumari Waiba, who wrote under the pen name of Parijat, was a leading literary figure in the 1960s and 1970s. Two of her popular writings are her novel *Sirish ko Phool* (The Blue Mimosa) and her short story *Mero Najanmieko Chora* (The Son Not Born to Me). Her works can be divided into two time periods for easier reference. In the earlier period of her fiction writing, she focused on nihilism, sex, and sexual perversions, while in her later works, she became more progressive and drew on Marxist philosophy. Some of the other well-known writers of today and those who come together to write about the many issues pertaining to women are Bhagirathi Shrestha, Bhuvan Dhungana, Maya Thakuri, Jaleshwari Shrestha, and Sushmita Nepal. They no longer write along the masculinist modes but have moved toward self-discovery and exploration of the inner space of woman's experience. But in their literary works can still be found traces of "bitterness aimed at men" that tell of a wounded psyche.[34] They have today a common literary organization called Gunjan, a forum to speak their minds and write their ideas.

In the period between the thirteenth and seventeenth centuries, bhakti songs were prevalent throughout the subcontinent. Then from the mid-seventeenth century onward, the British imperialists began to make their presence felt in every aspect of life. Peoples' lives changed. By the mid-eighteenth century, the imperialists had already set up bases across the major cities. The social reformer Rammohan Roy's efforts in the 1820s to eliminate the sati system were making headway. Women's education was the central issue at this time. Major changes were taking place in the agrarian structure. In other words, there was a huge paradigm shift from this time onward. Gender was not marginalized in the process. Instead, "it had a major role to play in the structuring of a whole range of social institutions and practices."[35] Thus whenever women wrote, their subjectivity was interlinked with the historical as well as the political happenings of the times in which they lived. Women understood their worth as individuals, and thus autobiographies and personal testimonials of their own interests and activities were written. But again in these testimonials was embedded disillusionment with the "promises of liberalism held out to colonized women. These life stories are therefore historical documents of how women worked out these conundrums."[36]

India

In India, writings by women started early. Rassundari Devi was the first woman in Bengal to write an autobiography in the Bengali language. Born in 1809, she was married at the age of 12 and taught herself to read and write by scratching letters on the blackened walls of her kitchen. A few lines from her writings read thus:

> I was angry with myself for wanting to read books. Girls did not read . . .
> Anyway, I was pleased I was able to perform this impossible feat
> at least in a dream. My life was blessed![37]

The words are poignant. They exemplify the physical state and psychological frame of mind of an upper-class married woman of the time. The orthodox notion was that if a woman was educated, she was bound to become a widow at an early age. That was the only social stigma Rassundari Devi carried after she became a widow at the age of 58. Her autobiography was published the same year (in 1868), and at the age of 88, she revised and lengthened the autobiography.

There were two leading women writers: Binodini Dasi (1863–1941) and Hamsa Wadkar (1923–1972) who struggled to survive in the male-dominated world of theatre and cinema but were forced to back track many times. Binodini's *Amar Katha* (My Story), is her biographical account of the troubles and travails of setting up a theater. There were several other auto-biographical writings in the form of letters to her mentor, which were later published in 1913. *Amar Abhinetri Jiban* (My Life as an Actress) was published in a literary journal *Rup aur Ranga* (Beauty and Color), which was edited by Saratchandra Chatterjee, a well-known literary figure of the time, in a series between January 1924 and May 1925. Wadker, unlike Binodini, reached the heights of fame as a cinema actor. When compared to that of Binodini, her personal life may not have been as bad, but nevertheless, it was full of traumatic events. Her memoir *Sangatye Aika* (I'm Telling You, Listen), looks at the life of an independent woman. In 1971, a year before she died, she was honored by the state as an actor.

In the nineteenth century, the oral tradition of folksongs and dances continued to evoke creative instincts in female writers. Folk forms such as *tarja* and *jhumur* were sung ad-lib, using very fast colloquial language, and evoked rampant problems that existed among the poor people. The themes of their songs and poems were primarily about the oppressive laws and restrictions that had a direct impact on the lives of the poor.[38] Bhabani is one such folk artist of the early nineteenth century who captured such themes in her compositions. But her troupes very often came under attack, especially by the urban middle class who felt her songs and dances were performed by women of easy virtue. This particular oral folk form suddenly declined toward the middle of the nineteenth century.

The literary compositions of women were found in such oral traditions of folksongs, in proverbs, and in dramatic compositions. They sang and performed during weddings and festivals such as Durga Puja (worship of the goddess Durga) and when celebrating Krishna and Radha, commemorating Radha's grief on having to part with Krishna. These kinds of women's folk traditions were visible in the nineteenth century, primarily in Bengal.[39] Kolkata, which is in Bengal, was a cultural hub until the late twentieth century. Literary artists from Nepal and many parts of India visited Calcutta for long months, learning and absorbing the literary culture that flourished there. In Bengal alone between 1860 and 1910, there were almost 190 women who wrote poems, novels, essays, and plays, and acted as editors of journals that primarily focused on women's issues written about by women.[40]

During this time, movements for social reform began, and most of the issues taken up were those regarding women such as education, child marriage, sati, and the right of remarriage for upper-class Hindu women. There was a countrywide demonstration known as the swadeshi movement (1905–1908), which means "of one's own country." This movement brought about much cultural transformation because the aim of the movement was to refuse to use any goods from the West. Women carried this movement forward by boycotting the use of foreign goods and literally making use of home-made products. The women organized programs, songs, and discussions to take the movement forward. Culturally, the Indian subcontinent became vibrant. It was around the time of this swadeshi movement, in 1909, that Rameshwari Nehru launched a journal, *Stree Darpan* (Woman's Mirror), and soon another journal called *Kumari Darpan* (Girl's Mirror) followed. These magazines were forums for women's issues during the anti-imperialist struggle. They raised questions and carried rebuttals about women's education, the *purdah* system, and the oppression of women by men.[41]

In 1930, the Congress Party launched the civil disobedience movement and in 1942, the Quit India call was made. These were all movements against the British imperialists. On August 15, 1947, the British imperialists pulled out of India. The country was now independent. But there was not much to celebrate. The British had left behind a country torn by Hindu-Muslim factions. Amrita Pritam, a Punjabi who is well known as a Partition writer, wrote: "What I am against is religion—the partition saw to that. Everything I had been taught—about morals, values and the importance of religion—were shattered. I saw, heard and read about so many atrocities committed in the name of religion that it turned me against any kind of religion."[42]

Amrita Pritam lived in Lahore and in 1947 moved to Delhi. The literary worlds of India and Pakistan both respect her as a strong literary artist. Lines from her much celebrated Partition poem goes thus:

> Get up, you who sympathize with our grief, get up and see your Punjab.
> Today there are corpses everywhere, and the Chenab is filled with blood.
> Somebody has mixed poison in all the five rivers.[43]

In scholarly writings, one can read the depiction of violence and displacement and its impact on millions of people, including women and children. Vivid descriptions can be found of divided families, wailing abducted women, and the "plights of migrants and the harrowing experiences of countless people who boarded the train that took them to realization of their dream, but of whom not a man, woman or child survived the journey."[44] Ritu Menon and Kamala Bhasin, two well-known Indian scholars on women, describe the trauma suffered by women during the time of Partition. They describe how the process of abduction of women was religiously motivated, and families' as well as societies' honor and sentiments were involved. The family members and the women themselves were so afraid of being abducted that many women committed suicide, while many others were even killed by their own families. Some women also carried poison in their pockets so that if captured by the enemy, they could consume it. Even after being released, many of those women committed suicide because they could not accept the fact that they had been "used" by the enemy.[45]

After Partition and years later, stories about these abducted women continued to inspire writers. Several kinds of works have been written to document the times. Some are clearly documentations of different perspectives of the same event or events; others are writings based on historical research that focus on the politics of the leading parties, the Muslim League and the Indian National Congress, and consequences of the friction between them. Since the 1960s, stories that express the memories of the trauma and anguish of the times have proliferated. More recently, writings have been transcribed from oral stories, which tell of previously untold realities. Many of these stories have been camouflaged as fiction, perhaps because the memories were too traumatic and they did not want the readers to relate those so-called fictitious elements to the lives of themselves, the writers.[46] One example is Attia Hosain, another woman writer of the Partition era. In her *Sunlight on a Broken Column*, she writes about the wounded societies, the splits within families on ideological grounds, and the fear and doubts in the minds of people.

Pakistan

After the Partition of India, Urdu literature in Pakistan took up an identity of its own while still maintaining sociolinguistic ties with India. Women's writings that came to the foreground, either in their original form or translated from regional languages, were until then limited to Urdu language and academic journals. Aamer Hussein says that "the space given to women writers is negligible, particularly when one considers the major contribution they have made to experiments in form and subject over the last half century, equaling and often surpassing their male contemporaries."[47]

Two twentieth-century writers are A. R. Khatun and Hijab Imtiaz, who are known for their novels *Afshan* and *Cruel Love*, respectively, but are better remembered for their short stories. Khatun unfailingly chronicles the history of her times, which includes World War II, the freedom movement, decolonization, Partition, and postindependence Pakistan. Hijab is less interested in documenting the historical events of her time, and in the 1960s, she focused on issues of gender. Hussein describes her as being a "highly self-conscious novelist, a post-modernist *avant la lettre*, concerned with the self reflexive narration of memory and desire and the slippages of language which involuntarily reveal repressions, evasions and lack."[48]

It was in the 1930s and 1940s, before the Partition, that Urdu had begun to flourish, though it was increasingly being recognized in India as a "minority" language. In fact, it was during these years in India's literary history that more short stories, rather than longer novels, were being written, and Urdu as a language became significant in South Asia because many short stories in the language flourished after Partition.[49]

Bangladesh

Similar to the feminist magazine *Seito* in Japan, which became a literary springboard for women in the early years of the twentieth century, in Bangladesh too, a women's magazine—known as *Begum*—turned out to be a forum where upcoming female writers could get their literary works compiled and published. This magazine was started in 1947 in Kolkata and later was moved to Dhaka. This was the time women's literature started to blossom. The genres and themes were varied. Short stories and poetry were very popular among the literary genres, which generally included themes of politics, health, and scientific debates. *Begum* provided a forum for them all. It is through these writings that the history of Bangladeshi women can be traced.

Rokeya Sakhawat Hossain's novella *Sultana's Dream* was first published in 1905 and was written originally in English. She is considered the pioneer of women's writings in India, Bangladesh and Pakistan. *Sultana's Dream* is a woman's vision of a world where the roles of men and women are reversed. Men are made to occupy the interior space while women are given the exterior. The world she creates is a utopian world where all the desires of freedom and capabilities of women find expression.

The 1950s and 1960s was a period when the theme of social realism was explicit in the novels and short stories of women writers. To name a few, Razia Mehbub, Helena Khan, and Rabeya Khatun were those who profusely wrote for *Begum*.

But it was only after the War of Liberation in 1971, when Bangladesh separated from Pakistan and became an independent country, that the literary works began to really flourish. *Begum* has lost its literary touch today, but in its place women have started writing for daily newspapers. Postcolonial writings to poetry, fiction, and literary criticism have been the forte of Bangladeshi women these last few decades. The common themes in works of these writers such as Selina Hossain and Makbula Manzoor, and the younger ones like Shaheen Akhtar, Papri Rehman, Purabi Basu, Jharna Rehman, and Nuzhat Amin Mannan, are all about bringing out the cultural wealth of the nation. The literature of Bangladesh is also undergoing great change, especially because the writers have begun to dip into the rural settings. Thus the writings also reflect the changes the country is going through.[50]

Nepal, though never under colonial rule at any time in its history, has indirectly inherited the colonial legacy. Kolkata, a city in West Bengal, was a cultural hub for Nepali literary artists between the 1940s and 1970s, but almost all were male. Whatever literature was created by women writers in Nepal was mainly self-expression or defiance, rooted either in the home or the physical body of the self. In 1991, a group of Nepali women writers established a literary forum called *Gunjan*. Even today, they organize literary seminars and programs to give impetus to fledgling female writers. They compile selections of the works of female writers writing in Nepali and publish them. One such collection is *Nepali Women Literatuers* (2012), edited by Lila Luitel. It provides a detailed chronological survey from the early nineteenth century up to the present of the works of women writers, their stories, poetry, and biography, works that have never been documented or addressed, or writings that have been published only in daily newspapers. She chronicles the background of the oral songs with themes drawn from royal weddings and coronations, love stories of aristocracies down to the present times of political turmoil.

In India, Rashid Jahan, a young medical doctor, wrote two short stories in Urdu around 1931—*Dilli ki Sair* (A Visit to Delhi) and *Parde ke Peeche* (Behind the Veil)—which were included in the Urdu anthology *Angare* (Burning Embers). *Angare* was a forum to bring to the audience the issues and problems of abortion, domesticity, patriarchal oppressions, and women's sexuality. But its main objective was also to try and bring about social justice. Rashid soon became quite well known in literary circles because her stories uncovered the evils of patriarchy and domesticity. And her works, "as a woman and as a doctor writing about gender, medicine and the politics of space, became an icon of the literary radicalism of *Angare* itself, decried by some and celebrated by others."[51] Many years later, in 1986, another Urdu writer who was strongly influenced by and valorized Rashid's works took women's issues still further and made a sensual representation of homoeroticism in her short story *Lihaf* (Quilt). Even though she was writing in the final decades of the twentieth century, Ismat Chugtai still caused a stir with her story.

Unlike the previous period, it was around the mid-twentieth century that the works of women (and men) were surprisingly devoid of the "birth of the history that shaped them."[52] Some of the other well-known writers of the mid-1950s and 1960s who have attained national and international fame are Krishna Sobti, Raji Seth, Sajida Zaidi, Kabita Sinha Sugatha Kumari, Gauri Deshpande, and Anita Desai. Malati Pattanshetti, a Kannada writer born in 1940 who started her literary career with the publication of a collection of poetry, writes, "A woman need not depend on anyone else to make her life a happy one . . . . In spite of tragedies, in spite of disappointments, life is beautiful."[53]

The image that has been built of postcolonial women has become a subject of great attention for feminist studies in the West as well as in developing countries. The images of women of developing countries, especially of many parts of Asia and Africa, have been fore-grounded in feminist studies. The "other" women of the developing countries have been projected in a way that makes them distinctly different from women of the West. Constructed myths have developed around these women. Orientalists make sweeping generalizations some of which may be correct, but others are too farfetched to be even remotely at par with the realities of these women. Or else these Orientalist scholars give blatant examples of male approaches to women's problems.[54]

Several other forms of oral folk tradition have continued to the present times with the transcription of orality into texts—poetry, novels, and short stories. Mahasweta Devi, a Bengali writer of the post-Partition era, was always attracted to, as the postcolonial theorist Gayatri Chkravorty Spivak, terms it, "the individual in history."[55] Mahasweta's novels, which she started writing in the 1950s, are a nostalgic representation of Bengali society, for example, *Hajar Chaurashir Ma* (Mother of 1084), and *Standayini* (Breast Giver). In 1977, with the publication of *Aranyer Adhikar* (Rights of Forest), her position as a writer of the subaltern was established. In almost all her stories, including *Rudali*, facts and fiction merge in a subjective manner as she takes the individual from a historical context and gives it a form and face; in other words, she makes them appear real. Her characters are a class of people who have gone unidentified by history, or whose voices go unheard, for example, landless laborers, individuals from tribal communities, people of the lower caste, and the classless—in other words, those who are subordinates. Thus in the period after the 1960s and 1970s, subaltern studies in Asia, primarily in South Asia, became a focus of learning in the academia.

LITERATURE OF THE DIASPORA

There is a huge Asian diaspora spread across the world. For various reasons, Asians have migrated to the United States, Europe, Australia, and other areas. They may be socially and politically assimilated in these other countries, but the various other complexities of sensitivity have kept them

Writer Jhumpa Lahiri arrives at the Fox Searchlight New York premiere of the movie *Namesake*, March 6, 2007. (Associated Press)

connected to their countries of birth, the essence of which are pronounced in the diasporic literatures. When moving to America and other countries, these people carry with them "their multicultural histories."[56] Therefore, most of their stories carry nostalgia of time experienced, seen, or heard about in the past. They are depicted in the themes of alienation and assimilation, culinary delights, clothes, and visits to those far off, one time homes. Jhumpa Lahiri and Chitra Bannerjee depict the problems of assimilation for Asians in the West, the search for identity, and the crisis of dual identity, for example, as depicted in the search for identity in *Namesake* by Jhumpa Lahiri and her Pulitzer prize winner *Interpreter of Maladies*. Similar themes can be seen in Bharati Mukherji's novels of the 1970s, *The Tiger's Daughters* and *Wife*, which were written during her time of alienation in Canada. Another example is Monica Ali's *Brick Lane*, which is the story of the quest of one woman of Bangladesh trying to make sense of her life in an alien world.

Shirley Lim's memoir of homelands, *Among the White Moon Faces,* captures the troubled world of a Malaysian woman caught between the memories of her homeland and the new world she chooses as her new home. Lim's works have been "Recognized for their poetic exploration of the ironies of finding a voice in a borrowed tongue, the disorientation of living with each foot in a different culture, and the travail of actualizing a female self in a male dominated society . . ."[57] Hilary Tham, another well-known diasporic writer, did not write for 10 long years after she went to the United States from Malaysia after marrying an American Peace Corps volunteer, for she felt alienated and in a state of complete cultural shock so that she could not bring herself to write. The title of her famous book *Lane with no Name: Memoirs and Poems of a Malaysian-Chinese Girlhood* says it all. It is considered a postcolonial writing full of cultural hybrids and the succinct use of English language within the context of postcolonial Malaysian nationalism.

Wild Swans: Three Daughters of China was published in 1991 and won the Booker Prize Award in 1993. It was written by a Chinese woman named Jung Chang. This book narrates "the tale of three generations of Chinese women in twentieth-century China—Jung Chang, her mother and grandmother—spanning from the warlord period, the civil war intervened by the chaos of the Japanese invasion, to the Communist period." *Wild Swans*, with more than 10 million copies sold, has received many acclaims and critiques.[58] Another well-known Chinese woman in the diaspora is Xinran, the writer of autobiographical narratives *The Good Women of China* and *Sky Burial*. They were originally written in Chinese and later translated into English. Three other lesser known yet diasporic writers are Hong Ying, a controversial writer known well in mainland China, Anchee Min, and Adeline Yen Mah.[59]

The works of Asian writers in the present go beyond domesticity and patriarchal oppression. Writer and activist Mahasweta Devi takes up the issues of the tribal society and the lower class in stories like *Rudali* and *Hunt*. She writes about their oral culture, haunting episodes of their exploitation and struggle, and their self-respect and honor. She transcribes their stories into text from the songs that tell those stories because many tribals and people in the lower class do not write. Arundhati Roy wrote the *The God of Small Things*, which was published in 1996. She captures the prudery of the elite class, the small things that lie within the caste system, and political callings of modern day India. She was awarded the Booker Prize in 1997. Bangladeshi writer Taslima Nasrin gained fame, or rather notoriety, for her outspokenness and secular views after the publication of her book *Lazza* in 1994. A *fatwa* (religious ostracization) by Islamic fundamentalists was decreed against her, and the Bangladeshi government banned the book in Bangladesh. In 2003, Ayu Utami, an Indonesian writer, published *Si Parasit Lajang, Seks, Sketsa and Cerita* (The Single Parasite, Sex, Sketches and Stories), in which she uses her feminist perceptions to challenge patriarchal norms and satirizes Indonesians' sexual double standards. Through depictions of sexual promiscuity, young and up-coming Japanese women writers portray the dissatisfaction of contemporary youth with university education and their protest against social norms. Novels like *Of Breasts and Eggs* by Kawakamai Mieko trace the road to divorce and single womanhood while also raising questions about the standard of women's beauty, like breast augmentation and obsession with appearance. In their writings of the 1980s, like they had never done before, Chinese female writers focused on the crisis of gender conflict and psychosexual dilemmas. And slowly a move toward focusing on coexistence and mutual understanding emerged rather than just emphasizing the conflicts. One such writer of the time is Zhang Jie, whose popular works are *Love Must Not Be Forgotten*, *Emerald*, and *The Ark*, which trace the transformative journey of the women writers of the time. Nevertheless, across the region, the present-day literature of and by women mostly appears to be literature of self-expression, protest, defiance, and negation through explicit portrayals of body and expressions of body language, in various narrative forms. Thus women in literature seem to recast the roles of women in society.

NOTES

1. Elaine Showalter, *A Literature of Their Own* (Princeton, NJ: Princeton University Press, 1977), 13.
2. Shirely Geok-lin Lim and Cheng Lok Chua, eds., *Tilting the Continent: South East Asian American Writing* (Minneapolis: New Rivers Press, 2000), xi.
3. Pankaj K Singh and Jaidev, "Decentering a Patriarchal Myth: Bhisham Sahni's *Madhavi*," in *From Myths to Markets. Essays on Gender*, Kumkum Sangari and Uma Chakravarti, eds. (Shimla, India: Manohar Publishers, Indian Institute of Advanced Study, 2001), 3–17
4. Ibid.
5. Madhu Khanna, "The Goddess Woman Equation in Sakta Tantras," in *Faces of the Feminine in Ancient Medieval and Modern India*, Mandakranta Bose, ed. (New Delhi: Oxford University Press, 2000), 109.
6. Susan Mann, "Myths of Asian Womanhood," *Journal of Asian Studies* 59, no. 4 (November 2000): 836.
7. Barbara Hatley, "Theatrical Imagery and Gender Ideology in Java," *in Power and Difference: Gender in Island Southeast Asia*, Jane Monnig Atkinson and Shelly Errington, eds. (Stanford, CA: Stanford University Press 1990), 192.
8. Ketu H. Katrak, *Politics of the Female Body: Post Colonial Women Writers of the Third World* (New Brunswick, NJ: Rutgers University Press, 2006), 87.
9. Mann, "Myths of Asian Womanhood," 835–62.
10. Bettina Knapp, "The New Era for Women Writers in China," *World Literature Today* 65, no. 3 (Summer 1991): 432–40.
11. GuoYanli, "An Introduction to Modern Chinese Female Literature," *Sungkyun Journal of East Asian Studies* 3 (2003): 109–22.
12. Yasuko Claremont, "Modernising Japanese Women through Literary Journals," *Hecate: An Interdisciplinary Journal of Women's Liberation* 35, no. 1/2 (2009): 42–56.
13. Fukuko Kobayashi, "Women Writers and Feminist Consciousness in Early Twentieth-Century Japan," *Feminist Issues* 11, no. 2 (Fall 1991): 43–64.
14. Knapp, "The New Era for Women Writers in China," 432–40.
15. Kobayashi, "Women Writers and Feminist Consciousness in Early Twentieth-Century Japan," 43–64.

16. Kumari Jayawardena, *Feminism and Nationalism in the Third World* (London: Zed Books, 1986), 246.

17. Jayawardena, *Feminism and Nationalism in the Third World*, 247.

18. Kobayashi, "Women Writers and Feminist Consciousness in Early Twentieth-Century Japan," 55.

19. When Suharto became president, he initiated a new policy called the New Order, which had to do with economic rehabilitation.

20. Laine Berman, *Speaking through the Silence: Narratives, Social Conventions, and Power in Java* (New York: Oxford University Press, 1998).

21. Tineke Hellwig, *In the Shadow of Change: Images of Women in Indonesian Literature* (Berkeley: University of California Press, 1994).

22. Marching, Soe Tjen. "The Representation of the Female Body in Two Contemporary Indonesian Novels: Ayu Utami's *Saman* and Fira Basuki's *Jendela-Jendela*," *Indonesia and the Malay World* 35, no. 102 (July 2007): 231–45.

23. Rebekah Clements, "Suematsu Kencho and the First English Translation of *Genji monogatari*: Translation, Tactics, and the 'Women's Question,'" *Japan Forum* 23, no. 1 (2011): 25–47.

24. Katrak, *Politics of the Female Body. Post Colonial Women Writers of the Third World*, xi.

25. A female monkey addressed as "miss" in a Nepali folktale, "The Story of *Bandarni Maiya*." According to the tale, a beautiful princess was cursed to this state of a monkey and is waiting for prince charming to lift the curse and bring her back to her original state of a princess.

26. Sangita Rayamajhi, *Can a Woman Rebel?* (Kathmandu: Across Publication, 2003), 14.

27. Rayamajhi, *Can a Woman Rebel?*, 14.

28. Vijaya Ramaswamy, "Women and the 'Domestic' in Tamil Folksongs," in *From Myths to Markets. Essays on Gender*, Kumkum Sangari and Uma Chakravarti, eds. (Shimla, India: Indian Institute of Advanced Study 2001), 39–55.

29. Ibid.

30. A festival in Nepal and some parts of India where the wife fasts for the long life of her husband or an unmarried girl fasts and prays to Shiva so that she may get a good husband.

31. Susie Tharu and K. Lalita, eds. *Women Writing in India: 600 BC to the Present* (Delhi: Oxford University Press, 1993), 65–66.

32. Tharu and Lalita, *Women Writing in India*.

33. Lila Luitel, ed., *Nepali Women Litterateurs* (Kathmandu: Gunjan, 2012), 49.

34. Rayamajhi, *Can a Woman Rebel?*, 123.

35. Tharu and Lalita, *Women Writing in India*, 153.

36. Tharu and Lalita, *Women Writing in India*, 160.

37. Rassundari Devi, "Amar Jiban," in *Women Writing in India: 600 BC to the Present*, Susie Tharu and K. Lalita, eds. (Delhi: Oxford University Press, 1993), 190.

38. Tharu and Lalita, *Women Writing in India, Vol. I*, 188.

39. Sumanta Banerjee, "Marginalization of Women's Popular Culture in Nineteenth Century Bengal," in *Recasting Women: Essays in Colonial History*, Kumkum Sangari and Sudesh Vaid, eds. (New Delhi: Zubaan, 1989), 132–33.

40. Usha Chakrabarty, *Condition of Bengali Women around the Second Half of the Nineteenth Century* (Calcutta: Usha Chakrabarty, 1963), 97.

41. Vir Bharat Talwar, "Feminist Consciousness in Women's Journals in Hindi, 1910–20," in *Recasting Women: Essays in Colonial History*, Kumkum Sangari and Sudesh Vaid, eds., (New Delhi: Zubaan, 1989), 205–6.

42. Amrita Pritam, "Femina (Bombay: August 1, 1997)," in *Memories of a Fragmented Nation: Rewriting the Histories of India's Partition*, Mushirul Hasan, ed. (Edinburgh: Centre for South Asian Studies, School of Social and Political Studies, University of Edinburgh, 1998), 3.

43. Amrita Pritam, "Today, I Call Waris Shah, 'Speak from Your Grave,' " in *Memories of a Fragmented Nation: Rewriting the Histories of India's Partition*, Mushirul Hasan, ed. (Edinburgh: Centre for South Asian Studies, School of Social and Political Studies, University of Edinburgh, 1998), 2.

44. Mushirul Hasan, ed., "Introduction," in *Inventing Boundaries: Gender Politics and the Partition of India* (New Delhi: Oxford University Press, 2000), 26.

45. Hasan, *Inventing Boundaries*, 212.

46. Trivesh Singh Maini, "Traces of Humanity," in *Indo-Pak History: Journal of Religion Conflict and Peace* 4, no. 2 (Spring 2011).

47. Aamer Hussein, "Preface," *Kahani: Short Stories by Pakistani Women* (London: Stanza, 2007), 15–20.

48. Hussein, "Preface," 15–20.

49. Partha Chatterjee and Pradeep Jeganathan, eds., *Community, Gender, and Violence: Subaltern Studies XI* (Delhi: Permanent Black, 2000).

50. Niaz Zaman and Firdous Azim, eds., "Introduction," in *Galpa: Short Stories by Women from Bangladesh* (London: Stanza, 2007), 7–15.

51. Priyamvada Gopal, *Literary Radicalism in India* (New Delhi: Routledge, 2001).

52. Tharu and Lalita, *Women Writing in India*, 91.

53. Tharu and Lalita, *Women Writing in India*, 460.

54. Rayamajhi, *Can a Woman Rebel?*, 168.

55. Gayatri Chakravorty Spivak, "A Literary Representation of the Subaltern: Mahasweta Devi's 'Standayini,'" *Subaltern Studies: Writings on South Asian History*, vol. 5, ed. Ranajit Guha (New Delhi: Oxford University Press, 1987), 95.

56. Lim and Chua, *Tilting the Continent*, xii.

57. Ibid., xix.

58. Amy Tak-yee Lai, *Chinese Women Writers in Diaspora: Jung Chang, Xinran, Hong Ying, Anchee Min, Adeline Yen Mah* (Newcastle, UK: Cambridge Scholars Publishing, 2007), 2.

59. Ibid., 6–7.

SUGGESTED READING

Ahmad, Rukhsana. *We Sinful Women: Contemporary Urdu Feminist Poetry*. London: Women's Press, 1991.

Chang, Jung. *Wild Swans: Three Daughters of China*. New York: Flamingo, 1993.

Hiltebeitel Alf, and Kathleen M. Erndl, eds. *Is the Goddess a Feminist? The Politics of South Asian Goddesses*. New Delhi: Oxford University Press, 2000.

Schmidt, Johannes Dragsbaek, and Torsten Rodel Berg, eds. *Gender, Social Change and the Media*. New Delhi: Rawat Publications, 2012.

Shikibu, Murasaki. The Tale of Genji, *trans*. Arthur Waley (Modern Library Edition). New York: Random House, 1960.

Shimkhada, Deepak. *Nepal, Nostalgia and Modernity*. New Delhi: Marga Foundation, 2011.

Shrestha, Tara Lal. "The Naivety of Subaltern Heroes in Oral Nepali Texts." *Cross Currents: A Journal of Language, Literature and Literary Theory* 1, no. 1 (2011): 273–79.

6

—⊗⊗⊗—

Women and Cultural Change

Asian women have performed and continue to perform an important role in the development of the dynamic and changing societies and cultures of South Asia, Southeast Asia, and East Asia. The social, cultural, economic, political, and environmental changes that have occurred in the lives and roles of women in these three major geographical and cultural regions have occurred against the backdrop of complex histories. Many of the challenges Asian women face cannot be understood without first understanding the different historical changes that have impacted their lives. European colonial processes and later Japanese colonization often had a negative and debilitating effect on the societies and cultures of the region. Beginning in the 1400s, the European colonial powers set out to control the societies along the Asian trade routes and their rich natural resources, having already impoverished their own societies and cultures. The Portuguese and Spanish were the earliest European colonizers to take control of the spice trade routes, along the South Indian coastline and around Southeast Asia. They conquered numerous islands and coastal communities, and brought colonial Catholicism to the region. By the time of their arrival, Hinduism, Buddhism, and Islam were already well established in most of these communities and societies. Then came the Dutch East India Company, a multinational corporation that took over Indonesia. The British established control from India through Burma, into Hong Kong and Singapore, while the French colonized IndoChina (Vietnam, Cambodia, and Laos). By the turn of the twentieth century, the United States took the Philippines from Spain, and Japan invaded and colonized Korea. Natural resources as well as

Japanese artist Yayoi Kusama sits in front of one of her newly finished paintings in her studio, on January 25, 2012, in Tokyo, Japan. Yayoi Kusama, who has mental health problems and lives in a hospital near her studio, is one of today's most highly revered and popular of Japanese artists. She is one of the world's greatest selling female artists. (Jeremy Sutton-Hibbert/Getty Images)

contingent cultural and indigenous knowledge systems that were developed and controlled by local people were suddenly being absconded and controlled by outside foreign colonizers, who grew richer while local cultural communities and societies grew poorer.

During World War I, Germany, Austria-Hungry, Turkey, and Bulgaria invaded neighboring European countries, and the European colonial powers recruited troops and requested supplies from their colonies. World War II broke out in Asia in 1941, when Japan set out to "liberate" the colonies from European and American colonial domination by bringing them under its Great Asian Economic Prosperity Sphere. However, while the Japanese imperial army and emperor claimed to be freeing the colonies and creating a new society for the full benefit of Asians, the hidden agenda was to extend its colonial reach over the whole region. Japan had brutally colonized Korea in 1905, around the same time that the United States cruelly pacified the Philippines. In the nineteenth and early twentieth centuries, various European powers were vying for trade in goods, land, and influence in East Asia. Japan sought to join the major economic and political world powers. Under Japanese colonial rule, Korean children were forced, under threat of harsh punishment for them and their families, into adopting Japanese language and culture. However, no matter how fluent in Japanese they became, they were never accorded equal treatment and status on par with their Japanese counterparts. Even today, Koreans living in Japan are treated as second-class citizens. Japanese Korean women are given lower social and family status than men in East Asia. Japanese Koreans generally suffer from lack of economic, educational, and employment opportunities; job discrimination in the workplace; and false stereotyping and stigmatizing, even though many of them have lived and made their home in Japan for generations, and are fully conversant in Japanese language and culture. In Japanese colonial Korea, during World War II, Korean men were forcibly conscripted into the bottom ranks of the military and factory war work, while countless Korean women, especially virgins and barely pubescent girls, were rounded up at schools, or otherwise abducted or falsely recruited, and forced into military prostitution. During World War II, the Japanese conducted themselves around Asia and created much animosity and resentment among many local people and prisoners of war in their colonies. Consequently, Japan was defeated due to the strong resistance of local people, men and women, who supported and fought alongside the allied forces against German Nazism and Japanese imperialism. A groundswell of independence movements soon followed but often became embroiled in internal fighting between capitalist advocates and communist proponents, which usually were backed by either the U.S. military or that of the Soviet Union, and were turned into civil wars. The communists ultimately gained control in China, North Korea, Vietnam, Burma, Laos, and much of India. However, since the breakup of the Soviet Union (1989–1991), China and India have become the new Asian economic dragons and tigers in league with Japan, South Korea, Taiwan, and Singapore in the new world capitalist arena.

Today, the cultural and economic colonization of Asia also takes the form of golden arches and swoosh signs morphing all over the region. Whether the cultures where these are being imported need them or not, these commodities are being touted as symbols of progress, democracy, and free trade. The culture of conspicuous consumption in the United States, for example, ignited and fueled rapidly by free market enterprise, often is the single identifying factor for U.S. values in Asia, not human rights, women's and gay people's rights, constitutional freedom, or civil equality, but fast food and materialism. The United States, with its vast resources of corporate giants and patent pools, poses a formidable challenge for those who want to protect indigenous intellectual property rights. India has one of the oldest Ayurveda and herbal medical systems in the world but is faced with expensive legal and implementation hurdles when it comes to protecting indigenous knowledge systems from being used by global pharmaceutical and other commercial companies. Indian farmers have long used their own traditional varieties of seeds and seed preservation methods to sprout better crops, but the *Center for Media and Democracy* reports that in 1998, the neoliberal structural adjustment policies of the World Bank coerced India into opening up its seed market to global corporations such as Cargill, Monsanto, and Syngenta.[1] These corporations make and sell genetically engineered seed organisms, known in the industry as GMOs, which are pesticide-saturated seeds that are higher priced and come with conditions attached that bar resale and reuse, and no scientific assistance of any kind, known as customer service in commodity sales, to help an illiterate farmer understand the best way to maximize output. There also is little known about the possible risks GMOs pose to human health as they make their way deeper into the food chain.

Traditional Asian seed crops are in jeopardy of being overtaken and destroyed by GMOs that are picked up and dropped by birds and winds on non-GMO fields. While India focuses on rapid urbanization and industrialization, 58.4 percent of its population works in agriculture; half or more of these farmers are women.[2] According to Indian custom, only men can hold land in their own right, but the bulk of the agricultural work is still done by women. After the imposition of the outside neoliberal reform package, one of the highest incidences in human history of recorded suicides occurred in the Indian countryside. Between 1997 and 2007, a staggering figure of 182,836 Indians committed suicide. Close to two-thirds of these recorded suicides were committed by farmers. Most of these farmers were deeply in debt. Indebted farmers, including women, also, were being compelled to sell their kidneys.[3] According to Indian journalist Palagummi Sainath, "peasant households in debt doubled in the first decade of the neoliberal economic reforms, from 26% of farm households to 48.6%."[4] Most suicides were committed by cash crop growing farmers who were producing coffee, cotton, groundnut, sugarcane, and vanilla; suicides were fewer among food crop farmers of rice, wheat, and maize. Also, Sainath explains, the government figures do not account for women farmer suicide deaths because women farmers who have committed suicide are recorded as suicide deaths, rather than farmer deaths, because they are considered farmer's wives, even though women do the bulk of farm work.

Most Asian countries today, despite ongoing internal ideological divisions and struggles, are still predominantly based on the capitalist economic production mode, exceptions being North Korea, Burma, Laos, and Vietnam, although the latter today has a more mixed economy. Over the twentieth century, millions of people were killed or displaced by civil wars and conflicts in the region. War and conflict bring widespread suffering and deprivations such as land lying fallow over long periods and food shortages, which decrease women's options for making a living. In desperation to feed their families, women sometimes turn to prostitution in times of warfare and poverty. Many social, cultural, and economic transformations have occurred throughout Asian history, which is composed of many peoples who speak different languages and have different cultural and historical experiences.

Traditionally, Tibetan women enjoyed a higher social status than many of their female counterparts in South and East Asia. They actively participated in the outside public affairs of society and had strong roles in the family. However, according to the *National Report on Tibetan Women* presented by the Tibetan Administration in Dharamsala, India, in 1995, at the *United Nation's Fourth International Women's Conference* held in Beijing, since the occupation of Tibet by the Chinese military forces, women have suffered oppression, subjugation, exploitation, and oppression. They continue to be subjected to forced abortions and sterilizations designed to reduce the Tibetan population and wipe out Tibetan ethnic identity. Abortions and sterilizations are done without adequate medical facilities and often in unhygienic conditions. Tibetan children are not allowed by the Chinese administrator teachers to speak their own languages in the schools, where they are taught in Chinese about Chinese history, culture, and society. Opportunities for girls to get an education in Tibet are limited due to high costs and parental preference for educating sons before daughters. Also, the medium of instruction for Tibetan children is in Chinese. Many young Tibetan women have escaped into India to get an education. Historically and presently, Tibetan women continue to play a strong role in the resistance movement against the Chinese occupation. They are at the forefront of organizing protest movements and are vocal in denouncing the colonization of Tibet by China. Due to their strong presence in resistance movements, Tibetan women have been arbitrarily searched, interrogated, and subjected to arrests and prolonged imprisonment. They have undergone unspeakable torture in the jails. Many have suffered rape and sexual violence, which sometimes results in death.

Many poor women in the Philippines, Bangladesh, Thailand, Burma, Cambodia, Malaysia, India, and China live in squatter settlements without security, which makes them vulnerable to diseases of poverty, including HIV/AIDS and tuberculosis, malnutrition, and sexual violence. The burden of poverty usually falls hardest on women, who typically are the ones responsible for feeding and clothing the children and providing for the family's emotional needs. On the other hand, women who claim independence through divorce, particularly in the Muslim communities of Indonesia, Malaysia, and the southern Philippines, often experience social stigma and discrimination in their communities. Southeast Asian Muslim women, in particular, often enjoy more freedoms and rights than their sisters in the Middle East. They can get an education and are allowed to work outside the home but often are taught that they are inferior to men, and are expected to behave submissively and obediently toward men, especially in public. Opening up more equal opportunities for women to get an education and employment, as well as providing access to fresh nutritious food and a comfortable and safe place to live in a clean environment are gateways to promoting women's health and that of their families while alleviating poverty in Asia.

In most of Asia, men still enjoy preferential treatment and preferred status over women, whether at home or at work. In Confucian Korea and Japan, women are addressed less respectfully in relation to men in the public and domestic domains. And there is inordinate pressure on young couples to produce male heirs, which results in a greater number of aborted female fetuses.[5] In Buddhist and Hindu societies such as Sri Lanka, India, and Nepal, females traditionally have been less valued than males.[6] While males and females are accorded a more equal status in many Southeast Asian contexts, women still have to struggle for greater equal protection under the law.[7] For example, there is no divorce in the Philippines, and Indonesian marriage law considers men the head of the household, even though if they are divorced, their ex-wives are responsible for feeding their children. Once divorced, women can no longer receive vital government subsidies and aid, unless their ex-husbands represent them. Males can also have more than one wife, according to Islamic law. Islamic law does allow for divorce, but the Indonesian family code requires a woman's divorce to be formally recognized in a civil court if she is to receive the many benefits offered by the government to heads of households.

In India, Hindu divorced women and widows are particularly harshly discriminated against and maltreated. According to local customary codes, divorced and widowed women are not allowed to remarry. In the past, a widow was expected to commit *sati* (suicide) upon the death of her husband by jumping into his flaming funeral pyre. In the Ramayana, one of two great Indian epic adventure stories (the other being the Mahabharata), after Prince Adjuna rescues his wife, Princess Sita, from Ravenna, the evil king of Lanka, Sita is asked by her devoted husband to commit suicide by jumping into the fire to prove her fidelity and love for him. Since she had been captured, she had technically been sleeping in the house of another man. Adjuna refused to take her back into his household, although in some modern renditions of this story, he does forgive her after she proves her loyalty by surviving the trial by fire. Interestingly, however, Ravenna only tried to use his powers of seduction; he never successfully wooed Sita into his marriage bed. When looked at from a feminist perspective, this can be read as an example of women's powerful political and social skills and influences in the context of ancient society. Today, this archaic and outdated practice of committing suicide, or sati, is illegal and considered by most people in India to be a particularly heinous and vicious crime, which is punishable by law. Most Indian women today continue to value the importance of being a good wife and mother by taking care of the home, but they no longer consider Princess Sita to be a viable role model for their lives because they see themselves as strong, independent women capable of making their own decisions, in charge of their own actions. Although rare, there are a few cases of wife burning and women who have committed sati reported in the local and international press.[8] Many Indian widows are pushed out of the home and abandoned by greedy and selfish in-laws, and left to fend for themselves. Sometimes they must live on the street, where women are vulnerable to a host of poverty problems, including being recruited into prostitution.

There also are many sad cases of Muslim women and girls in Pakistan (as well as Afghanistan, Bangladesh, and India), and Buddhist women and men in Cambodia who have had acid thrown on their faces by abusive husbands and in-laws after a family squabble, or for being so-called disrespectful of family honor by refusing a marriage proposal; or, in the case of Taliban regions in north Pakistan and Afghanistan, for being girls who have personally made or been encouraged by their family to make the difficult and courageous decision to risk their lives to get an education by walking or bussing to school. The BBC, for example, reported that as many as 150 women have acid thrown on them per year and that acid attacks are increasing, despite the passage of the 2010 Acid Control and Acid Crime Prevention Bill that imposes a lifetime sentence on offenders.[9] This law is rarely enforced, especially in rural areas. Maimed girls and women find it difficult, if not impossible, to find witnesses to help prosecute and prove their attackers are guilty in court. Even in cases in which the attackers are known, rarely will a witness step forward for fear of possible acts of violent revenge against their lives.

However, women in Asia have made some highly significant and remarkable achievements. Women have suffered and given their lives struggling against colonization, war, and dictatorships, as well as top-down development ventures that benefit the rich but often adversely impact the health and quality of life of ordinary people, who form the local majority. Women have been at the forefront, fighting to alleviate poverty and doing relief work in times of natural disasters. They have engaged in legal and parliamentary means of struggle as advocates for civic and political rights. Women have designed and implemented new policies for and on behalf of the rights of women and children, as well as indigenous peoples, gays and lesbians, immigrants, those in poverty, animals, and the natural environment. Today, women continue to actively participate in new social movements that unite people across classes, castes, ethnicities, genders, nations, and societal work sectors in their common struggle for the total and integral transformation of their communities—in all of their local, global, cultural, economic, political, and environmental aspects—into more equitable and just societies overall.

Asian women play important roles in all sectors and on all levels of society. They are doctors, lawyers, teachers, social workers, engineers, computer analysts, scientific researchers, and presidents. Women in Asia are not only often in charge of managing the household budget, some also manage small household businesses. In rural areas, women work primarily in agriculture and do household chores but also take on side jobs like washing the clothes of nearby townspeople. In cities, women engage in different types of work. Their employment opportunities often are influenced by factors such as where they were raised in relation to good schools and a strong economy, class or caste, and educational level. Women today are breaking the glass ceiling and entering jobs that traditionally were reserved only for men but still, their job opportunities are limited. While women can be found at work in every level of society, they often are underrepresented at the upper levels of administration, law, universities, and governance, although Southeast Asian women often fare better than Korean and Japanese women in this regard. Out of desperation, women often have to take temporary jobs that offer low pay, poor working conditions, and no social security benefits.

POVERTY AND MIGRATION

In the twenty-first century, the diverse societies and cultures of Asia have moved from being largely agricultural to predominantly urban, although millions of women work directly and indirectly in agriculture, especially in South Asia and Southeast Asia, and also in China. News researcher for the *Wall Street Journal* Sky Canaves explains that 90 percent of the poverty in China is in rural areas.[10] The most impoverished areas are in the western regions of China, although under the mixed communist and capitalist economy, poverty at the national level is becoming more dispersed as some households are growing richer and other households poorer. While the local government experiments with and adapts different approaches in an effort to help relieve the poverty and suffering of the poor by targeting individual households for assistance, for example, there remains little difference in the poverty factors of poor male and female adults and older adults in rural China. Poor girls below 16 years of age, however, are at more risk than their male counterparts of becoming poor adults. Many poor young women migrate from rural areas to work, for example, for low pay and long hours under seemingly slave-like conditions in global factories, where they are supervised by male bosses and housed in female dormitories that are put under curfew, lock and key. The situation is similarly dire in the South Asian countries of Nepal, India, and Sri Lanka, where most rural people work as subsistence agriculturalists. Despite India being rich, highly urbanized, industrialized, and running neck-and-neck with China as one of the fastest growing economies in the world, the rural poverty there is profound.

Chinese children stand in front of a wall with a propaganda slogan saying "Enrich the People" in Cha Shang village, Shanxi, central China on January 16, 2003. Despite an economic boom in many Chinese cities, widespread poverty remains in the majority of the countryside. (Associated Press/Wide World Photo)

According to the 2011 report "Rural Poverty in Asia and the Pacific Region" published by the International Fund for Agricultural Development (IFAD), rural poverty in South Asia is more prevalent than in any other region of the world. While parts of South Asia are leaping ahead economically, other areas are falling deeper into poverty. Mumbai, where the movie *Slumdog Millionaire* was filmed, is a rich, bustling, cosmopolitan metropolis and strong business hub in the region. It is also home to one of the largest slums in the world. Parts of Southeast Asia also are showing adverse health indicators and other signs of deeper decline into poverty. Southeast Asia's poorest people, who include women, ethnic minorities, landless and marginal farmers in upland areas, and coastal fishers on remote islands, lack access to essential services, safe drinking water, and basic sanitation. Tuberculosis and HIV rates are increasing, according to IFAD. Living conditions of large portions of poor people in Cambodia, Laos, and the Philippines, in particular, are lagging behind those in neighboring countries.

In the rural coastal communities of the Philippines, many natural beaches are vanishing into tourist resorts and cement-encased fishponds that ruin rural reefs and mangroves. Many coastal areas are beach lined into neatly partitioned resort areas. Beach lining involves blasting coral beds, bulldozing coastal beaches flat, and then partitioning them by cement seawalls that serve as catchments for privately owned sandbeds or beaches. Visitors arriving from North America, Japan, Taiwan, South Korea, Australia, and Europe are sometimes sex tourists attracted to prostitutes and mail order brides who are advertised in pen pal and erotic magazines, and online.[11] Throughout South and Southeast Asia, and in parts of China, poverty remains largely a rural phenomenon and is often directly linked to low agricultural productivity. Poverty is usually more severe for women, who face greater hardships in providing for themselves and their children. They generally have fewer employment opportunities, and less access to education and training. In South Asia and China, for example, poor rural parents usually send a boy to school, while girls are kept back to help with the work at home. Young women are at more risk than their male counterparts of being falsely recruiting by fraudulent recruitment agents who may coerce them into prostitution or domestic servitude. They are also vulnerable to being raped by abusive employers, and contracting HIV/AIDS.

Economic transformations and urban processes have brought new social and cultural changes as traditional gender roles continue to be reinvented and transformed. Globalization has created new employment opportunities for mobile female workers, which often challenge traditional gender roles within the family and society. Examples are when daughters and mothers work the night shift at urban call centers in India or the Philippines, or migrate to work abroad in an effort to help support their families back home. The function of the family changes when working mothers come home to sleep when children are awake, or mothers migrate to work overseas and leave behind husbands to take care of their children. The traditional family structure changes as children are cared for by sisters, aunts, and grandparents, and the husband's traditional role as breadwinner is threatened.

Rachael Parrenas explains that typically, overseas working mothers assume a double gender role within the family as breadwinner (formerly the male role) and emotional caregiver (traditionally the female role).[12] Her children (largely) blame her for not being physically at home when they do poorly in school or in other areas, even as most mothers overcompensate for their absence by amply providing for the material needs and education of their children. Likewise, husbands prefer their wives to be in the home but for the sake of the financial survival of the family, let them go. Not many husbands assume the role of househusbands and childcare mainly falls on elder sisters, aunts, and grandmothers. This mass migration of mothers in search of work has other consequences. Many couples endure issues of marital strife and infidelity, and their children suffer in the process.

Until the 1970s in the Philippines, for example, individuals or families usually migrated with the aim of permanently settling in the United States or Canada, which offered them landed status. The 1970s oil crisis combined with then president Ferdinand Marcos's illicit use of foreign aid monies for his own self-aggrandizement and that of his cronies, gave rise to an economic crisis and high unemployment rate. At the same time, there arose a high demand for contract migrant workers in the oil rich Gulf states that began to attract large numbers of Filipinos, mostly males. Marcos capitalized on this migration flow by establishing an overseas employment program. This program, intended as a temporary stopgap measure, has yet to be disbanded by subsequent administrations due to economic indebtedness to first-world lending organizations. Ongoing economic crises, increasing militarization, and corporate-led globalization processes have converged in the new millennium to increase international employment opportunities for overseas Asian migrant workers, especially females coming from the poorer countries of Sri Lanka, Nepal, Indonesia, Thailand, and the Philippines. The new type of migration is patterned after and facilitated by expanding international networks based on the family, as the transnational family is rapidly becoming the norm in many parts of Asia.

The transnational family traverses class lines, and migrant parents work in a variety of labor sectors in the global market. Parrenas found that families with fathers working overseas fare better than those with mothers working abroad. This is because stay at home moms typically perform the role of mother and father to their children. They do what is expected of them as caregivers and housekeepers, plus they take on the (traditionally male) task of disciplining their children. In contrast, fathers who work abroad are acting out their traditional role as breadwinner. Many of the children that Parrenas interviewed talked about a gap developing between children and migrant fathers. However, the family unit still remains intact at the nuclear level. By contrast, when mothers are absent, their children still expect them to perform their traditional gender role, even as they understand why their mothers had to leave to support the family. All their woes are blamed on their mother for not being there physically to support them emotionally in times of need. Yet in many of these transnational families, mothers and children have found creative ways to bridge the divide. Most mothers call their children routinely, if not daily, to maintain strong emotional ties.

In short, when fathers work away from home, the nuclear family tends to stay intact. This is because mothers do what is traditionally expected of them, plus they take on the male role of disciplinarian. However, when mothers migrate to work abroad, children often are sent out to relatives; or fathers sometimes hire domestic helpers to help raise their children at home and clean house, while elder daughters often perform the role of surrogate mother. Men often still find it difficult to assume a traditional female role within the household, even as they are supported by kith and kin. The transnational family has become the new normative family structure in many of the diverse societies of South Asia, Southeast Asia, and East Asia, while the closeness of the family and strong extended family ties continue to be most highly valued across the region and into the new millennium.

TRANSNATIONAL MARRIAGE AND TOURISM

Since the 1990s, international marriages involving Asian brides have been on the rise. Many of these marriages are being arranged through web-based matchmaking services. Most, however, still reflect an earlier pattern of women migrating from poorer countries, for example, the Philippines, Thailand, and impoverished areas of China, to marry men in wealthier industrialized countries of Australia, the United States, Canada, and Western Europe. After World War II, and subsequent wars in Korea and Vietnam, a large body of literature appeared on marriages between U.S. servicemen and Asian brides. These studies often aimed to develop cross-cultural counseling theories to address issues such as miscommunication derived from cultural misunderstandings. However, there have always been a broader range of international marriages occurring in the region.

Eligible Vietnamese American bachelors have long been returning to Vietnam to find brides.[13] While there are more Vietnamese American men than women in the United States, there are more women than men in Vietnam. This is because many men died during the Vietnamese-American war. Also, usually sons were sent by parents to the United States to help support the family by sending remittances back home. This led to an interesting development. Women in Vietnam tend to want to marry up, but there are too few eligible men. Also, these daughters often are well placed and highly educated because their families receive outside remittances, which enabled them to go to school. In contrast, many (but not all) first-generation Vietnamese American men had to give up their dreams to work in low-paying jobs in the United States. They made significant sacrifices for the sake of their families back home. These men, when looked at from the Vietnamese perspective, are good sons of high social standing because they are fulfilling their family obligations. However, in the context of their work and lives in the United States, they experience a big drop in status. In effect, explains sociologist Hung Cam Thai, they seek to regain their self-esteem by marrying "traditional" Vietnamese brides who will behave in accordance with the Confucian idea of the man as the sole head of the household. Highly educated Vietnamese women, in contrast, view these men as desirable marriage partners because they imagine them to represent what it means to be modern.

Women participate in making decisions in an effort to protect their own and their family's best interests even as traditional courtship and marriage rituals are rapidly changing as a result of globalization. Hmong American men have joined group tours to visit upland Miao communities in China to participate in local courtship and marriage rituals, even as some are legally married in the United States but pretend otherwise.[14] While the Miao produce cultural courtship rituals and dances to entertain the Hmong guests, the Hmong men's ulterior motive is to find a suitable marriage partner for their daughters, sisters, and selves to improve their economic and social status. The Miao consider marrying an American Hmong to be a step up the social hierarchy because these transnational brides send money and status goods back to help to support their families. However, how can women and men participate in a highly orchestrated traditional dance ritual, where couples talk with their eyes, when couples are complete strangers? Also, what happens to Miao women who are deceived by men whose only goal is a "one-night stand"?

Asian women involved in international marriages are making carefully thought out and difficult decisions within the strictures of their social, cultural, and economic circumstances. As Nicole Constable explains, international marriages and transnational marriages are best understood as "marriage-scapes that are shaped and limited by the existing and emerging cultural, social, historical, and political-economic factors."[15] These marriages are influenced not only by individual economic interests, but imagined human desires that include notions of emotionality, sexuality, gender, tradition, and modernity. The contemporary rise of cross-cultural marriages is taking place not only between Asian and non-Asian spouses, but also between Asians and Asians within the broader Asia-Pacific region.

Although Asian women often seek to marry men of foreign countries to escape the patriarchal structures of their own family and society, the underlying bases around which gender roles are constructed in Southeast Asia differ substantially from those of East Asia. The Confucian family system underlying many societies of East Asia, locally and abroad, often places females in roles subordinate to males, while this is not so in the traditional constructions of the Indonesian and Philippine family, where traditionally, men's roles and women's roles were more horizontally aligned than in the ideal-typical Confucian family model, though there are always exceptions that elude generalization. For example, Chinese men's roles and women's roles within the family domain were, theoretically, turned upside-down and inside-out in an effort to make them more horizontal during Chairman Mao's communist regime due to what he considered to be some of the excesses of Confucianism, such as foot-binding and keeping nonpeasant women out of the workforce. These changing gender relations within the structure of mainland Chinese families continue to transform in relation to globalization; modernizing China in the twenty-first century has assumed a prominent position on the stage of world capitalism.

Asian mail order brides and women who marry U.S. soldiers often are stereotyped by members of their own societies and outsiders as being women who have sold themselves as sex objects to more domineering men. However, these women often are acting independently on their own behalf in the face of constricting circumstances and constraining structures. They are making decisions that often take into consideration their need to meet family obligations while at the same time fulfilling their own personal and economic desires. Even in worst case scenarios, as when Naxi women are kidnapped and confined in remote rural households, the women typically are making decisions that promote their own best interests and those of their children, if they have any.[16] While tragically in the past, Korean comfort women were kidnapped or deceived by recruiters who sold them into military prostitution, even then, there were cases of some women who naively volunteered in an effort to escape servitude in the context of the domineering patriarchal family system of traditional Korean society, which offered women no real choices other than to be arranged into a marriage, become a kaisang, or go crazy and thereby accept the "call" of becoming an out-casted shaman. Sociologist Grace Cho laments that such history of military prostitution often fails to acknowledge the human faces of the women involved or euphemistically glosses over the actual unmentionable role of the camp follower by labeling these women who marry U.S. soldiers yang-gongja, or "war brides."[17] These women are prone to posttraumatic stress syndrome due to not talking about it, which affects the way they raise their children even as their earlier decisions often were made altruistically to give their children an opportunity for a future better than their own.

Grace Cho also challenges taken-for-granted narratives of the family, assimilation, and United States–Korea relations, all of which she suggests make up the fantasy of the American dream. She likens the "silences" present in her childhood home with the unnamable emptiness of a harrowing cave, while also recollecting her mother's selfless devotion to family and community. Her mother was a consummate cook and housewife as well as a prolific gardener who supplied their small town market with fresh produce. Still, silence and lack of verbal communication characterizes her mother's answers to questions regarding her earlier wartime experiences, in addition to the words that went unspoken in the household, words like "prostitute" and "western princess" (yonggongju). Western princess is an allegorical and satirical Korean expression used to refer to female entertainers and prostitutes working around U.S. military bases in Korea. Employing a plethora of sources, including published interviews conducted not only by herself but others, fieldwork, films, plays, novels, newscasts, and scholarly articles, Cho is not as interested in having her mother or any of these women lay bare their secret past lives. Rather, she aims to reconstruct the circumstances of the war and poverty that brought them to their knees. She notes that history either fails to acknowledge the human face of wartime prostitution or glosses over the unmentionable role of military prostitution by giving those who were prostituted a proper role, if they were "lucky" enough to marry a soldier, by labeling them "wartime brides." This misrepresentation of the truth in which the figure of the sex worker is transformed into that of a loving wife is what makes the formerly prostituted women into virtual spirits and hovering ghosts who belie the integral role they play in contributing to the support of family members and bringing them within reach of the American dream.[18]

WOMEN'S AGENCY IN THE NEW MILLENNIUM

Women's decision making and in turn how women's individual and collective decisions challenge or reinforce existing patriarchal structures of power and domie are influenced by their historical and individual experiences in the context of specific cultures, societies, economies, and histories that are informed and constrained by prevailing world politics and global changes. In 1991, the Soviet Union was officially disbanded and the Cold War ended, which brought new socioeconomic and political changes and opportunities to women in India and China and, more broadly, Asia.

Novel situations and contexts prompted women to make decisions such as working outside the home and migrating to urban centers that challenged traditional norms. Changes to family and society have led many Asian women to make decisions that were not commonplace or socially acceptable in the past. The Asian economic crisis of the 1990s prompted more Asian women to work overseas, leaving their families behind. These and other developments influenced women to make decisions that brought about changes that transformed their lives.

After the bombing the of the World Trade Center in New York City on September 11, 2001, another paradigmatic shift shocked the Asian region when President George Bush Jr. declared war on terrorism and invaded Afghanistan and Iraq. The war on terrorism spilled over into nearby South Asian and Southeast Asian countries, particularly northern Pakistan. The Philippine government, for example, allowed the U.S. military to use its ports, and U.S. armed forces conducted war exercises and trainings in the southern Philippines. Women living in war and conflict areas often become the new heads of households as men go off to fight, but these women have limited or no access to education, health care, and food. They also often are restricted from farming as a means to grow food because war zones are unsafe and farmlands usually are bombed out of existence, especially in bombing zones. Natural disasters, for example, the 2004 tsunami that swept

Chinese woman chatting on mobile phone and smoking in modern redeveloped Xintiandi, Shanghai, China, 2008. (Tim Graham/Getty Images)

over and around the Indian coastline onto Southeast Asia, killing over 200,000 people, are another major change factor that can alter the terrain in which women navigate and make decisions.

Recent studies have explored the multiple overlapping and particular contexts in which women, past and present, make life-changing decisions within the structural constraints of their societies in a variety of Asian cultures. While global and historical processes impact material conditions that structure women's lives in different locations, leeway remains for bargaining and negotiating greater power or for mitigating one's sense of powerlessness. Women can act to enhance their value or subvert the dominant social order.

Yet exercising agency in the complex circumstances of changing lives may result in unforeseen and even unspeakable consequences. Anthropologist Sarah Soh critically explored some of the structural causal factors and personal circumstances of agency among young unmarried women.[19] She focused on subordinate voices among the comfort women and Chongsindae (Women's Volunteer Corps) of colonial Korea under Japanese rule (1910–1945). Their life stories reveal that as young women, they sought emancipation from oppressive political and home environments through an education and modern wage labor offered by the political, social, and economic institutions of Japanese-controlled Korea. Prior to colonization, Korea was largely a male-oriented agrarian Confucian society that offered women little opportunity beyond the confines of the family. To escape poverty, illiteracy, familial strife, or an arranged marriage, some women chose to accept offers for factory jobs abroad; others decided to join the Women's Volunteer Corps. Tragically, how-ever, many of these seekers of autonomy and financial independence as modern gendered selves were cruelly and inhumanely duped by Japanese and Korean crony recruiters into military prostitution and sexual slavery. In con-trast, some Chongsindae members were able to save wages and use their war-time experience of industrial labor for further self-promotion after liberation. By looking at the historical interstices of women's lives in relation to issues of class, gender, and labor in late colonial Korea, Soh adds a deeper layer of under-standing to modern Korean women's history of crafting gender under patri-archy, colonial industrialization, and total war.

Without denying the historical, cultural, and socioeconomic particularities of the structural forces that shape gender relations, evidence indicates that women can negotiate many aspects of their lives and through these negotia-tions can shape their destinies. In Thailand, high numbers of women migrate to urban centers in search of employment opportunities with better pay. This mobility stands in sharp contrast to women's lifestyles in the mid-twentieth century, when women's movements were restricted and chaperoned. It is often noted that women's engagement in paid work may increase their autonomy and decision-making power within their households. However, less is known about how women's autonomy and decision making is affected when women cease to earn wages, as often occurs when women marry and start their own families. Anthropologist Pilapa Esara focuses on this question from the per-spective of a group of married females in a migrant community in Bangkok.[20] Once married, women found it even more challenging to manage their com-peting roles as wives, mothers, daughters, and workers. Their collective deci-sion to contest and renegotiate the conditions under which they live with the household contribute to the broader changes in mobility patterns, gender norms, life course expectations, and family organization.

Sociologist Ligaya Lindio-McGovern offers an alternative perspective on theories of rational choice and calculating individualism that attribute migration to the individual decisions of migrants.[21] Individualist approaches ignore the deep structures of poverty that push massive outflows of labor from the Philippines. She argues that labor export in the context of globalization creates contexts of alienation for migrant workers in the host societies. While these women, individually and collectively, attempt to resist being turned into commodities by capitalism through participating in community building and engaging in active protest movements, their resistances are not without contexts. Lindio-McGovern explains that their problems can be solved by human agency at the more complex structural level, not the individual level.

Women's choices are influenced and constrained by the local realities in which they live. At the same time, these choices influence those realities by reinforcing existing cultural expectations for women or undermining them and creating new ideas. Structural and global forces can constrict and shape women's decision-making processes. Significant moments of choice in women's lives reveal how these forces manifest to constrain their options. These moments of choice also reveal how gender ideology shapes and can be altered by women's decisions in Asia.

For example, traditionally, the Lahu of Lancang, Southwest China, have enjoyed a uniquely egalitarian gender relationship, one that pervades Lahu institutions, cosmology, myths, religion, and spirituality, which includes long-held beliefs in reincarnation. Their gender ideology depends on stable and monogamous married relationships. These relationships are challenged by new outside ideas coming in through the media and tourism of romantic love and marriage, which contradict the traditional concept of arranged marriage as consisting of a stable lifelong partnership. Anthropologist Shanshan Du explains that the traditional concept of marriage among the Lahu is challenged by the emotional desires and ties that develop between two people who cannot marry because one or both are already married.[22] However, rather than challenge the traditional notion of marriage by eloping or simply remarrying in this world, Lahu star-crossed couples often express their desires by reinforcing the traditional idea of marriage, committing love-pack suicides in order to remarry in the next life after death.

In contrast, many women living in Taiwan are making a deliberate choice not to get married by taking a vow of chastity and entering the Buddhist nunneries These women are defying the traditional expectation that women are supposed to get married. While in the past entering a Buddhist nunnery was viewed by Taiwanese society as the choice of last resort, mainly taken by so-called fallen women or those who failed at marriage, today, an unprecedented number of young females are entering monasteries to avoid what they see as the onerous responsibilities of marriage. Married women in Confucian-influenced societies such as Taiwan often are considered subservient to men and perform their duties in an extended family structure, even when households are nuclear, under the watchful eyes of mother-in-laws. They are often pressured to give birth to sons and are blamed if they fail to produce them. Much to the consternation of their parents, many marriageable young women in Taiwan today are embarking on a spiritual path by rejecting mundane female roles that subsume them under their husband's dictates. In the process, rather than challenging the traditional gender ideology, they stop identifying themselves as women, a category that they perceive to be created and defined in the context of familial roles, and instead identify themselves as men on par with male Buddhist monks.

Asian feminist intellectuals and educators are also experimenting with new teaching strategies that incorporate and engage ideas about women's liberation and postcolonial theory in the classroom, as well as in the community. Filipino students and professors often get involved in teaching literacy skills and doing other kinds of educational outreach work in urban and rural poor communities in mutually reciprocal ways that empower the people from whom they also are learning. Singaporean college professors Chitra Sankaran and Chng Huang Hoon co-facilitate classroom discussions with their students about what it means from a Singaporean perspective to be a modern feminist and woman. As professors engaged in applied work, they develop new ways of looking at gender relations and marriage by critically analyzing Western textbooks and films that may not be applicable to actual Singaporean women's issues and concerns. As is common practice in many Asian classrooms, they also experiment with participatory teaching and learning modules that involve students in rethinking gender matters through the analysis of local texts instead of canonical, Western texts. Through this process, they hope to empower young women to contest the negativism of global images that depict them in terms of stereotypical models and create a locally meaningful feminism.

WOMEN'S NONGOVERNMENTAL ORGANIZATIONS AND MOBILIZATION

For most of the twentieth century, women's organizations, awareness groups, and individuals in virtually all of the countries of Asia were educating and organizing local people to fight for freedom and independence from colonialism and authoritarian regimes. Women formed protective barriers between the police and protesters in the actively nonviolent revolution led by Gandhi for independence from British colonialism. Female warriors fought and sacrificed their lives, alongside men, in the nationalist communist independence struggles led by Ho Chi Min in Vietnam and Mao Tse Tsung in China. The contemporary National League for Democracy in Myanmar (Burma) was founded in 1988, largely as a result of the leadership skills of a woman, Aung San Suu Kyi. Her famous walk into the soldiers' guns

As leader of the National League for Democracy, Aung San Suu Kyi
was placed under house arrest by the Myanmarese government in
1989. Aung San Suu Kyi was awarded the Nobel Peace Prize in 1991,
but the resultant international attention failed to win her release.
(Reuters/Apichart Weerawong/Hulton Archive)

is reflective of the strength and courage of other revolutionary women. She
was awarded the Nobel Peace Prize in 1991.[23] Another woman, this time in
Indonesia, Sukarnoputri Megawati, similarly attracted a large following
composed of young people, mothers and homemakers, religious people,
teachers, students, laborers, and a host of other people coming from
all walks of life for the Democratic Party that toppled the Suharto regime (1965–1998). She became president of this nation in 2001. In the
Philippines, Corazon Aquino, backed by the People's Power revolution,
defeated the dictator Ferdinand Marcos (1965–1986) for the presidency
as nuns and women helped to guard ballot boxes to ensure the election
was fair.[24]

Women's organizations and groups have participated in educating and mobilizing local people to oppose large-scale dam constructions, mining operations, logging concessions, and the building of golf courses, hotels, and tourist resorts, as well as big off-shore trawling. Large-scale development projects often are built over traditional farmlands and forested areas that for generations have provided a way of life for whole communities that are being displaced by development. Women have formed blockades to stop logging concessions in Sarawak, Indonesia, and mining operations in Mindanao, Philippines.[25] A female journalist, Tai Qing, who criticized the construction of the Three Gorges Dam on the Zhang River in her book *The River Zang, The River Zang*, in 1989 was subsequently arrested at Tiananmen Square while participating in the mass protest movement that was squelched by the Chinese government's military police. Although Tai Qing was released from prison in 1991, her book was banned locally, and she was not allowed to criticize the government.[26] Another woman, Meda Patkar, organized a nationwide protest movement that succeeded in putting a stop to the construction of the Narmada Dam project in India, which would have displaced 1 million residents from their homes, most of whom were tribal minorities.[27]

In Thailand, Malaysia, Indonesia, the Philippines, Sri Lanka, India, and Nepal, villagers often receive support from local and international nongovernmental organizations (NGOs) promoting an alternative, participatory bottom-up development approach by way of small-scale income-generating projects such as raising small livestock and developing organic farming techniques, including the production of medicinal herbs and multicropping to better meet the nutritional and health needs of families. Nongovernmental organizations run by women also have organized credit unions and cooperatives such as the Gramean Bank in Bangladesh. Also, Christian church-led and Buddhist temple–led village ecology movements for agricultural sustainability and environmental stewardship are prevalent around Asia. Anthropologist Susan Darlington explains that the reinterpretation of religion and culture for ecology is "an effort to put the basic ideas of religion in terms that meet the needs of the modern world."[28] For example, Buddhist ethical values and principles include loving kindness, respect, and compassion for one another and "every form of sentient life, which participates in the karmic continuum."[29] Buddhism seeks to end human suffering, and some of the most pressing causes of human suffering are directly connected with the destruction of the environment brought on by large-scale and top-down capitalist development projects. For example, Darlington explains that the rate of deforestation in Thailand is higher than anywhere else in the pan-Asian region except Nepal and possibly Borneo.[30] This deforestation and destruction is caused by human vices such as selfishness, greed, and desire, which ironically are values apparent in capitalism. The most toxic environmental problems result from the practice of capitalist globalization, which is largely responsible for increasing gender discrimination, economic inequality, environmental degradation, and war.[31] Because Buddhist nuns and monks perceive the causes of human suffering to be derived from capitalist development processes that degrade nature, they feel bound by duty to oppose them.

As the global political and cultural economy transforms relations between nation-states, women's nongovernmental organizations also bring new forms of discrimination into public view. Such discrimination can range from how Filipina women are ethnically stereotyped as being suitable for domestic work in Hong Kong, to how racism combines with socioeconomic restructuring to justify bringing in poor women from less developed countries in Southeast and South Asia to work in Middle Eastern homes. Social and cultural changes come about from an array of exceedingly complex and diverse circumstances and trends that often form uneven contradictions in the sites of development. The Philippine government's deployment of overseas contract workers is illustrative of a highly contentious and contested strategy for national economic development. The maltreatment of poor Asian women working overseas on temporary contract visas as domestic helpers, service industry workers, and entertainers in Thailand, Japan, South Korea, Singapore, Taiwan, the Middle East, and elsewhere in the European Union and North America was widely publicized in the international media in 1996 when two domestic workers—Flor Contemplacion in Singapore and Sarah Balabagan in the United Arab Emirates—were convicted of murder and sentenced to death. It is widely believed that Contemplacion had been wrongly accused and that Balabagan was sexually assaulted by her employer. NGO activists helped to organize mass vigils and protest movements that united feminists, women, and men around the world to petition for new court hearings. Despite proof of her innocence, however, Contemplacion was denied an appeal by the Singaporean government and was subsequently executed. Balabagan's death sentence, on the other hand, was later appealed. Activists around the world used these cases to highlight the adverse effects of a liberalized and outward-looking economy on women. Both stories highlighted the plight of overseas domestic workers in the international media, although this issue already had long been debated in Asia.

Nongovernmental organizations offer a variety of services, including counseling for overseas female migrant workers in distress; legal advise on working conditions, immigration requirements, and the termination of contracts; and temporary shelter for women who are between jobs and therefore without accommodation. They also collect data and conduct research, which usually takes the form of advocacy campaigns directed either against the host country or the concerned government. In the 1990s, women's

NGOs, working out of South Korea, Thailand, Cambodia, and the Philippines, among other Asia-Pacific rim countries, also analyzed the role of APEC (Asia Pacific Economic Cooperation) in facilitating particular kinds of labor migration streams in the region. As Law and Nadeau explain, women's NGOs in Asia have been developing unique bodies of knowledge about women in transnational migration that synthesizes women's experiences, which also include their own experiences as women working in NGOs based overseas and across several cultures.[32]

Finally, women's emancipation involves their own individual psychological struggles, as well as the creative ways in which they respond to new problems. Women have to adapt to the existing social system in which they find themselves and their immediate circumstances, about which they sometimes can feel helpless to change. The women's movement has come to support these women, and one another, by increasing women's awareness and raising the public's consciousness about the structural roots of gender discrimination and poverty. Women's self-actualization and appreciation of their self-worth and strength is a vital part of women's emancipation. However, women's liberation can come about only with men's liberation and the development of new social, economic, political, and environmental relationships that are locally and culturally oriented toward a genuine ethics of care for each other, animals, and mother earth.

NOTES

1. Center for Media and Democracy, "Monsanto in India," *SourceWatch*, May 10, 2012.

2. India's National Statistics Office, "Agriculture," India.gov.in (New Delhi, India, 2012).

3. Center for Media and Democracy, "Monsanto in India," 1.

4. Palagummi Sainath, "The Largest Wave of Suicides in History," *ZNet: A Community of People Committed to Social Change* (February 13, 2009), 1.

5. William LaFleur, *Liquid Life: Abortions and Buddhism in Japan* (Princeton, NJ: Princeton University Press, 1994).

6. Carla Risseeuw, *Gender Transformation, Power, and Resistance among Women in Sri Lanka: The Fish Don't Talk about the Water* (New York: E. J. Brill, 1988).

7. Jane Monnig Atkinson and Shelly Errington, *Power and Difference in Island Southeast Asia* (Stanford, CA: Stanford University Press, 1990).

8. Catherine Weinberger-Thomas, "Widow Burning," in *Encyclopedia of Death and Dying*, Dana Cassell, ed. (New York: Infobase Publication, 2005).

9. BBC News, "Pakistani Women's Lives Destroyed by Acid Attacks" BBC News Blog (April 9, 2012).

10. Sky Canaves, "Facts about Poverty in China Challenge Conventional Wisdom," *Wall Street Journal* (China edition, November 9, 2012), 1.

11. Kathleen Nadeau, *Liberation Theology in the Philippines, Faith in a Revolution* (Denver, CO: Praeger Press, 2002), 42.

12. Rhacel Parrenas, *Children of Globalization, Transnational Families and Gendered Woes* (Stanford, CA: Stanford University Press, 2005).

13. Cam Hung Thai, "Clashing Dreams in the Vietnamese Diaspora: Highly Educated Overseas Brides of Low Wage U.S. Husbands," in *Cross-Border Marriages, Gender and Mobility in Transnational Asia*, Nicole Constable, ed. (Philadelphia: University of Pennsylvania Press, 2005), Chapter 8.

14. Louisa Schein, "Marrying Out of Place: Hmong/Miao Women across and beyond China," in *Cross-Border Marriages, Gender and Mobility in Transnational Asia*, Nicole Constable, ed. (Philadelphia: University of Pennsylvania Press, 2005), Chapter 4.

15. Nicole Constable, ed., *Cross-Border Marriages, Gender and Mobility in Transnational Asia* (Philadelphia: University of Pennsylvania Press, 2005), 4.

16. Emily Cho, "Cautionary Tales: Marriage Strategies, State Discourse, and Women's Agency in Naxi Village in Southwest China," in *Cross-Border Marriages, Gender and Mobility in Transnational Asia*, Nicole Constable, ed. (Philadelphia: University of Pennsylvania Press, 2005), Chapter 3.

17. Grace Cho, *Haunting the Korean Diaspora: Shame, Secrecy, and the Forgotten War* (Minneapolis: Minnesota Press, 2008).

18. Ibid., 23.

19. Sarah Soh, "Aspiring to Craft Modern Gendered Selves: 'Comfort Women' and Chongsindae in Late Colonial Korea," in *Critical Asian Studies*, special issue *Crafting Gender: Women Making Decisions in Asia*, Hillary Crane and Kathleen Nadeau, eds., 36 (2004): 175–98.

20. Pilapa Esara, " 'Women Will Keep the Household': The Mediation of Work and Family by Female Labor Migrants in Bangkok," in *Critical Asian Studies*, special issue *Crafting Gender: Women Making Decisions in Asia*, Hillary Crane and Kathleen Nadeau, eds., 36 (2004): 199–216.

21. Ligaya Lindio-McGovern, "Alienation and Labor Export in the Context of Globalization: Filipino Migrant Domestic Workers in Taiwan and Hong Kong," in *Critical Asian Studies*, special issue *Crafting Gender: Women Making Decisions in Asia*, Hillary Crane and Kathleen Nadeau, eds., 36 (2004): 217–38.

22. Shanshan Du, "Choosing between Life and Love: Negotiating Dyadic Gender Ideals Among the Lahu of Southwest China," in *Critical Asian Studies*, special issue *Crafting Gender: Women Making Decisions in Asia*, Hillary Crane and Kathleen Nadeau, eds., 36 (2004): 239–64.

23. Peter Popham, *The Lady and the Peacock: The Life of Aung San Suu Ky* (London: Rider Books, 2011).

24. Kathleen Nadeau, *The History of the Philippines* (Greenwood Press, 2008).

25. Regarding Indonesia, see Yayori Matsui, *Women in the New Asia: From Pain to Power* (London and New York: Zed Books, 1996). Regarding the Philippines, see William Holden and Daniel Jacobson, *Mining and Natural Hazard Vulnerability in the Philippines* (London: Anthem Press, 2012).

26. Matsui, *Women in the New Asia*, 109.

27. Ibid., 109.

28. Susan Darlington, "The Ordination of a Tree: The Buddhist Ecology Movement in Thailand," *Ethnology* 37, no. 1 (1998): 5.

29. Donald Swearer, "Principles and Poetry, Places and Stories: The Resources of Buddhist Ecology," *Daedalus* 130, no. 4 (2001): 227.

30. Darlington, "The Ordination of a Tree," 2.

31. Pierre Walter, "Activist Forest Monks, Adult Learning and the Buddhist Environmental Movement in Thailand," *International Journal of Lifelong Education* 26, no. 3 (2007): 331.

32. Lisa Law and Kathleen Nadeau, "Globalization, Migration and Class Struggles: NGO Mobilization for Filipino Domestic Workers,"*Kasarinlan, Philippine Journal of Third World Studies* 14, no. 1–2 (1999): 51–68.

Glossary

Arya Samaj: A Hindu reformist sect founded in 1875 in order to re-establish the Vedas. It opposes sacrifice and idol worship, and gives credence to the caste system based on birthright alone.

Aswangs: Philippine folkloric and colloquial term for witch.

Ayurveda: Hindu system of traditional medicine.

Barong: Balinese folkloric term for lion-like creature and character in mythology.

Bhikkuni: Honorific term for a fully ordained female Buddhist monastic nun equivalent to fully ordained monk.

Bilateral: Kinship term for tracing the family line through both mother and father.

Bride-price: Payment made to the bride's family by the groom's before the wedding.

Bruja: Spanish colloquial term for witch.

Calonarang: Colon Arang is a character in Hindu Balinese and Javanese folklore.

Ch'i: Life force or energy is a fundamental element in Chinese philosophy and culture.

Concubinage: The state of cohabitation with a man without being legally married to him.

Consanguineal: Kinship term for blood relationship or being descended from the same ancestor as another person.

Devadasi: Hindu term for girls dedicated to a deity.

Diaspora: The migration of a people away from an established ancestral homeland.

Dowry: Money or property given to the daughter to take to her husband's home at the time of marriage.

Feudalism: A social system in which vassals were protected and maintained by their lords, usually through the granting of fiefs. They were also required to serve under the lords. Feudalism developed at different historical times in different countries or regions. (Also known as the feudal system.)

Geisha: Traditional female entertainers who act like hostesses and sometimes prostitutes in Japan.

Kisaeng: Traditional female entertainers who act like hostesses and sometimes prostitutes in Korea.

Lineage: Kinship term for direct line of descent from an ancestor.

Mahabharata: One of the two great epics of the Hindus, originally written in Sanskrit.

Manananggal: Tagalog term for a witch in the Philippines.

Mara: Hindu term referring to the world of illusion.

Matrilineal: Kinship term for tracing family descent through the mother's line.

Mujahidin: Muslims who are engaged in a *jihad* or struggle in devotion to Islam. (Also known as Mujahideen.)

Natraj: Hindu term referring to the god of dance.

Nautch: Anglicized word for Hindu term referring to girls who dance, or devadasis.

Nirvana: Transcendental state of enlightenment.

Orientalization: The objectification of Asian women as exotic oriental woman.

Patrilineal: Kinship term for tracing family descent through the father's line.

Patrilocal: Custom in which married couple resides with or nearby the husband's kin group.

Penanggalan: Malaysian term for witch.

Polygyny: Marriage practice of husband having more than one wife.

Purdah: A social Islamic practice to keep women in seclusion.

Quran: The sacred writings of Islam revealed by God to prophet Muhammad.

Ramayana: One of the two great epics of the Hindus, originally written in Sanskrit.

Rangda: Balinese Hindu term for the witch who is the daughter of Durgha, the Queen of witches.

Roh: Balinese Hindu term for soul.

Sakti: Balinese Hindu term for spiritual power.

Sangha: Buddhist temple community.

Sati: Archaic and no longer customary practice in India in which the wife was burned in the ashes of her deceased husband's funeral pyre.

Sharia: Sacred law of Islam. (Also known as Muslim law.)

Suffrage: The exercise of the right to vote.

Swadeshi   Term used in South Asia to mean produced in one's own country, not imported.

Talaq: Islamic term for divorce.

Untouchables: People of the lowest class in the Hindu caste hierarchy. (Also known as dalits.)

Vedas: Oldest scriptures of Hinduism, composed in Sanskrit.

Vedic period: Period in history when the Vedas were composed.

Yang: The bright force opposing Yin in traditional Chinese philosophy and medicine. Refers to that which is bright, dry, growing, light, warm, hard, and masculine.

Yanggongja: Korean colloquial term for war brides, or Korean brides of American soldiers.

Yin: The dark force opposing yang in traditional Chinese philosophy and medicine. Refers to that which is dark, moist, inert, turbid, cold, soft, and feminine, the womb.

Yonggongju: Korean term for "Western Princess," which is a colloquial term for Korean prostitutes who service American soldiers.

Selected Bibliography

Abinales, Patricio, and Donna Amoroso. *State and Society in the Philippines*. New York: Rowman and Littlefield, 2005.

Abrera-Mangahas, Alcestis. 1998. "Violence against Women Migrant Workers: The Philippine Experience." In *Filipino Workers on the Move: Trends, Dilemmas, and Policy Options*, edited by Benjamin Carino, 45–80. Quezon City: Philippine Migration Research Network, 1998.

Addelton, Jonathan. "The Impact of the Gulf War on Migration and Remittances in Asia and the Middle East." *International Migration* 29, no. 4 (1991): 509–26.

Aguilar, Filomeno. "The Philippine Peasant as Capitalist: Beyond the Categories of Ideal-Typical Capitalism." *Journal of Peasant Studies* 17, no. 1 (1989): 41–67.

Ahmad, Rukhsana. *We Sinful Women: Contemporary Urdu Feminist Poetry*. London: Women's Press, 1991.

Andaya-Watson, Barbara. *The Flaming Womb: Repositioning Women in Early Modern Southeast Asia*. Honolulu: University of Hawaii Press, 2006.

Atkinson, Jane Monnig, and Shelly Errington, eds. *Power and Difference in Island Southeast Asia*. Stanford, CA: Stanford University Press, 1990.

Bennet, Lynn. *Dangerous Wives and Sacred Sisters: Social and Symbolic Roles of High Caste Women in Nepal*. New York: Columbia University Press, 1983.

Berman, Laine. *Speaking through the Silence: Narratives, Social Conventions, and Power in Java*. New York: Oxford University Press, 1998.

Bishop, Ryan, and Lillian Robinson. *Night Market: Sexual Cultures and the Thai Economic Miracle*. New York and London: Routledge, 1998.

Bose, Sugata, and Ayesha Jalal. *Modern South Asia: History, Culture, Political Economy*. New Delhi: Oxford University Press, 2004.

Broad, Robin. *Unequal Alliance: The World Bank, International Monetary Fund, and the Philippines*. Berkeley: University of California Press, 1988.

Cannell, Fenella. *Power and Intimacy in the Christian Philippines*. Cambridge: Cambridge University Press, 1999.

Chakrabarty, Usha. *Condition of Bengali Women around the Second Half of the Nineteenth Century*. Calcutta: Usha Chakrabarty, 1963.

Chakravarti, Uma, and Preeti Gill, eds. *Shadow Lives: Writings on Widowhood*. New Delhi: Zubaan, 2001.

Chang, Jung. *Wild Swans: Three Daughters of China*. New York: Flamingo, 1993.

Cho, Grace. *Haunting the Korean Diaspora: Shame, Secrecy, and the Forgotten War*. Minneapolis: University of Minnesota Press, 2008.

Clements, Alan. *The Voice of Hope: Aung San Suu Kyi*. London: Penguin Books, 1997.

Constable, Nicole, ed. *Cross-Border Marriages, Gender and Mobility in Transnational Asia*. Philadelphia: University of Pennsylvania Press, 2005.

Crane, Hillary, and Kathleen Nadeau, eds. "Crafting Gender: Women Making Decisions in Asia." Special issue, *Critical Asian Studies* 36 (2004).

Darlington, Susan. "The Ordination of a Tree: The Buddhist Ecology Movement in Thailand." *Ethnology* 37, no. 1 (1998): 1–15, see 5.

Eaton, Heather, and Lois Ann Lorentzen. *Ecofeminism and Globalization: Exploring Religion, Culture, and Context*. Lanham, Maryland: Rowman and Littlefield, 2003.

Ebert, Teresa. *Ludic Feminism and After*. Ann Arbor: University of Michigan Press, 1996.

Ehrenreich, Barbara, and Arlie Russell Hoschschild. *Global Women: Nannies, Maids, and Sex Workers in the New Economy*. New York: Metropolitan Books, 2003.

Fukuko Kobayashi. "Women Writers and Feminist Consciousness in Early Twentieth-Century Japan." *Feminist Issues* 11, no. 2 (Fall 1991): 43–64.

Go, Susan. "Mothers, Maids, and the Creatures of the Night: The Persistence of Philippine Folk Religion." *Philippine Quarterly of Culture and Society* 7 (1979): 186–203.

Harvey, Youngsook Kim. *Six Korean Women: The Socialization of Shamans*. San Francisco: West Publishing, 1979.

Hellwig, Tineke. *In the Shadow of Change: Images of Women in Indonesian Literature*. Berkeley: University of California Press, 1994.

Heyzer, Noeleen. *Working Women in South-East Asia: Development, Subordination, and Emancipation*. Philadelphia and Milton Keynes, UK: Open University Press, 1986.

Hiltebeitel, Alf, and Kathleen M. Erndl, eds. *Is the Goddess a Feminist? The Politics of South Asian Goddesses*. New Delhi: Oxford University Press, 2000.

Howe, Brenden, Vesselin Popovski, et al., *Democracy in the South: Participation, the State and the People*. Tokyo, United Nations University Press, 2010.

Jeffery, Patricia, and Amrita Basu, eds. *Appropriating Gender: Women's Activism and Politicized Religion in South Asia*. New York: Routledge, 1998.

Jordon, Kay. *From Sacred Servants to Profane Prostitute: A History of Changing Legal Status of the Devadasis in India, 1857–1947*. Oxford: Oxford University Press, 2003.

Junker, Laura Lee. "Networks of Power and Political Trajectories in Early Southeast Asian Complex Societies." *Philippine Quarterly of Culture and Society* 27, nos. 1–2 (1999): 59–104.

Katrak, Ketu H. *Politics of the Female Body: Post Colonial Women Writers of the Third World*. New Brunswick, NJ: Rutgers University Press, 2006.

Knapp, Bettina. "The New Era for Women Writers in China." *World Literature Today* 65, no. 3 (Summer 1991): 432–40.

Koyama, Takashi. *The Changing Social position of Women in Japan*, UNESCO 1961.

Kumari, Jayawardena. *Feminism and Nationalism in the Third World*. London: Zed Books, 1986.

LaFleur, William. *Liquid Life: Abortions and Buddhism in Japan*. Princeton, NJ: Princeton University Press, 1994.

Lai, Amy Tak-yee. *Chinese Women Writers in Diaspora: Jung Chang, Xinran, Hong Ying, Anchee Min, Adeline Yen Mah*. Cambridge: Cambridge Scholars Publishing, 2007.

Lansing, Stephen. *The Balinese*. New York: Harcourt Brace, 1995.

Lanzona, Vina. *Amazons of the Huk Rebellion: Gender, Sex, and Revolution in the Philippines*. Madison: University of Wisconsin Press, 2009.

Law, Lisa. *Sex Work in Southeast Asia: The Place of Desire in a Time of AIDS*. London and New York: Routledge, 2000.

Law, Lisa, and Kathleen Nadeau. "Globalization, Migration and Class Struggles: NGO Mobilization for Filipino Domestic Workers." *Kasarinlan: Philippine Journal of Third World Studies* 14, nos. 1–2 (1999): 51–68.

Levine, Philippa. *Prostitution, Race, and Politics: Policing Venereal Disease in the British Empire*. New York: Routledge, 2003.

Lindio-McGovern, Ligaya. *Filipino Peasant Women: Exploitation and Resistance*. Philadelphia: University of Pennsylvania Press, 1997.

Mann, Susan, and Yu-Yin Cheng, eds. *Under Confucian Eyes: Writings on Gender in Chinese History*. Los Angeles: University of California Press, 2001.

Marching, SoeTjen. "The Representation of the Female Body in Two Contemporary Indonesian Novels: Ayu Utami's *Saman* and Fira Basuki's *Jendela-jendela*." *Indonesia and the Malay World* 35, no. 102 (July 2007): 231–45.

Matsui, Yayori. *Women in the New Asia: From Pain to Power*. London and New York: Zed Books, 1996.

Menez, Hermina. *Explorations in Philippine Folklore*. Quezon City: Ateneo de Manila Press, 1996.

Miralao, Virginia. "The Family, Traditional Values and Sociocultural Transformation of Philippine Society." *Philippine Sociological Review* 45, nos. 1–4 (1997): 189–215.

Moon, Katherine, H. S. *Sex among Allies: Military Prostitution in U. S.-Korea Relations*. New York: Columbia University Press, 1997.

Nadeau, Kathleen. *The History of the Philippines*. Westport, CT: Greenwood Press, 2008.

Nadeau, Kathleen. *Liberation Theology in the Philippines: Faith in a Revolution*. Westport, CT: Praeger Press, 2002.

Nair, P. R. Gopinathan. "Return of Overseas Contract Workers and Their Rehabilitation and Development in Kerala India: A Critical Account of Policies, Performance and Prospects." *International Migration* 37, no. 1 (1999): 209–42.

Ogasawara, Yuko. *Office Ladies and Salaried Men: Power Gender and Work in Japanese Companies*. Los Angeles: University of California Press, 1998.

Orr, Leslie. *Donors, Devotees, and Daughters of God: Temple Women in Medieval Tamilnadu*. New York: Oxford University Press, 2000.

Parker, Lynette. "The Power of Letters in the Female Body: Female Literacy in Bali." *Women Studies International Forum* 25, no. 1 (2002): 79–96.

Parrenas, Rhacel. *Children of Globalization, Transnational Families and Gendered Woes*. Stanford, CA: Stanford University Press, 2005.

Patel, Rashida. *Woman versus Man: Socio-Legal Gender Inequality in Pakistan*. Karachi: Oxford University Press, 2003.

Perez, Rosa Maria. "The Rhetoric of Empire: Gender Representations in Portuguese India." *Portuguese Studies*, January 1, 2005, 1–19.

Pieris, Aloysious S. J. *An Asian Theology of Liberation*. New York: Orbis Books, 1988.

Popham, Peter. *The Lady and the Peacock: The Life of Aung San Suu Kyi*. London: Rider Books, 2011.

Ramaswamy, Vijaya. "Women and the 'Domestic' in Tamil Folk Songs." In *From Myths to Markets: Essays on Gender*, edited by Kumkum Sangari and Uma Chakravarti, 39–55. Shimla, India: Indian Institute of Advanced Study, 2001.

Rayamajhi, Sangita. *Can a Woman Rebel?* Kathmandu: Across Publication, 2003.

Reynolds, Craig. *Seditious Histories: Contesting Thai and Southeast Asian Pasts*. Seattle: University of Washington Press, 2006.

Risseeuw, Carla. *Gender Transformation, Power, and Resistance among Women in Sri Lanka: The Fish Don't Talk about the Water*. New York: E. J. Brill, 1988.

Sanbonmatsu, Kira. "Gender-Related Political Knowledge and the Representation of Women." *Political Behavior* 25, no. 4 (2003): 367–88.

Sangari, Kumkum, and Uma Chakravarti, eds. *From Myths to Markets: Essays on Gender*. Shimla, India: Indian Institute of Advanced Study, 1999.

Sarkar, Tanika. "Strishiksha, or Education for Women." *Women's Studies in India: A Reader*, edited by Mary E. John. New Delhi: Penguin Books, 2008.

Saunders, Kriemild, ed. *Feminist Post Development Thought: Rethinking Modernity, Post-Colonialism and Representation*. New Delhi, India: Zubaan Books, 2004.

Schlegel, Stuart. *Wisdom from a Rainfores: Spiritual Journey of an Anthropologist*. Quezon City: Ateneo de Manila Press, 1999.

Schmidt, Johannes Dragsbaek, and TorstenRodel Berg, eds. *Gender, Social Change and the Media*. New Delhi: Rawat Publications, 2012.

Sen, Uditi. *Spinster, Prostitute or Pioneer?: Images of Refugee Women in Post-Partition Calcutta*. San Domenico di Fiesole, Italy: European University Institute, 2011.

Seth, Mira. *Women and Development: The Indian Experience*. New Delhi: Sage Publications, 2001.

Shafer, Ingrid. "From Confucius through Ecofeminism to Partnership Ethics." In *The Sage and the Second Sex: Confucianism, Ethics, and Gender*, edited by C. Li, 97–112. Chicago: Open Court, 2000.

Shankar, Jogan. *Devadasi Cult: A Sociological Analysis*. New Delhi: Ashish Publishing House, 1994.

Shikibu, Murasaki. The Tale of Genji, trans. Arthur Waley (The Modern Library Edition). New York: Random House, 1960.

Shimkhada, Deepak. *Nepal, Nostalgia and Modernity*. New Delhi: Marga Foundation, 2011.

Showalter, Elaine. *A Literature of Their Own*. Princeton, NJ: Princeton University Press, 1977.

Shrestha, Tara Lal. "The Naivety of Subaltern Heroes in Oral Nepali Texts." *Cross Currents: A Journal of Language, Literature and Literary Theory* 1, no. 1 (2011): 273–79.

Singh, Pankaj K., and Jaidev. "Decentering a Patriarchal Myth: Bhisham Sahni's *Madhavi*." In *From Myths to Markets: Essays on Gender*, edited by Kumkum Sangari and Uma Chakravarti, 3–17. Shimla, India: Manohar Publishers, Indian Institute of Advanced Study, 2001.

Siu, Helen F., ed. *Merchants' Daughters: Women, Commerce, and Regional Culture in South China*. Hong Kong: Hong Kong University Press, 2010.

Soh, Sarah. *The Comfort Women: Sexual Violence and Postcolonial Memory in Korea and Japan*. Chicago: University of Chicago Press, 2008.

Stoler, Ann Laura. *Capitalism and Confrontation in Sumatra's Plantation Belt, 1870–1979*. New Haven, CT: Yale University Press, 1985.

Stranahan, Patricia. "Opening the Books on China's Leadership." *Critical Asian Studies* 33, no. 1 (2001): 136–159.

Sturdevant, Saundra, and Brenda Stoltzfus. *Let the Good Times Roll: Prostitution and the U. S. Military Bases*. New York: New Press, 1992.

Sumanta Banerjee. "Marginalization of Women's Popular Culture in Nineteenth Century Bengal." In *Recasting Women: Essays in Colonial History*, edited by Kumkum Sangari and Sudesh Vaid, 132–33. New Delhi: Zubaan, 1989.

Talwar, Vir Bharat. "Feminist Consciousness in Women's Journals in Hindi, 1910–20." In *Recasting Women: Essays in Colonial History*, edited by Kumkum Sangari and Sudesh Vaid, 205–6. New Delhi: Zubaan, 1989.

Weitz, Rose, ed. *The Politics of Women's Bodies: Sexuality, Appearance and Behavior*. New York: Oxford University Press, 1998.

Unaiza, Niaz, and Sehar Hassan. "Culture and Mental Health of Women in South East Asia." *World Psychiatry* 5 (June 2006): 118–20.

Ward, Kathryn. *Women Workers and Global Restructuring*. Ithaca, NY: School of Industrial and Labor Relations, 1990.

Watson, James, ed. *Asian and African Systems of Slavery*. Berkeley: University of California Press, 1980.

Weatherford, Jack. *The Secret History of the Mongol Queens*. New York: Crown Publishers, 2010.

Yan, Yunxiang. "Girl Power and the Waning of Patriarchy in Rural North China." *Ethnology* 45 (Spring 2006): 105–23.

Yanli, Guo. "An Introduction to Modern Chinese Female Literature." *Sungkyun Journal of East Asian Studies* 3 (2003): 109–22.

Yasuko, Claremont. "Modernising Japanese Women through Literary Journals." *Hecate: An Interdisciplinary Journal of Women's Liberation* 35, nos. 1–2 (2009): 42–56.

Index

Bahinabai (poet), 147
Bahrain, 66
Bajang of Malaysia, 30
Balabagan, Sarah, 182
Bali, Indonesia, 55, 138; Calonarang
   dance in, 30–31; spirit children in,
   32–33
Bandaranaike, Sirimavo, 7, 109
Bangladesh, 2, 96, 112, 126, 136; dowry
   system in, 95; Grameen Bank in, 181;
   literature and women of, 152–53,
   156; War of Liberation (1971), 122,
   125–26, 128, 152; widowhood in,
   101; women politicians in, 109,
   122–23, 128–29, 130; women's
   work in, 99
Bangladesh National Party, 128
Bannerjee, Chitra, 155
Ban Zhao, 138
Barong (Balinese folkloric
   creature), 31, 33
Basic ecclesial communities (BECs),
   36–37, 38, 39, 41–42, 47
Basuki, Fira, 143
BECs. See Basic ecclesial communities
   (BECs)
Begum, Ferdous Ara, 100
Begum (women's magazine), 152
Beijing Platform for Action Conference
   (1995), 119
Besant, Anne, 90
Bhabani (folk artist), 149
Bhagavad Gita, 13, 14
Bhakti (devotion) movement,
   146–47, 148
Bhasin, Kamala, 151
Bhutto, Benazir, 7, 109, 127–28, 130
Bible, 37, 39, 84; Old Testament, 49
Birth control, 97–98, 100
Bishop, Ryan, 72
Blanc-Szanton, Cristina, 4, 27
Boff, Leonardo, 38
Book of Rites, 47
Brahma (god), 12, 13, 14

Brahmans (priests), 11, 85, 88, 147
Bride-price, 24, 84, 112. See also Dowry;
   Marriage
British imperialists, 71, 121; in India,
   21–22, 113, 125, 148, 150, 161
Broad, Robin, 42
Buddhism, 6, 13, 39; ecology movement
   in, 16, 42, 45, 181; escape from
   suffering in, 17, 43, 44, 181;
   Hinduism and, 9; in Korea, 86; stupa
   mounds in, 16; in Thailand, 23,
   43–45; Theravada, 16, 45; women
   and, 14–17, 166
Buddhist nuns and monks, 15–16,
   42–47, 125; deforestation and, 43,
   44–45, 182; poetry of, 146; in Taiwan,
   178–79
Burma (Myanmar), 7, 45, 109, 179–80
Bush, George, Jr., 175
Bush, George, Sr., 71

Cabangbang, Randolph, 40
Cadbury, Deborah, 44
Calcutta School Society, 89
Call center industry, 75–77, 79
Calonarang dance (Bali), 30–31
Canaves, Sky, 168
Cannell, Fanella, 33, 34–35
Capitalism, 60–61, 163; deforestation
   and, 43–44, 181; globalization
   and, 8, 42, 46, 74, 178, 182;
   modernization, 35
Capitalism and Confrontation in
   Sumatra's Plantation Belt (Stoler),
   60, 62
Caste system, 9, 11–12, 93, 97, 147; four
   varnas of, 11, 85, 88
Castillo, Gelia, 103
Catedral, Romeo, 41
Catholicism, 38; in Philippines, 28, 34,
   37, 84. See also Liberation theology
Catt, Carrie Chapman, 116
Center for Media and Democracy, 164
Chang, Jung, 156

About the Authors

KATHLEEN NADEAU, PhD, is a professor of anthropology at California State University, San Bernardino. Her published works include ABC-CLIO's *Encyclopedia of Asian American Folklore and Folklife*, Greenwood's *The History of the Philippines*, and Praeger's *Liberation Theology in the Philippines*.

SANGITA RAYAMAJHI, PhD, is a professor of literature and women's studies at the Central Department of English, Tribhuvan University, Kathmandu, Nepal. At present she is teaching Asian and world literature at the Asian University for Women in Bangladesh. She is the author of *All Mothers Are Working Mothers*, *Women in Politics: Semantics of Capacity Enhancement*, and *Can a Woman Rebel?*